GOD, GOLD & GLORY!

God, Gold & Glory!

Revealing the Truth — A journal of
"THE CALIFORNIA CONTRIBUTION"
to global outpourings and the end-time harvest

Henry Falany

Outskirts Press, Inc.
Denver, Colorado

The opinions expressed in this manuscript are solely the opinions of the author and do not represent the opinions or thoughts of the publisher. The author has represented and warranted full ownership and/or legal right to publish all the materials in this book.

Unless otherwise indicated, all scripture quotations are from the King James Version of the Bible.

God, Gold & Glory!
The California Contribution
All Rights Reserved.
Copyright © 2010 Henry Falany
V3.0 R1.1

"Due diligence"
Please note: Great care has been taken to locate and/or acknowledge all owners of copyrighted material in this book. If any such owner has inadvertently been omitted, acknowledgment will gladly be made in future editions.

Cover photo by Vladimir Fanning

Yosemite's Horsetail Falls: At sunset in late winter Horsetail Falls resembles the famous Yosemite Firefalls. See chapter 13

This book may not be reproduced, transmitted, or stored in whole or in part by any means, including graphic, electronic, or mechanical without the express written consent of the publisher except in the case of brief quotations embodied in critical articles and reviews.

Outskirts Press, Inc.
http://www.outskirtspress.com

ISBN: 978-1-4327-5209-5

Library of Congress Control Number: 2009940771

Outskirts Press and the "OP" logo are trademarks belonging to Outskirts Press, Inc.

PRINTED IN THE UNITED STATES OF AMERICA

California
GROUND ZERO FOR AN EXPLOSION IN THE SPIRIT

As Grace and I travel and minister around the world, we find that California is highly thought of as a desired place to live, especially amongst the younger adults. We meet a lot of people that are downright envious when we tell them we live in California. Some of them jokingly ask us to take them home with us.

On the other hand, we know that California is also well-known for its liberalism and perversions. Many in the world, including many California Christians, have given up on California as too far gone. As a California minister of the Gospel, I also have to admit that there is indeed an evil veil over the state. By a veil I mean that the evil reality is all that most people see. But the veil is not the reality. The fact is that under all that evil there lies the most fruitful place on the planet for propagating the Gospel of Jesus Christ.

We must remember this principle: "You can always tell what God is doing by what satan fights the hardest." California is ground zero for so much darkness only because it is ground zero for explosions of God's light.

CALIFORNIA HAS NEVER BEEN JUST ABOUT CALIFORNIA

From its very beginning when ships were sailing out through the Golden Gate laden with so much gold it was changing the economy of other nations California has been anointed with an export or Apostolic mantle.

With its agriculture, technology (Silicon Valley), media (Hollywood) and many other exports, California has always been about the nations.

Now for over 100 years California has been launching more ministries with global impact than any place on earth.

This book is not about worshipping a state or place, but in recognizing the plan of God. As we realize His plan more clearly it will increase our prayer focus and bring the body into agreement … thus facilitating bringing the world into its spiritual fullness.

Table of Contents

An encouraging word ~ "The Church's Finest Hour" i
Endorsements iii
Acknowledgments ix
Introduction .... God, Gold & Glory ~ From Myth to Reality xi
Chapter 1 .... The Seed of "Original Intent" 1
    "The Law of the First Sent" 1
    A word given by prophet Dr. Chuck Pierce 3
    The Vision 4
Chapter 2 .... Fire Fishing! 11
    This is revival ~ by Owen Murphy 17
Chapter 3 .... California: Special Real Estate 19
    Origin of the Name California 19
Chapter 4 .... California: Young Land of Abundance 23
    Windsor Castle 23
    "The Land of Milk & Honey" & Harvest 24
    California food & fiber statistics 25
    Prophetic symbols from California realities 25
    Where California is number one ~
    Exposing the Texas myth! 26
Chapter 5 .... America By The Hand Of God 29
    The Mayflower Compact 30
    John Winthrop 31
    "A City Upon a Hill" 34
Chapter 6 .... California By The Hand Of God 37
    Early Indian and Spanish History 37
    The first Europeans 37
    Father Junipero Serra 38
    California, "The vineyard of the Lord" 41
    The Spanish colonization and the Mexican period 41
Chapter 7 .... Jedediah Smith ~ "Beloved of Jehovah" 43
Chapter 8 .... The Gold "Hidden in Plain Sight" 47
Chapter 9 .... John Charles Fremont 49
    A spiritual encounter 50
    "Manifest Destiny" 54
    The Bear Flag Revolt 55
    The Golden Gate ~ Prophetic Act 56
    God, Gold & Glory! ~ 2 57

                    The British are coming! 58
                    Senora Donna Bernard Ruiz 60
                    Seeds of Equality 62
                    Conquest complete 62
                    Campo de Cahuenga to Azusa Street ~
                    10 miles and 60 years 63
                    More on Freemont..63
                    A quote from Kit Carson 64

Chapter 10......Eureka! ~ The Blinds are Removed ~
                Gold is Discovered! 67
                    A prophetic Don...69

Chapter 11......The World Rushed In ~ The 49'ers....................71
                    California Dream Article 72
                    Statehood & multi-million dollar economy 74
                    California's gold and the Civil War 75

Chapter 12......The Gold is Still Here 77
                    "The gold is Mine" says the Lord!................................78
                    So, the long and the short of it.....................................78
                    God, Gold & Glory! 3 78

Chapter 13......Yosemite Firefalls 81
                    Fire on Azusa Street 84
                    Headwaters of the "River of Mercy"..............................85
                    God's Own Fire Falls 85

Chapter 14......California's Apostolic Mantle ~
                "The Spiritual Mother Lode" 87
                    Azusa Street Revival ~ Preview....................................88
                    Church of God in Christ ~ Preview 88
                    The Assemblies of God 88
                    Aimee Semple McPherson and the Foursquare Church ~
                    Preview..89
                    Dr. Charles Price 89
                    Henrietta Mears 89
                    West Angeles Church Of God in Christ 90
                    Franklin Hall 90
                    Dr. Billy Graham 91
                    Full Gospel Business Men's Fellowship 92
                    Bill Bright and Campus Crusade for Christ.....................92
                    Crystal Cathedral ~ Robert Schuller............................92
                    Youth With A Mission~ Loren Cunningham 93
                    Calvary Chapel & Chuck Smith ~ Preview....................93
                    The Jesus Movement..94
                    Church On The Way ~ Jack Hayford...........................94

        Trinity Broadcasting Network ~ Paul & Jan Crouch..........94
        Crenshaw Christian Center ~ Fred Price.........................95
        The Vineyard Movement ~ John Wimber ~ Preview........95
        U.S. Center for World Mission ~ Dr. Ralph D. Winter 95
        Focus on the Family ~ Dr. James Dobson......................96
        The Call ~ Lou Engle 96
        Hollywood Presbyterian Church 96
        Rick Warren ~ Purpose Driven Life ~
        Saddleback Church 97

Chapter 15......Fire on Azusa Street 99
Chapter 16......The Church of God in Christ 125
Chapter 17......Aimee Semple McPherson and the
                Foursquare Church 129
Chapter 18......Calvary Chapel, Jesus Movement, Vineyard 139
        Chuck Smith and Calvary Chapel 139
        Lonnie Frisbee ~ Hippie Preacher 139
        John Wimber and the Vineyard movement 141
Chapter 19......Seeking the Double Portion 143
Chapter 20......Revival Comes to Mariposa 147
Chapter 21......Mariposa's Feast of Fire Revival 153
Chapter 22......Why Mariposa? 159
Chapter 23......Minerva & The California Seal 171
        The California state seal 173
        A curse 174
        An unholy trinity 177
        Mount Diablo 180
Chapter 24......The Wilderness Tabernacle & America 181
Chapter 25......Pray For California 185
        The day I saw prayer...185
        California needs prayers 189
        Financial crisis..190
        Water wars 190
        Gay marriage 192
        California burning!...193
        The good news! God is Stirring the Waters 193
Chapter 26......First, a Birthing in the Spirit............................ 195
        The Portland Vision...195
        All I know is, We were hungry......................................196
        Sometimes you just have to go fishing 196
        The Issachar anointing...197

Chapter 27......So, what now? ~
            Back to the ministry of Jesus!..........................199
                Jesus didn't pray for the sick 200
                In summary..203
Appendix 1.....Prophetic Words Over California......................205
                Dr. Chuck Pierce 205
                The Author's Vision....................................205
                Kim Clement..206
                Shawn Bolz...210
                Doug Addison..215
                Chad Taylor..218
Appendix 2......California agriculture chart 223
Epilogue 1.......California, a story still untold..........................225
Epilogue 2.......Re-dig your wells 227
A Decree and Prophecy Over California 229
About Henry & Grace Falany 231
Source notes..235

An Encouraging Word
The Church's Finest Hour!

This book is being released at a time in history when America and the world are in great turmoil. We have just experienced a major collapse of the global financial markets and institutions. Worldwide epidemics are being forecast by governments. The threat of attack by foreign powers that hate this country increases almost daily.

However, I believe that if the "Body of Christ" in California, or any other place in the earth, stirs itself up and takes its position on the wall to pray, instead of disaster we will experience the greatest move of God in history.

Second Chronicles chapter 7 verses 14 & 15 state:

"If my people, which are called by my name, shall humble themselves, and pray, and seek my face, and turn from their wicked ways; then will I hear from heaven, and will forgive their sin, and will heal their land. Now mine eyes shall be open, and mine ears attent unto the prayer that is made in this place."

In other words God puts blessing and revival for the land in the believer's hands. If we as the church will take this opportunity to repent and seek Him like never before, we can by-pass the hatemongers, the sinners, the politicians and even the voters, and put our region, state or nation directly into the hands of God. It's a promise from God!

Saints, the Church's finest hour is just ahead!

"If My People" ~ "If My People" ~ "If My People"

Endorsements

What William Booth was to London and Charles Wesley was to Bristol - Henry Falany is to California. As the din of doom and gloom seems to amass over the horizon of this great state, Pastor Henry's voice is a clear clarion call for its hope and future. The timing of this book is impeccable and will be mortar in the cannons of intercession as the Holy Spirit wages all out war on the powers of darkness. It is a lamp and torch on the front lines! Read it carefully.
Chad Taylor, Author of "Why Revival Still Tarries" & "The Cry of the Harvest"

~~~~~~~~~~~~~~~~~~

I recently had the opportunity to read Henry Falany's new book "GGG". Expecting possibly a dry fact-driven book, I was pleasantly surprised to find it to be a very interesting and informative read. Myself a native Californian, I learned more about California history than I ever knew, thanks to Henry's exhaustive and careful research. I found the spiritual observations and insight in regard to California's place in prophecy to be responsible and thought-provoking.

I highly recommend this book to all, but especially to Californians who may need a spiritual boost in these troubling times.
Chuck Girard, Contemporary Christian Music Pioneer, Chuck Girard Ministries, www.chuckgirard.com, Granada Hills, CA

~~~~~~~~~~~~~~~~~~

The book you are about to read will probably cause you to repent or rejoice. I found myself doing both. As a fifty-three year resident of California, I have seen both the good and the bad of this great state. At times I have fallen into the deceptive trap of limited and slanted information that comes through the media or other sources of news. While there is truth to some of these reports, the divine calling and purpose of this state and people were somewhat obscure to me.

I believe this book is a prophetic word. I believe that the Holy Spirit has truly revealed the prophetic purpose and destiny for California to Pastor Henry Falany. I plan to encourage everyone in our ministry to read it.

I pray that as you read "God, Gold & Glory" you will praise the Lord. Praise Him for not only what He has done but for what he is about to do in this great state. The prophetic time clock is ticking and God will establish the spiritual purpose and destiny for California.

He will reveal it not only to its people but to our generation. There's going to be another "California Gold Rush" but this time the people will come running to the GLORY!
Pastor John Pursell, Believer's Church of Madera, California

~~~~~~~~~~~~~~~~~~

I commend Henry Falany for giving us such a bold, anointed and powerful look at the prophetic history of California and a look into revival with all its potential for the day in which we live. This profound study is filled with insights and grace that are sure to powerfully impact all who read it.
Bob Brasset, Extreme Healing Ministries, Victoria, BC, Canada

~~~~~~~~~~~~~~~~~~

Henry and Gracie have prepared our hearts for another great move of GOD! Great and insightful material! I could not put it down. This book should be read by all who seek revival and reformation in the nations of the world. God has done it more than once from California and will do it again. This book will help you grow in the knowledge of HIM who brings revival and reformation. Read it and be revived.
Fred Berry, Azusa Street Mission, Los Angeles, California

~~~~~~~~~~~~~~~~~~

I wholeheartedly support his book. It is a prophetic word for the hour in which we live.

Henry has truly revealed the prophetic plan of God for California. I highly recommend that every Christian read God, Gold & Glory!

Peggy Cole, Peggy Cole Ministries International, Cambria, California

~~~~~~~~~~~~~~~~~

As Pastor Henry gave me the opportunity of reading the manuscript for his new book, my mind went back over my 84 ½ years of life, and especially my very early years living on a cattle ranch in the Gold Rush town of Julian, California.

I spent my early years hearing of the whirlwind activities of the 1860's in the little one- horse town, which in the gold fever days came within three votes of becoming the county seat for San Diego County. I well remembered that in one year they had 75 killings by six shooter and stabbings and I had walked in the boot hill cemetery to prove it.

Now my friend Henry was having me read his fact-filled manuscript depicting not only those same early times in this great State, but with words that kept me wanting to continue reading all night.

Perhaps the most interesting thing is that before my own eyes I have seen this rough gem of a man, raised in the marshes of Florida, moving West and spending years traveling down the Colorado River and many other world rivers on a raft, then ending up living in and raising a great family in Mariposa. Here I first met this river-shaped nugget, who when called by God somewhat reluctantly changed course, but eventually said, "Here I am, Lord," and honored me by allowing me to be one of the ones to lay hands on him during his ordination so many years ago.

Now, this sparkling nugget of a man, along with his dear wife Grace, have not only evangelized around the world, but he has written a book about what God has and is doing in the great State of California.

You will be captivated by the stories Henry will unfold for you in his book, "God, Gold & Glory."

Dr. Robert W. Christensen, Pastor, Covenant Marriages Ministry, Golden, Colorado

Every land and every people need watchmen. Where America and the so-called "free western world" are heading is alarming. While we may look in vain to our politicians, it needs a man of Godly insight to see what lies deep to the moves of men, even to what lies buried in the ground of God's promises, waiting to be rediscovered and taken hold of. Jesus rescues, and just as God determined to bring Israel through the wilderness to the Promised Land, despite their stubbornness and waywardness, so there is clear evidence that God has invested his intent in California. This has awesome significance for the future for California, for America and potentially for the world.

It needs painstaking research to gather together so many facts of history and find in them a chain of Godly links, as Henry Falany has done. Right from the roots, from that boatload of founding fathers, John Winthrop, the mighty exploits of John Fremont, the California gold rush, the establishment of the United States Constitution and the prophetic significance of the famous Yosemite Firefalls, the reader will find a revealing sequence of events, blessings and promises in which California has played lead roles in the development of America. California has certainly had its share of preachers too, as well as a great outpouring of the Holy Spirit in the Azusa Street Revival. Indeed, Henry and Grace Falany have themselves seen genuine revival spring from their home church in Mariposa, involving 20 churches and 30 ministries. At the same time, the inception of God's victories will always be opposed and Henry highlights these areas also, such as San Francisco, homosexual capital of the world. Even the emblem in the Great Seal of the State of California is not as innocent as it looks.

History shows that true revival, by the power of the Holy Spirit, can turn a nation. It has happened several times here in Wales, where I live. We therefore share the keenest expectation in our respective countries, based on precedent and a reading of what has gone before. Whatever our desperate times, God has not changed, neither is his arm shortened. Henry and Grace are revivalists – and Californians from the heart. This book is written as naturally as they speak. It is compelling.

Dr. & Rev. Richard Parkhouse, Revivalist/Welsh Revival Historian, Wales, UK

~~~~~~~~~~~~~~~~~

I am honored to place my support, endorsement, encouragement to Henry's historical and timely book for the state of California. I encourage every Californian to read it from cover to cover as an assignment. This book will encourage you, bless you, and give you accurate historical information that enforces God's plan for this state, as a state, and then as a catalyst for the nation and even to the nations. God works in his time and it is clear in Henry's research that there is definitely a timeline established by the King of the Universe over California, and Henry has caught that timeline and labored intently to put it on pages so that thousands can glean, learn and take their place in the army of God for these end times and for the state of California.

Dr. Candi MacAlpine, Founder and senior leader of Destiny Training – A Christian International Apostolic Ministry ~ Founder High Sierra Epicenter Prayer Room Oakhurst, California

~~~~~~~~~~~~~~~~~

If one would think that it takes a colorful pastor with cowboy hat and boots preaching from his horse, as if a modern day "circuit rider," then Henry Falany would be the perfect instrument for revival. However, we know that is not a requirement for a move of God.

Henry Falany has, though, an unmatched passion to see a move of God in his lifetime, and the conviction that he will see it. Passion for revival, intimate knowledge of the person of the Holy Spirit - a friendship developed over many hours of walking and conversing with the Holy Ghost by the creeks and paths in the mountains of California - and an unmovable stance on the Word of God, combined with the will to follow the Spirit wherever He leads, that is a sure path toward revival.

His passion for revival and his dedication to the land where God planted them took him into long hours of research and prayer: one looking into what it was, and the other looking into what is coming, leading him under the grace of the Holy Spirit to write this book, which we could say is "dripping fire."

This book is more than encouraging. It inflames the reader with a desire to call fire from heaven to revive the nation and the world. It will lead you to cry out very much like the crier down in the valley in Yosemite National Park: "Let the fire fall!" - responded immediately by the one on top of the mountain: "The fire is falling."

Julio Conrad Lampan, Pastor – Missionary, Revival Highway, Argentina – Wales – U.S.A.

Acknowledgments

My first and foremost appreciation goes to the Lord Himself. It is through His inspiration and leading that this work was accomplished. I can personally testify that He is the source and resource for this book. He was with me every step of the way.

Next I must acknowledge my wife **Grace.** I can truly say, "I found favor with God, because I was given **'Grace!'"** Big smile!

Although I did the writing, this book is very much a joint effort of both her and me. For the months I was writing she was running interference for me and covering many of my other ministry duties while she continued her own busy domestic and ministry schedule. She even did a lot of the Sunday preaching at the church in order to free me up to focus on the book. She also spoke into the book with ideas and recollecting stories and events that pertained to the different subjects. On top of that she did many hours of typing, proof-reading and research, and, she was right there on all the research trips we had to take for the project. Yes, this book has been Graced!

I also want to thank my daughter **Bernadette Davis** who bailed me out of a lot of computer situations. On several occasions, because of her technical rescuing ability, I'm still saved and on my way to heaven. She put in many hours of computer help and research. Even her daughter, my six-year-old Granddaughter, **Bayleigh Davis**, brought me coffee and a sandwich from time to time.

More thanks also goes to these incredible folks that gave a lot of themselves to the endeavor. There was **Dave Breemer**, who helped immensely with research, grammar and the general flow of the book. Dave's wife **Mirabai Breemer** also helped with proof reading. **Barbara Wehman** was a key proof reader. She went through the book with a fine-tooth comb and corrected a lot of punctuation and typos. **Nita Berquist** spent a great deal of time coaching us on the format and publishing issues. **Peggy Cole** encouraged us and sent us material to use in the book. **Sandy Tobias** was also a great help as she did a lot of onsite investigation for us in the southern California area ~ My Argentine revivalist friend, **Julio Conrad Lampan**, advised and provided information. **Fred Berry** also spoke into the book and provided us with some key information. **Marilyn Noorda** was an awesome inspiration and encourager to us, and she spoke prophetically of its importance and timing, and that it should be written from the heart of California. She also sent drafts of the book to key prophetic people for review. **Shawn Bolz** met with us about the book and, by direction from the Lord, he became a supporter and counselor of the project. Historian **Leroy Radanovich** provided historic art-work of the Yosemite Firefalls. His knowledge of Mariposa history was also very useful. **Tommy Welchel** spent a whole afternoon and half the next morning with us in Los Angeles telling us the Azusa Street stories and history. **Heidi Whiteside** was a great help as a proof reader. **J.R. Miller** spent a lot of time helping put the text into a useable software program. **Vladimir Fanning** was very helpful in providing the cover photo of Horsetail Falls in Yosemite. **Dave Hamlett** was a big help with proof reading.

Other readers that commented and encouraged include: **Chuck Cooper, Lois Wahl, John Pursell, Dennis McCourt, Chad Taylor, Candi MacAlpine, and Vicki Norhden.**

More importantly, besides their physical help, all of the above have been praying for the book. Their hearts are in agreement for a move of God in the land, and they see "God, Gold & Glory" as an instrument of the Lord for that purpose.

An Introduction
GOD, GOLD & GLORY!
from
Myth to Reality

The story of California truly transforms the term "God, Gold & Glory" from myth to reality. The phrase has been around for ages, but, for the most part, every endeavor that laid claim to it failed to live up to one or all of its promises. Indeed, it is a sad reality that most attempts to live out the phrase "God, Gold & Glory" have in fact been guided by the opposing spirits of imperialism and greed.

In the early 1600's the Virginia Company of London sponsored a voyage to the New World with the purpose of establishing a colony for God, Gold & Glory! But the fact was, the enterprise was not of God, there was no gold and its quick demise was the opposite of glory.

Before that, there were Spanish Conquistadors, like Hernando Cortez, who searched futilely in Mexico and the southwest for the imaginary El Dorado, or the city of gold. On the other side of the continent Juan Ponce de León struggled through Florida looking for the "Fountain of Youth." Both were deceived into chasing myths, and neither came close to capturing the promises of "God, Gold, & Glory."

Those promises have come to life, however, in one more recent campaign. Although the phrase "God, Gold & Glory," has rarely, if ever, been consciously used to describe the history and evolution of California, it is an accurate description. Today, just by studying the history and looking at the facts, it is easy for me to apply the phrase to California and to this book. **God** proved He had a plan for California. **Gold** is its backbone (literally). His **Glory** radiates forth from California!

God, Gold & Glory became reality in California!

- God commissioned California for His purpose in America and the world

- Gold is the symbol of the state. The mineral gold, and the gold of His Spirit are a reality in California

- Glory is easy to see when you look at the incredible landscape, the "milk & honey" (agriculture & wealth), and the unmatched ministry that California represents

A spiritual observation, or over romanticizing?

Right from the beginning let's get one thing straight, I am a romantic. When I watch a good western, at the end of the movie the cowboy better get the girl or I'm sorry I watched. That's when I would offer to rewrite the ending for the director.

The purpose of this book is to show the secular and spiritual history of California from the view of a master plan from the Creator Himself. It is my desire in this book to unveil and clarify the full nature of California as it relates to God and His end-time plan for the world. At the same time I never want to purposely remove the embedded romance from a good story. As we grasp the plan of God and allow the prophetic reality of His vision to become our vision, it strengthens our ability to stand in the gap.

Now, with that said, God Himself wrote the story of California with a heart burning with romance for His people. Therefore, by nature, it is a very romantic story. I am merely the messenger that is doing my best to research and reveal the reality of God's hand. I am trying to write it down in a simple and chronological order to encourage the church and energize the intercessors.

I am addressing this issue because, from a strictly secular view, this book could be seen as over-romanticizing an age-old pattern of the human race merely continuing to capture and conquer for worldly reasons.

But, as the Bible tells us, spiritual things are spiritually discerned:

"But the natural man receiveth not the things of the Spirit of God: for they are foolishness unto him: neither can he know them, because they are spiritually

discerned. But he that is spiritual judgeth all things, ..." (1 Cor 2:14-15)

I truly hope that as you read this book, you will see the thread of the Holy Spirit through the entire story. If you do, I believe it will help stimulate your heart to the exciting and victorious plan of God for California, the world, and your life.

"If My People ..."

CHAPTER 1

THE SEED OF "ORIGINAL INTENT"

My intent in writing this book is to reveal God's intent to use California in a very special way to touch the nations. There is a term we sometimes use as Bible teachers in defining God's emphasis on the definition of a particular word in Scripture called "The Law of First Mention." This principle basically means that the first place a particular word is used in Scripture is probably God's emphasis on the definition of the word. For instance, the word "glory" is first found in Genesis 31:1, and in that verse it refers to Jacob's wealth. So, under the principle of "The law of First Mention" we consider that wealth and glory are at least closely related in God's opinion.

"The Law of the First Sent"

Using a similar principle I believe there is a direct connection to the first people, or first use, that God uses to establish His ultimate purpose. For the intent of this writing, let's call it "The Law of the First Sent." When Abraham was sent to Israel, God established His plan and precedence for that land. Others were there before and others came in later, but that did not change God's plan for the end time. God's first man was Abraham, the father of our faith. Although millions in this world do not agree, and blood has been running in the streets over the issue, and it doesn't look anything like the "City of Peace," the fact remains: Israel and Jerusalem are Ground Zero as The Lord's throne. Jerusalem is "the City of Peace," and it is the base of His operation for the ages to come. That was established, once and for all, when God sent His first man, Abraham, to "The Promised Land."

I believe the same principle holds true for America. On his discovery voyage Columbus wrote that he was guided by the Holy Spirit. Then the first body politic for America was the little band of Pilgrims on board the Mayflower. Their clear intent and purpose was to establish a Christian community in the New World. That purpose was clear to everyone everywhere and it was confirmed in the words of the Mayflower Compact.

Likewise, God established these firsts in California's history:

- He sent **Father Junipero Serra** to establish missions and evangelize California. He was establishing an uncommon plan for an uncommon purpose, in an uncommon place. Serra proclaimed California as "The Vineyard of the Lord." See Chapter 6.

- Then He sent His mountain man, **Jedediah Smith**, who's name means "beloved of Jehovah" as the first overland explorer. Jedediah read His Bible and prayed through California from bottom to top. See Chapter 7.

- Then "The Conqueror of California," **John Fremont**, a devout believer, was hand-picked by God to establish California as American soil. See Chapter 9.

- **The Yosemite Firefalls** ~ A strategic prophetic act ~ See Chapter 13.

- **The 1906 Azusa Street Revival** ~ A global outpouring ~ See Chapter 15.

- Even **Hollywood,** which greatly impacts the world, was birthed as a Bible-based community. In 1887 Horace & Daeida Wilcox laid out the first development of Hollywood and planned it to be a Christian community.[1]

- **The first feature film** produced in Hollywood was made by the young producer, Cecil B. DeMille. DeMille was a praying believer, and the son of an ordained minister. His famous quote was "I have found the greatest power in the world is the power of prayer."

    His works include; "The King of Kings," "The Ten Commandments," "The Sign of the Cross," and "Samson & Delilah."

- **Grauman's Chinese Theatre**, the Historic Landmark Theater on Hollywood Boulevard that premiers many major movies, was used by God in 1927 for its first film release. It was Cecil B. DeMille's production, "The King of Kings."[2]

Bringing some of these things to light, to me, is overwhelming confirmation that the theme of "the California Contribution" is not fantasy, but revelation; that God, indeed, is working a master plan to the world through California.

A word given by prophet Dr. Chuck Pierce ~ May 31, 2008
Glory of Zion International Ministries ~ Denton, Texas

In a prophetic conference in California in June of 2009, well known prophet Dr. Chuck Pierce reiterated a prophetic word that he received from the Lord on May 31, 2008.

I transcribed the below from an audio recording of the June 2009 meeting. This portion of his message is unedited. The entire below text is a prophetic word by Chuck. All the emphases are mine.

> The Lord showed me that California has two distinct root systems. The state that will be contending for the course of the nation in the days ahead will be California.
>
> And then He showed me that how the "Glory realm (root)" in California was greater than the "evil root" that most people judge California from.
>
> Now I'm not saying that because I'm here in California, but I will tell you this ~ All minds are linked with the concept of tasting and seeing that the Lord is good. What that means is this … it means we must discern correctly. And I believe we have been a people who have discerned wrongly. Because constantly all you hear is … "Well, California, they're so liberal they need to fall off in the ocean." That was not how God saw this state or its people at all.
>
> Now hear me ~ He actually said "the Glory realm" in California will overtake the evil root that is trying to distort covenant in this entire nation. And, how California wins this battle in covenant will begin to be a movement that shifts throughout the nation.
>
> He actually said, "How you (California) win your wars will create a rift throughout this nation." Now, that was on May 31. Therefore it has never even been a doubt in my mind how you would vote on Proposition 8.

This word goes directly to the heart of the reason for this book. In my spirit, the reason for this book is to reveal and bring to the surface God's awesome plan for California as it pertains to the nation and the world. There is a very prophetic California that the enemy has tried to pull a veil over. Even many Spirit-filled leaders in California are pleasantly surprised when I share with them some of the spiritual history and the present prayer movements that are so sincere and active in the state now.

I sincerely believe that the Lord has shown me clearly that California has a key role in the end-time harvest. California is a revival state and it desperately needs a fresh move of the Spirit. Furthermore, more than ever before, the world needs California to get that move of the Spirit and arise to its destiny.

A good decree right here is Psalm 125:3 (NIV):

"The scepter of the wicked will not remain over the land allotted to the righteous …"

As you read the lines of this book, and between the lines of this book, you will hear our cry, "… as California prays for the peace of Jerusalem and the nations, we are asking the nations to intercede for California!"

The Vision

To further understand why I am intent on exposing California's glorious natural and spiritual inheritance, I must share a vision I had a few years ago. It is foundational to this book.

As the first step toward our vision of 24/7 prayer move in Mariposa, we began a "Tabernacle of David" time of twenty-four hour prayer, one day a week, in early 2000. It continues to this day. It was the first night of that endeavor that the vision or "visitation" came.

The experience came in the early hours of the morning, just after midnight, as I was alone lying on the floor at the altar praying. It was just as clear to me as watching it on a movie screen.

CALIFORNIA, A PLACE OF ACCELERATED TIME ON GOD'S CLOCK!
February 2000

> I saw a light hover over the Holy Land in the Middle East. The light then moved to Europe for a long period of time, then to the east coast of America, and then on to California and the west coast. When it hit

California it immediately exploded like fireworks with shafts of fire shooting all over the globe. Those shafts were like lightning. I immediately knew that they represented the mighty world-changing outpouring of the Holy Ghost at Azusa Street in Los Angeles in 1906. The shafts of lightning shooting out of California in all directions were symbolic of the "tongues like as of fire" on the day of Pentecost in Acts chapter 2. That outpouring became known as "Fire on Azusa Street," and it literally reignited the mighty baptism in the Holy Ghost back into the earth and immediately exported it to the nations.

After dwelling in Europe for centuries, in the 1600's, the Light of God which had begun millennia before in the Holy Land, moved across the Atlantic to the "New World." Time seemed to accelerate each time it moved. We all know the history. The light of the Gospel began and dwelt in the Holy Land, then it moved to Europe for centuries. Then through the Pilgrims and Puritans it moved to the east coast of America. Making a long story very short, early America quickly became the place of spiritual freedom, invention, industry, free trade and prosperity and evangelism.

What took millenniums in the old countries only took a couple of centuries in early America. But even early America's east coast grew at a much slower rate than California and the west. For more than 200 years America consisted mostly of only the eastern seaboard. Compared to the opening of the west, early America grew slowly and steadily into her destiny.

California and the west, on the other hand, lay in waiting, practically untouched until the Lord was ready. In stark contrast to the standard of long slow growth, California exploded onto the scene within a matter of months. It was only one year after California became American soil that gold was discovered in January of 1848 and "The Great California Gold Rush" was on. It was in full swing by late 1849 and a state with a multi-million dollar economy by 1850.

Now, it wasn't just America but "the world rushed in." Instantly California had the attention of the whole world. They came on foot, by sailing ships, by mule or ox and wagon or on horseback. They came from every country and the islands of the sea. Great cities exploded onto the scene. It was a different time. The goldfields were alive and crawling with people from every continent on the planet. Consequently, California almost immediately became the wealthiest state of the wealthiest nation in the world.

A SPIRIT OF EXPORT AND DISTRIBUTION

Then within 56 years of California's expedited birth into statehood in1850, the great Azusa Street Revival of Los Angeles in 1906 was sent from heaven. That revival dramatically changed the entire world spiritually, and it did it practically overnight.

As a latter-day Pentecost, California's mighty Azusa Street Revival, that became known as **"Fire on Azusa Street"** took the recent re-birth of the mighty baptism in the Holy Ghost and exploded it to the world. Today every Pentecostal church and Spirit-filled or charismatic movement in the world can trace its roots back to Azusa Street.

Then the subjects below came to my mind during the vision and the Lord witnessed to me to write them down and tell the people. With a bit of research added, the vision included these subjects.

Almost instantly California became a world leader in many important arenas.

Spiritual "ground zero": California has birthed, or launched (exported), more global moves of God than any other place in the world. The list includes but is not limited to: The Azusa Street Revival, The Church of God in Christ, The Foursquare Church, Assemblies of God roots to Azusa, The Billy Graham Evangelistic Association, Youth With A Mission, Campus Crusade for Christ, Calvary Chapel, Vineyard USA, The Jesus Movement, "The Call" prayer movement, The Full Gospel Business Men, Trinity Broadcasting Network, and the list goes on.

The Economy: With a 2007 $1.8 trillion dollar GDP (Gross Domestic Product) California as a nation would rank number 7 in the world economically.

The Agriculture: Literally "the Land of Milk and Honey" California is the world's undisputed leader in the agricultural output of food and fiber production.

War/defense support: With its aircraft and aerospace industry, nuclear labs, software production, huge naval harbors and air bases, California is a world leader in military power.

Knowledge and learning: With its University of California system, plus the University of Southern California, Stanford, and the California State University system, plus many other private and community colleges, California stands alone in available education. It is also the home of the Silicon Valley, which is ground zero for technology and the computer and software industry.

The Arts: The world's eyes are focused on Hollywood and the motion picture industry. Hollywood is the undisputed world leader in the motion picture industry, and it became such while California was still very young in the early 1900's. What comes out of Hollywood goes around the world. Because of Hollywood, the nations know more about America and its culture than they know about almost any other nation. I believe the prophets when they say Hollywood will become Holy Wood, and God plans to use it for His glory and the end-time harvest.

On the negative, but in keeping with the principle of "what God is doing, the adversary is trying to divert and pervert."

California gave the world **hippies** and **free sex**. **San Francisco** is the homosexual capital of the world. It is also the environmentalist's capital of the world (Worshiping the created more than the Creator). One source I read said that the porn capital of the world is the San Fernando Valley in southern California. And that list goes on. " ... *But where sin abounded, grace did much more abound!*"

"THE GOLDEN STATE" PRECEDENCE IS ESTABLISHED
In summary, God often sets a precedence in the natural history of a land or people that is actually prophetic to HIS spiritual plans for them in the years to come. So, with the prophetic words that have come forth about revival in California, and with what I believe God showed me in this vision, I believe that God has saved California, "The Golden State," for the Great Finale, an explosion in the Spirit!

What satan has tried to derail and do to the world through this great state, God is going to turn it, right at the end, and use it for His glory and the great end-time world harvest.

Get ready! Get ready! Get ready!
It's getting close to explosion time again for California and the west, but this time, it will be an outpouring of HIS Spirit like the world has never seen. Daddy Seymour, the father of the Azusa Street Revival, prophesied in 1909 that in about 100 years God is going to send another revival to California that would be far

more powerful than the revival he experienced. Our more modern day prophets have also released prophetic words over the state (see Appendix 1 "Prophetic words over California") that confirm the spirit of Seymour's prophecy. So look out California, you are about to receive new marching orders! ... Revival is imminent!

The world will rush in one more time, and again, the Gold of the California Mother Lode, The Lord of Glory Himself, will be poured out to the entire globe!

"Even so, come, Lord Jesus"

The same night that I had the vision, the Lord gave me Isaiah 45: 1-3

"Thus saith the LORD to his anointed, to Cyrus, whose right hand I have holden, to subdue nations before him; and I will loose the loins of kings, to open before him the two leaved gates; and the gates shall not be shut; I will go before thee, and make the crooked places straight: I will break in pieces the gates of brass, and cut in sunder the bars of iron: And I will give thee the treasures of darkness, and hidden riches of secret places, that thou mayest know that I, the LORD, which call thee by thy name, am the God of Israel."

As you will see as you negotiate this book, the Lord truly went before America and opened the gates of California, subduing the adversary. The gold in the heart of the state, the natural oil being pumped, and the agricultural production, are only symbolic of the true "treasures of darkness, and hidden riches." The true treasures and riches of California are the oil of anointing, the glory of His presence, the miracles, and the outpouring of the Holy Spirit ... and the resulting souls swept into the kingdom of God.

That's what the Lord has already done and continues to do through California. But the Lord that night encouraged me with those verses for the future. What makes this particularly interesting is that my heart and vision is for the entire state and region, as well as to the nations. The Lord knows that nothing else will fulfill me.

One of the things I like about those verses is the number of times He says "I," referring to Himself. I count six of them with several more referenced. Gold represents purity, which represents deity. The Holy of Holies was identified in gold. The Golden State is prophetic of outpourings of the Holy Spirit.

I believe it is essential that we perceive and esteem these things and then "decree" them over the land.

"Thou shalt also decree a thing, and it shall be established unto thee: and the light shall shine upon thy ways." (Job 22:28)

I would ask intercessors everywhere to decree Isaiah 45:1-3 over California often.

<u>It is of global importance!</u>

"If My People ..."

CHAPTER 2

FIRE FISHING! *Waiting for the Dark Night*

Fire fishing in the bayou ~ This sketch by Mariposa artist, Larry Potter, was created especially for this book.

This book is about California's spiritual mantle. But in the initial pages, I want to set a "spirit" of *"edification, exhortation, and comfort."* I believe that is always the will and Spirit of the Lord. He always encourages us to *"fear not,"* or, *"be not afraid."* We are to *"cast our cares upon Him,"* and to always walk in a *"peace that passes understanding,"* with the *"joy of the Lord"* in our hearts.

This principle is more important today than at any time in our history. We are living in very different times in California and the world. I sincerely believe that the end is near. Jesus is coming soon!

This chapter is a sermon that I have been preaching to churches around the world lately. While it may not seem directly related to this book's California focus, believe me it is. God's plans are to prosper California in the natural and spiritual. Yet, as the following message attests, His light may not be clearly seen or grasped until it gets dark enough to see the glow.

Most of the world was shocked on September 11, 2001. The Twin Towers of The World Trade Center in New York City went down in a cloud of smoke. On December 26, 2004 the Indian Ocean Tsunami became the deadliest natural disaster in history. Also in 2004 four hurricanes hit Florida six times. Then in 2005 Hurricane Katrina hit New Orleans and for the first time in history, a major American city looked like a devastated third world country. Right behind it Rita went up through Texas and Louisiana. Tornados and floods have also increased. Last year in 2008, Hurricanes Gustav and Ike hammered Louisiana and Texas again. On September 13 Hurricane Ike, because of its exceptional size, practically wiped out Galveston, Texas.

Then a couple of days later, while Galveston was still in devastation, the world practically forgot about her because of the world financial crash. Fannie Mae and Freddie Mac went into conservatorship, and on September 14, Lehman Brothers went bankrupt. That began a world-wide financial dominoes effect. You all know the stories. Next week (at the time of this writing) General Motors, the historic icon of American success, is filing bankruptcy, which is following Chrysler, who already has. Home foreclosures are at a record level while home values are in the cellar. The president is printing and spending money right now at a rate that, ten months ago, nobody in their wildest dreams would have ever thought possible. Are you depressed yet? Smile! Now, remember, I am trying to encourage you.

From all this I could get into the sins of the people, the filth on T.V. and the movies, the degradation of the family unit and all that, but I think you get the point. We are living in incredibly changing times. It is truly getting dark out there, and fast.

In Matthew 5:14-16 Jesus exhorts us, *"Ye are the light of the world. A city that is set on an hill cannot be hid. Neither do men light a candle, and put it under a bushel, but on a candlestick; and it giveth light unto all that are in the house. Let your light so shine before men, that they may see your good works, and glorify your Father which is in heaven."*

"Fire Fishing"

Let me give you a good illustration by telling you an encouraging story about "Fire Fishing." When I was growing up in my pre-teen years in the 40's & 50's in the little coastal town of New Port Richey, Florida, our family lived in the woods on a dirt road out in the bayous. New Port Richey was a small town in those days and we lived in the woods between the town and the Gulf of Mexico. Our house was less than a mile inland from the gulf right on a bayou. It was common to look out the window and see dozens of pink flamingos and white cranes in the shallows of the bayou feeding on fish and shell fish. We also had 'gators around there all the time. Dad and his friends used to hunt gators. My grandpa, dad's pop, was actually a professional swamp guide and hunting 'gators was just one of the things he did … when he wasn't making "shine" at the "still" he had hidden in the woods.

Now for you Yankee types, a coastal bayou is an inland saltwater creek, or lagoon, that flows with the tide. The bayous are all lined with mangroves and the water depth would range from inches deep to several feet deep, depending on the tide. At low tide the oyster bars, which were everywhere, would be exposed. Many times my mother would send me out with a pail to get oysters for dinner. I would wait for low tide and wade out to the oyster bar and turn that pail upside down and sit on it and shuck and eat raw oysters till I was stuffed. Then I would shuck them and fill the pail for Mama.

The bayous were also full of blue crabs, a delicacy in the stores and restaurants. When Mama sent me for crabs I took a large wash tub and tied a short cord to it and to my belt loop on my cut-offs. We had crab nets on a short pole that we used to dip up the crabs. I would wade around in the bayou at low tide with the wash tub floating behind me. With that net I would dip crabs and shake them out in the tub. Dad had a fire pit in the back yard close to the bayou that was built to fit the wash tub. We would boil the crabs right there in the tub. If y'all would have dropped by at the right time you could have joined us for a big time crab feed. And you couldn't beat the price!

Those bayous were also full of all kinds of fish; like red snapper, snook, flounder and a dozen other species. But the one I want to tell you about is the mullet. Most of the folks in those southern woods loved smoked mullet. But the thing about a mullet was, it wouldn't hit bait or a lure. So you couldn't fish for them like normal fish. You either had to net them or spear them.

Years ago my grandpa found out that the mullet would come to a light on a dark night. So he rigged up a boat to catch mullet. It was a flat-bottomed boat about sixteen feet long that was totally rectangular in shape. In other words it was not boat-shaped in the bow but straight across like the stern. The front did have a bevel on it so that it would not push water as you polled it through the bayou. On the top of the front of the boat Grandpa built a box that was only open forward. Kind of like an orange crate nailed so it was closed off to the sides and the back but open to the water in front of the boat. Then he put a large pot in that box and built a fire in it. Hence, "Fire Fishing." With that fire on the very front of the boat, and the box configured so the light only shined on the water and not in your eyes, he would then poll around in the bayous on a dark night. The sea-water in those bayous ran crystal clear and only dark nights would work.

He had a four or five-prong spear on an approximately ten-foot pole. He put a man in the back of the boat to poll the boat real easy and quiet around through the mangroves while he and another man stood in the front of the boat, one on each side of the fire box, with their spears handy. Many times the mullet would come to the light so fast and so excited they started jumping out of the water. More than once they jumped right into the boat. Once they swam into the light in front of the boat they become almost traumatized by the light. That's when he would ease that spear down into the water and quickly gig them. On a night's Fire Fishing adventure, lots of fish were caught and usually everybody took turns polling and spearing.

In later years when I was fishing with them my dad and uncles had gone hi-tech. Instead of the fire in the pot, they lined the inside of the box with aluminum foil for better reflection and hung a Coleman lantern in there. Otherwise they did it the same way Grandpa did.

Grandpa originally started "Fire Fishing" to catch mullet for smoking and eating, and, for selling to people. It was a necessity to him. But to my dad and his generation it became great sport. It was a lot of fun to go "Fire Fishing" at night. Every time you went out, you got a lot of mullet, and had a lot of fun doing it.

The Sea of Galilee

Little did my family know it, but archaeologists are finding out that Fire Fishing appears to have been around when Peter and the boys were fishing the Sea of Galilee. Underwater artifacts are revealing fire baskets and spears that indicate that they were on to this way back then. Remember Peter said to Jesus, *"… we have toiled all night …"* (Luke 5:5)

It must be a dark night

Now here's my point. Normally, fishing is over when it gets dark. But Fire Fishing is just the opposite. You are actually waiting for it to get dark. In fact it must be a dark night, the darker the better. By that I mean there can't be any sign of the moon. It was even better if there was a cloud cover so the stars didn't shine. The reason for that was that if there was any light at all, with that clear water the mullet could see to feed without your light. But on a real dark night they couldn't see and they were compelled to your light.

Even though we were mainly after mullet when we were "Fire Fishing," we would also spear snapper and flounder while we were at it. Dad would often take along a frying pan, and some oil and flour, and sometimes Mom would bring some hush puppies. Out there on the bank of the bayou in the middle of the night, we would fry up some fresh fish. It was good times!

Dad would watch the Almanac or calendar during the month, and note when there was no moon, and tell us kids that on a certain night, "Daddy's gonna take you Fire Fishing." That was big stuff to us in those days. That's when "the darker the night, the better." We waited for those dark nights!

Now lets read from Isaiah 60 ~ and read it with fire in your spirit!

"Arise, shine; for thy light is come, and the glory of the LORD is risen upon thee. For, behold, the darkness shall cover the earth, and gross darkness the people: but the LORD shall arise upon thee, and his glory shall be seen upon thee. And the <u>MULLET, oh I mean</u> Gentiles shall come to thy light, and kings to the brightness of thy rising. Lift up thine eyes round about, and see: all they gather themselves together, they come to thee: thy sons shall come from far, and thy daughters shall be nursed at thy side."

(Isaiah 60:1-4, Emphasis and humor mine)

Its "Arise Shine Time Folks!"

I sincerely believe that the darkness coming on the earth these days is not doomsday, it's our time. When the lights go out in the world, the sinners are going to be looking for the believers that have the light. Our job is to outfit our boat, and build our fire, and be ready!

In Luke 21 Jesus told us that these dark things would be happening. But he didn't say go hunker down in a survival cave somewhere, and wait for the end, He said *"... look up, and lift up your heads; for your redemption draweth nigh."* (Luke 21:28)

Jesus said, *"I am the light of the world,"* then He said, *"You are the light of the world."* Our light, which is the manifestation of Jesus, must shine. I believe our main objective should be to get back to the ministry of Jesus! That's what we must to do to get ready. He said, *"I am the way ... "* We need to get the Apostolic mantle, with all its power and anointing, back into the church. The "Gifts of the Spirit" and the person of the Holy Spirit must be featured in our services. And I don't mean just the "word," or "prophetic" gifts which are important, but we need the power, healing and manifested miracle gifts back in the church. In Luke 24 and Acts 1 Jesus actually forbids a "word only" gospel. He wouldn't release them into ministry without the "dunamis" power. Shout amen with me, somebody!

Paul said *"I don't come with excellency of speech .. or enticing words, ... but in demonstration of the Spirit and of power."* (1 Corinthians 2)

Psalm 110:3 says *"Thy people shall be willing in the day of thy power ... "* The world needs to see the power of the Holy Ghost back in the church. They are not impressed with a "Word only" Gospel.

Jesus came preaching, teaching, and healing, and He told us to do the same thing. (Matthew 4 & 10, & Luke 10)

So, when we stand with God, with a revelation of His Word in our hearts, we are not afraid of the darkness to come, we anticipate it. In fact, the darker the better!

Glory, Favor & Provision

Besides an increase in the anointing, and His Glory and favor coming on us, I see the faithful ministers and ministries actually prospering in crashing economic times. Isaiah 60:5 says *"the abundance of the sea and the wealth of the Gentiles will come to the church."* And Genesis 26 says *"Isaac sowed in time of famine and reaped a hundred fold!"* (both paraphrased)

Folks, it is harvest time! Jesus said, *"... Come ye after me, and I will make you to become fishers of men."* (Mark 1:17)

The world system is coming undone "like a two-dollar watch." But as a Bible-believing Christian, don't be taken back and getting confused like the world is; stand up and be encouraged! The whole plan of God is playing right into our hands. It's not doomsday, it's our time!

We are about to see a revival that is going to be a summation of all the revivals of the past. It's a promise, because Jesus is coming back for a glorious church!

> *"The Glory of this latter house shall be greater than of the former, saith the Lord of hosts:"* (Haggai 2:9)

The good news is: The Father is watching His calendar, so get ready saints of God, because real soon; **"Daddy's gonna take you Fire Fishing."**

"This is Revival" by Owen Murphy

What will revival and harvest look like when the lights go out and God's Glory rises in fullness? I do not know exactly, for God moves as He wills, but I hope and believe it should look like what Owen Murphy described in his classic: "This is Revival."

> *"When men in the streets are afraid to open their mouths and utter godless words lest the judgments of God should fall; when sinners, overawed by the Presence of God tremble in the streets and cry for mercy; when, without special meetings and sensational advertising, the Holy Ghost sweeps across cities and towns in Supernatural Power and holds men in the grip of terrifying Conviction; when every shop becomes a pulpit; every heart an altar; every home a sanctuary and people walk softly before God, this is Revival!*
>
> *Today the word Revival has largely lost its real meaning. Our present generation, never having witnessed the mighty movings of God in nation-wide spiritual awakening such as has taken place in past generations, has little conception of the magnitude of such a visitation.*

Heaven-sent revival is not religious entertainment, where crowds gather to hear outstanding preachers and musical programs; neither is it the result of sensational advertising - in a God-sent revival you don't spend money on advertising; people come because Revival is there!

Revival is an 'awareness of God' that grips the whole community, and the roadside, the tavern, as well as the church, become the places where men find Christ.

Here is the vast difference between our modern evangelistic campaigns and true revival. In the former, hundreds may be brought to a knowledge of Christ and churches experience seasons of blessings, but as far as the community is concerned little impact is made; the taverns, dance halls, and movies are still crowded, and the godlessness marches on.

In revival, the Spirit of God, like a cleansing flame, sweeps through the community. Divine conviction grips people everywhere; the strongholds of the devil tremble, and many close their doors, while multitudes turn to Christ!"

References Used: When God Stepped Down from Heaven by Owen Murphy

"If My People ..."

CHAPTER **3**

CALIFORNIA: A VERY SPECIAL PIECE OF REAL ESTATE

It may come as a surprise to some that God has designated California for a great revival. I can understand this on a natural level. When people ask me my real opinion of California I respond that I see two California's: the genuine one that God designed and created, and the social one, that man has tried to pervert and pollute. So, my answer is, God's California is as close to paradise as this world will ever see. The other California is what we are praying about.

Most Christians don't realize the rich natural and spiritual history of the Golden State.

"Howbeit that was not first which was spiritual, but that which was natural; and afterward that which was spiritual." (1 Corinthians 15:46)

"What has been will be again, what has been done will be done again …" (Ecclesiastes 1:9 NIV)

California is one of the most interesting and diverse pieces of real estate in the world. Its landscape includes beautiful sunny beaches and palm trees, hot dry deserts, north coast rain forests, high alpine meadows with snow capped peaks as well as beautiful rugged coastlines, and huge fertile agricultural valleys.

Although the west was America's last frontier to develop, California is the most populated state in the union with the largest economy.

Origin of the Name California
California was probably named by the Spanish. According to my good friend and Argentine revivalist, Julio Conrad Lampan, **Cali** means "hot" and **fornia** is old

Spanish for "little ovens." In other words it is Spanish for **"hot little ovens."** Although the early Spanish explorers were obviously referring to the summer temperatures of the southern reaches of the area, probably the southern tip of Baja California in Mexico, I believe that it is very prophetic in terms of God's plan and purposes. California is a land of many hot spots for God.

Rev. Lampan added that the Spanish Bible says in Malachi 4:1 *"the day of the Lord is coming hot as an oven,"* or, *"the day of the Lord is coming as Cali fornia."* It's a little play on words, but it works.

Queen Califia

Another suggested origin for the name California is the mystical terrestrial paradise island depicted in the romance novel written in 1510, "Las Sergas de Esplandian," by Garci Rodriguez de Montalvo. The book created a long-standing European belief in such a paradise called California. In the novel the island was peopled by strong black Amazonian women who were great warriors, with no men among them. Their ruler was the majestic and powerful "Queen Califia."

There is a mural that portrays California's history in the State Capitol entitled, "Origin and Development of the Name of the State of California," in which "Queen Califia" is the centerpiece at the top of the presentation. The painting is in the California Room which was recently rededicated as the John L. Burton Hearing Room (room 4203), on the fourth floor above the Governor's office.

Another theory for the name is "Kali-Forno," which is an Indian phrase meaning "high mountains."

The fact is, the historians and scholars do not agree on the actual origination of the name California. I find that to be very interesting as we don't have any argument about where New York, Virginia and Florida and Washington got their names. That gives me reason to believe even more than ever that God reserved that privilege to Himself.

California is a terrestrial paradise and a place of hot little ovens where God says, "the Fire is Falling!" Can I get an amen here?

A Special Plan

I believe that when you read this book you might agree that God has had a special plan and mission for the "Golden State." It might also become obvious why the adversary has tried so hard to pervert and divert it.

California is the richest state of the wealthiest country in history. The literal heart of the state is gold. The "Mother Lode" is a vein of gold-bearing quartz a half-mile wide and a hundred and twenty miles long that runs north and south just north of the center of the state.

It was this gold that sparked the largest migration in American history known as "the 49er Gold rush" or "The Great California Gold Rush." Eighteen months before the gold was discovered California was a very remote and unpopulated Mexican territory. This amazing history - of how quickly California became a natural and spiritual exporter to the world - is very interesting as seen under the hand of God. One must understand California's past and present to see its future.

"If My People ..."

CHAPTER 4

CALIFORNIA: YOUNG LAND OF ABUNDANCE AND GREATNESS

Windsor Castle in 1988

In 1988 Grace and I were on a vacation touring England and the UK. During the tour we were taking a private guided horse-drawn carriage ride at Windsor Castle near London. As we were talking to our carriage driver, who was also our guide, he told us that Windsor Castle was over 900 years old. Then he chuckled with a little humorous sarcasm and said "you Americans talk about old historical sites, but you don't really have any." I believe the Lord amusingly gave me a quick response and I said, "Yes, but buddy, we have trees practically in our back yard that are 3,000 years old and they aren't even dead yet." To that he subsided a bit. However, the guy had a point. If we have a building or structure in California reach a hundred years old, we declare it a historical site and register it with the National Historical Society. We even hang a plaque on it and have a big celebration over it.

A few days after Windsor Castle, Grace and I were having coffee in a pub in Dublin, Ireland when I saw a poster on the wall that they had recently celebrated the city's millennium. That is hard for a westerner to get his mind around. A European city, which itself is quite young compared to the ancient civilizations of the world, celebrating its thousand-year anniversary.

When I started thinking about how old some civilizations are and comparing it to California's history, it is mind blowing. California as a state just celebrated its sesquicentennial (150 years) in 2000. Outside of a handful of Spanish missions on the coast, there are no European structures in the entire state of California that date 200 years old. They do not exist. On the grand scale of time California is very young, and yet it has been a world leader in many major arenas, natural and spiritual.

"The Land of Milk & Honey" & Harvest

In a very short time, California has become the world leader in food production and agricultural prosperity. This reality has important spiritual ramifications. As the Word of God tells us in 1 Corinthians chapter 15, God moves first in the natural, then in the Spirit. The Word also declares:

"Behold, the days come, saith the LORD, that the plowman shall overtake the reaper, and the treader of grapes him that soweth seed; and the mountains shall drop sweet wine ... " (Amos 9:13)

A literal picture of California

California is where "the plowman" literally overtakes "the reaper" on an everyday basis.

The other day we observed this first hand, as Grace and I were driving home from Monterey after doing some research for this book. I said, "Honey, you are looking at Amos 9:13 in reality." As we drove through the Hollister area of the Salinas Valley, the crops were in every stage of production. Some were being harvested, some were being cultivated, while others were being planted. It was in June and many of the farms were already growing their second crops of the year. Planting and harvesting takes place there year round.

God literally created California to help feed the world. The state has several major agricultural areas, including the Imperial Valley in the very south of the state, the Salinas Valley and Monterey County on the central coast, the Napa Valley in the north, and the "Great Valley" in the center of the state. A combination of extremely fertile soil, the snow pack in the High Sierra Mountains, a long growing season and favorable weather patterns, plus a sophisticated reservoir and canal system, make these valleys and the state as a whole, the number one place of harvest on the planet.

California's unique variety of weather is especially important to California's agricultural productiveness. It has not only a sunny and long growing season, but as a rule it doesn't rain during the late spring and summer months. As high atmospheric pressure sets up on the west coast during those months, it actually protects the coast from rain storms. Irrigation then becomes the ideal source of watering. In general, if a crop needs so many acre feet of water every so many days for optimum growth, the goal is to give the crop exactly that amount. In California, the crops can be optimally watered because they grow without

CALIFORNIA: YOUNG LAND OF ABUNDANCE AND GREATNESS

the constant threat of rain storms that could follow the irrigation and hurt the crop.

California food & fiber statistics

Below are official government statistics that confirm California's agricultural productivity and the natural abundance of California's valleys. They also link California to important biblical and prophetic principles.

These statements and charts were taken from the California Department of Food and Agriculture, "California Agricultural Resource Directory 2008–2009"[1] (See Appendix 2)

- California's agricultural abundance includes 400 different commodities. Among these, <u>the state produces about half of U.S. – grown fruits, nuts & vegetables.</u>

- California's gross cash agriculture receipts in 2007 were $36.6 billion

- California's agricultural exports were $10.9 billion in 2007.

- California exported agricultural products to more than 156 countries worldwide in 2007.

Prophetic symbols from California natural realities

- **Gold** ~ The Mother Lode of Gold ~ speaks of His purity

- **Vineyards** ~ With over 90% of the U.S. vineyards, "The Vineyard of the Lord" speaks of fruitfulness

- **Wine** ~ With over 90% of the U.S. wine production ~ speaks of the New Wine or the Holy Spirit

- **Olive oil** ~ The Olive Capitol of the world is in California ~ speaks of His anointing oil & power

- **Harvest** ~ The world agriculture leader ~ speaks of His harvest

- **Almonds** ~ The nation's sole producer of almonds and 80% of the world's almonds ~ The almond tree symbolizes leadership and speedy fulfillment

GOD, GOLD & GLORY!

- **Milk & Honey** ~ The "Milk & Honey" production leader ~ speaks of "the promised land" & His peace and abundance

- **Good ground** ~ Fertile soil ~ speaks of the Word of God advancing the Kingdom of God

" ... Behold, I will send you corn (grain), and wine, and oil, and ye shall be satisfied therewith:" (Joel 2:19)

- California is a major **grain** producer

- California produces over 90% of America's **wine,** and is a world leader

- California is a world leader in **olive oil** production

"Thus saith the LORD, As the new wine is found in the cluster, and one saith, Destroy it not; for a blessing is in it ..." (Isaiah 65:8)

- As California produces almost all of the grapes and wine in America ~ the cluster is in California and *"a blessing is in it"*

- The "new wine" speaks of the Holy Spirit

Note: Please see the agriculture chart in Appendix 2 in the back of the book. It confirms the unmatched prominence of California's agricultural industries.

Where California is number one, or, Exposing the Texas myth!

Agriculture is not the only area where California excels. To the contrary, the State is characterized by greatness in many other areas, including geology, industry, art, spirituality, and more. For the benefit of my Texas preacher friends, I humorously call this list "Exposing the Texas myth."

Indeed, in the research for this book, I have verified that California has:

1. The most global Christian influence in the world
2. The biggest population of the 50 states ~ 36,700,000 people
3. The biggest budget ~ 1.7 trillion dollars in '07
4. The biggest international export distinction ~ $142.61 billion in '07 ~ U.S. Census
5. The Ag capitol of the world ~ The most agriculture production ~ Food & fiber

CALIFORNIA: YOUNG LAND OF ABUNDANCE AND GREATNESS

6. "The Land of Milk & Honey" ~ As the nations top milk producer, California is also a top honey producer ~ it is intermittently the number one honey producer.
7. The world's largest annual agricultural exposition ~ "The World Ag Expo" ~ Tulare
8. The richest and most productive agricultural county in the world ~ Fresno
9. The biggest winery in the world ~ Gallo ~ Modesto
10. The most wine production in the nation ~ over 90%
11. The most vineyards in the nation ~ over 90% of the U.S. grapes
12. The "Raisin capital of the world" ~ Selma (Fresno)
13. The "Olive capital of the world" ~ was Fresno, now Corning (anointing oil)
14. The "Garlic capital of the world" ~ Gilroy
15. The "Cowboy capital of the world" ~ Oakdale
16. The "Mule capital of the world" ~ Bishop ~ High country packers and guides
17. The biggest gold vein ~ the ½ mile wide by 120 mile long California Mother Lode
18. The biggest living things in the world ~ The California Redwoods
19. The oldest living things in the world ~ The Bristlecone Pine Trees
20. The continent's highest waterfall ~ Yosemite Falls ~ over 3,000 feet
21. The world's highest concentration of high waterfalls ~ Yosemite National Park
22. The most forest land in the lower 48 states & Hi.
23. The nation's most National Parks ~ 9 National Parks and a total of 23 NPS units
24. The movie & television filming capital of the world ~ Hollywood
25. The world's biggest county was Mariposa, now San Bernardino
26. The highest mountain in the lower 48 states & Hi. ~ Mt Whitney ~ 14,505 ft.
27. The lowest point in America ~ Death Valley ~ 282 ft. below sea-level
28. The home of the number one "Amusement Park System" ~ Disney
29. The first McDonalds ~ The world's leader and largest fast-food restaurant chain
30. The largest higher learning system ~ Universities and colleges
31. The world's technology center ~ Silicon Valley ~ San Jose
32. America's most famous golf course ~ Pebble Beach in Monterey
33. The continent's major fishery ~ Monterey Bay[2]
34. The greatest sardine fishery in the world in the 1930's ~ Monterey Bay[3]

GOD, GOLD & GLORY!

35. The largest water movement project in the U.S. ~ California State Water Project
36. The largest off-stream reservoir in the U. S. ~ San Luis Reservoir
37. The fastest transition from foreign soil (1846) to statehood (1850)
38. The first woman to preach on radio ~ Aimee Semple McPherson ~ 1922
39. The world's first Christian radio station ~ 1924 ~ A. S. McPherson's KFSG
40. Even in crude oil production, which California is not particularly known for, with up to 423.9 million barrels produced in a year, it ranks number four behind Louisiana, Texas and Alaska.[4]

These statistics are not just interesting trivia. They are a physical manifestation of God's plans for greatness in California. The state's prominence in natural things points to God's true will for the State in spiritual matters: greatness and prosperity. However, before we can consider and understand California's spiritual destiny in more detail, we must step back and look at California's geo-political position. The state is not an island; it is part of a nation: the United States of America. God's purpose for California is reflected, in part, by the reality that California was settled and developed as part of the United States.

"If My People ..."

CHAPTER **5**

AMERICA BY THE HAND OF GOD

The history of America has always amazed me as you look at it from the proper perspective. That perspective can only be seen as a major plan from heaven and directly executed by the hand of God.

I don't think it takes a lot of prophetic insight to understand that this great nation was planned for God's purpose and the glorious end-time harvest. Through the ages it literally sat here between two great oceans, totally protected and untouched, while most of the world developed ancient civilizations dating back thousands of years. When you study the early American history you will find miracle after miracle, and in some places split second timing from heaven that stopped the adversaries and kept the way open for God's people. That pattern is seen over and over in the adventures of Columbus in the 15th century, as well as the Pilgrims and Puritans in the 17th century, and the Continental Congress and George Washington with his tiny Continental Army in the 18th century. God used weather and all kinds of confusions and disturbances to guide and protect the birthing of America.

It is also interesting that America is the only other country except Israel that was established on a covenant with God. As a result of being blown off-course of their original destination of Virginia, where the colony had already failed terribly due to strife and corruption, the little band of believers called Pilgrims were faced with a plan B. It was then that they decided to end any confusion or mutinous ideas by making a covenant together and before the Lord of their clear intent. The Mayflower Compact was that covenant, which was signed and ratified by the Pilgrims (first called separatist) on board the Mayflower while anchored at Cape Cod.

The Mayflower Compact

> In the name of God, Amen. We whose names are underwritten, the loyal subjects of our dread sovereign lord King James, **by the grace of God**, of Great Britain, France and Ireland, King, defender of the faith, etc. **having undertaken for the glory of God, and advancement of the Christian faith,** and honor of our King and country, a voyage to plant the first colony in the northern parts of Virginia, **do by these presents solemnly and mutually, in the presence of God and one another, covenant and combine ourselves together** into a civil body politic, for our better ordering and preservation, and furtherance of the ends aforesaid; and by virtue hereof do enact, constitute and frame such just and equal laws, ordinances, acts, constitutions and offices, from time to time, as shall be thought most meet and convenient for the general good of the colony, unto which we promise all due submission and obedience.
>
> In witness whereof we have hereunder subscribed our names at Cape Cod, the 11th of November, in the year of the reign of our sovereign lord King James of England, France and Ireland the eighteenth, and of Scotland the fifty fourth, AD 1620. Emphasis added.[1]

Their intent was clearly to plant the New Colony based on biblical New Testament principles so that the New World would be a Godly community in accordance with the Holy Scriptures. The Mayflower Compact opens with the words ***"In the name of God, Amen .."*** and continues ***"by the Grace of God ... Having undertaken, for the Glory of God and advancement of the Christian Faith .."*** clearly establishes that our forefathers had a Godly plan for this nation.

The first colony was named Plymouth Plantation which became Massachusetts Bay Colony. From Massachusetts Bay Colony the New World grew to 13 colonies and finally to the 50 United States of America.

In its early history America saw the Spanish in Florida searching for gold and "the fountain of youth," and exploring up through the southwest searching for gold and treasures, as well as on the west coast. The French were in New Orleans as well as the French Fur traders across the mid-west and west. The Russians were on the west coast and, of course, there were our bouts with the British. But Saints of God, keep this in mind, our roots follow none of those trails. Our roots are directly tied to the little band of believers from the Mayflower and their descendants. In fact, our 6th president, John Quincy Adams, a descendant himself of Mayflower passenger John Alden, and son of the 2nd President who was a framer of the Constitution, called the Mayflower Compact the foundation of the U.S. Constitution in a speech given in 1802.

Understanding our roots as described here we can clearly see that the original intent for America was a Godly nation in covenant with God. With that understood it is not surprising that America is the wealthiest and most powerful nation in history. God has blessed America! It is a nation that stands for freedom and human rights around the world. It is the undisputed leader in missions and advancing the gospel of Jesus Christ around the world. It is also the primary supporter and protector of Israel, as well as the leader in financing the return of the Jews to Jerusalem.

As a quick side note, at this writing, on the issue of America and Israel, it is this writer's concern and prayer that our leaders never step outside of God's will and Biblical instructions for the nation of Israel. Indeed, our leaders need to repent from some of the offenses already committed, like land for peace. Can I get some agreement and an amen here?

JOHN WINTHROP
A prophetic American and my grandfather

John Winthrop leading prayer in the New World

In our home town of Mariposa, California, there is a great little museum that has been given favorable mention by the Smithsonian Institute. The museum features the history of the early mining days of the California Gold Rush, the Fremont story and the developing of Yosemite National Park. Interestingly, in the museum there is a portrait of John Winthrop, giving him tribute as a founding father of America.

My dad was a swamp rat and as I described in chapter two I grew up in the swamps and bayous of the Deep South. However, I was born in Boston, Massachusetts which is where my mom and her family are from. At the end of World War II, when Dad got out of the Navy, she and Dad lived there for the first several years after they were married. Dad moved us south when I was about two years old. My sister Susan was two years younger than I, and she was a small baby when we moved. My two younger brothers, Wade and Robin were born in Florida.

Nonetheless, through my mother's side I am a direct 12th grandson of John Winthrop. Our lineage comes down through the Dudleys and the Hiltons. Yes, this ol' country boy revival preacher, raised in the bayous of the south, and now in the mountains of California, is literally from one of the oldest families in Boston. God has a sense of humor, doesn't he!

Anyway, moving right along with my story here, Winthrop was unanimously elected the first Governor of the Massachusetts Bay Colony before he sailed to New England in 1630. He was re-elected several times from 1630 to the year of his death in 1649.

John Winthrop was a wealthy lawyer and preacher with the fire of God burning in his heart. He had a passion to see the New American Colony succeed as a New Testament community that lived and followed the teachings of his Lord Jesus Christ. His passion burned so strong that he not only governed the first years of our country, but also financed it from his fortunes in England. By popular demand from the New World, he came specifically to try to help save the badly failing and dying Christian colony. The word was, "they needed a Moses."

It may not be coincidence that here in the "last days" a direct grandson of the first elected ruler of America, and profound Christian advocate, is moving in an Apostolic anointing and standing for a move of God in the spiritual heart of California.

Excerpts from "The Light and the Glory" by Peter Marshall & David Manuel

> One of the most dedicated Puritans in England was John Winthrop. Cambridge-educated, the owner of a sizeable estate in Suffolk, Winthrop was an attorney in the Court of Wards, and a Justice of the Peace.[2]
>
> Time and again Winthrop would dig deeper into his own coffers to pay for desperately needed supplies. During this period, he was supporting the colony almost singlehandedly, and rapidly exhausting what remained of his own wealth to do so. But never once did he make the slightest complaint, not even in his private journal.[3]
>
> Without doubt, a miracle took place upon Winthrop's arrival: a nearly dead colony was resurrected. And from all reports, God's single instrument in this resurrection was John Winthrop. Cotton Mather would refer to Winthrop as Nehemias Americanus in reference to the Old Testament leader who had brought the Israelites back from their Babylonian exile to the Promised Land, and had directed the rebuilding of the walls of Jerusalem. But more important, Nehemiah had inspired them to resume their covenant with God.[4]
>
> Winthrop's love of his neighbors is exemplary in any age, and his commitment ranks second to none in the annals of this nation's history. One of the chroniclers of his own age sums him up thus: "His justice was impartial, his wisdom excellently tempered ... his courage made him dare to do right ... Accordingly, when the noble design of carrying

a colony of Chosen People into an American wilderness was by some eminent persons undertaken, this eminent person was, by the consent of all, chosen for the Moses." Another historian, of the early nineteenth century, ranks him second only to Washington in terms of stature among the founding fathers, and we would agree.[5]

Folks, these people are our direct forefathers. They are God's seed to the very beginning structure of America. The dream of the Puritans and Pilgrims was to pioneer and build a New Testament life in the New World. Their intention was never merely seeking "religious freedom." They were desperate to establish a life and a future based on the Holy Scriptures in the love of Jesus Christ. They were a courageous, devoted and lively people with a heart burning with love and compassion for the Lord and for each other.

Upon his arrival, as he viewed the tiny and sparse looking village of Salem from aboard his ship the Arbella, Winthrop penned his renowned sermon regarding the new settlement entitled *"A City Upon a Hill"* formally known as *"A Model of Christian Charity."* He used Jesus' words in Matthew 5 and prophesied America to be *"That City upon a Hill"* as a lighthouse to the world.

"A City Upon A Hill" Formally known as "A Model of Christian Charity"

> Now the only way to avoid this shipwreck, and to provide for our posterity, is to follow the counsel of Micah, to do justly, to love mercy, to walk humbly with our God. For this end, we must be knit together, in this work, as one man. We must entertain each other in brotherly affection. We must be willing to abridge ourselves of our superfluities, for the supply of others' necessities. We must uphold a familiar commerce together in all meekness, gentleness, patience and liberality. We must delight in each other; make others' conditions our own; rejoice together, mourn together, labor and suffer together, always having before our eyes our commission and community in the work, as members of the same body. So shall we keep the unity of the spirit in the bond of peace. The Lord will be our God, and delight to dwell among us, as His own people, and will command a blessing upon us in all our ways, so that we shall see much more of His wisdom, power, goodness and truth, than formerly we have been acquainted with. We shall find that the God of Israel is among us, when ten of us shall be able to resist a thousand of our enemies; when He shall make us a praise and glory that men shall say of succeeding

plantations, "may the Lord make it like that of New England." For we must consider that we shall be as 'a city upon a hill.'

The eyes of all people are upon us. **So that if we shall deal falsely with our God in this work we have undertaken, and so cause Him to withdraw His present help from us, we shall be made a story and a by-word through the world. We shall open the mouths of enemies to speak evil of the ways of God, and all professors for God's sake. We shall shame the faces of many of God's worthy servants, and cause their prayers to be turned into curses upon us till we be consumed out of the good land whither we are going.**

And to shut this discourse with that exhortation of Moses, that faithful servant of the Lord, in his last farewell to Israel, Deut. 30.

"Beloved, there is now set before us life and death, good and evil," in that we are commanded this day to love the Lord our God, and to love one another, to walk in his ways and to keep his Commandments and his ordinance and his laws, and the articles of our Covenant with Him, that we may live and be multiplied, and that the Lord our God may bless us in the land whither we go to possess it. But if our hearts shall turn away, so that we will not obey, but shall be seduced, and worship other gods, our pleasure and profits, and serve them; it is propounded unto us this day, we shall surely perish out of the good land whither we pass over this vast sea to possess it. Therefore let us choose life, that we and our seed may live, by obeying His voice and cleaving to Him, for He is our life and our prosperity.

Notice the prophetic warning from Winthrop in 1630. (which I bolded)

The above is said to be one of Ronald Reagan's favorite references. John Kennedy also said he was guided by the standard of John Winthrop.[6]

"Manifest Destiny" is rooted in the Puritan dream of a "nation under God."

It is this spirit that was willing to pay the price that established America as the greatest and most powerful country in the world. It is this same spirit that pioneered the light of Christ across the continent and brought America into its

◄ GOD, GOLD & GLORY!

"Manifest Destiny," a Godly nation "From Sea to Shining Sea."

I think it is appropriate that John Winthrop is acknowledged in the Mariposa Museum. Without him and others like him there would be no "California Contribution" to America or to global moves of God.

"If My People ..."

CHAPTER 6

CALIFORNIA BY THE HAND OF GOD

We have seen how the providence of God has miraculously guided the keeping and developing of the greatness of America. Now I want us to look at California in that same light. Understanding that although California is young even in New World terms it is the wealthiest, most populated state in America. It is also a world leader in moves of God and exporting the "good news" to the world.

Even most Californians are not aware of the incredible history of how California lay in waiting through the ages, then all of a sudden shot to the forefront as a world leader in so many arenas, including the spiritual arena. The near misses, coincidences and split-second timings involved in California becoming American soil are a story of miracles all by itself.

Early Indian and Spanish History

In the beginning the Indians had it right

When we think of early California as compared to back east or other civilized parts of the world, we think of a wilderness with no population to speak of. That is quite contrary to what people think when they think of California today. Although it has more wilderness, mountains and deserts than any other state but Alaska, today many people relate California to big cities, crowded beaches, Disneyland, and jammed freeways.

Well, it seems that the Native Americans figured out long ago that California was very inhabitable. According to my studies, before "white man" came to America, California had the highest density population of Native Americans on the continent. This was probably due to the California factors of temperate climate, fertile land, available water and abundance of fish and wildlife.[1]

The first Europeans

This is where my wife Grace gets to take a bow. She is full-blooded Portuguese.

◄ GOD, GOLD & GLORY!

Both of her parents were Portuguese from the Azores Islands off the coast of Portugal. I kid her from time to time and tell her that I married her for the linguica, which is that great Portuguese sausage. But she just smiles and gives me that "I know better" look.

So, anyway, moving right along, as history would have it, she gets the last laugh. The first European to explore the west coast was the Portuguese explorer Juan Rodriguez Cabrillo, in 1542. He was sailing for the Spanish Empire at the time. Then some 37 years later, in 1579, the English explorer Sir Francis Drake also explored and claimed an undefined portion of the California coast.

Enter the first preacher ~ Father Junipero Serra
1713 – 1784

Junípero Serra

CALIFORNIA BY THE HAND OF GOD

A California Spanish Mission

I believe I can safely say that Junipero Serra is an extremely important figure in the beginning of California's story. His influence was very prophetic to the real purpose of God's plan for the "Golden State." He literally marched up the west coast claiming the land for the kingdom of God. Today his trail is officially named "El Camino Real," the "Highway of the King." Yes, he was a Catholic priest and under the authority of the king of Spain, but his heart and personal mission was totally surrendered to the King of Glory!

It was in 1769 that this Spanish Franciscan Father, with a heart for souls, accompanied Governor Gaspar de Portolà on an expedition to Nueva California.

It was then that he and some of his fellow Franciscans began establishing the twenty-one California Missions.

If I ever thought I was a fiery preacher I am reconsidering after reading about Serra. In his zeal Serra would employ extraordinary and dramatic means in order to move the people to repentance. He would pound his breast with a stone while in the pulpit, then scourge himself, and even apply a lit torch to his bare chest.

I will submit to you that I have never done that. Nor am I thinking about doing anything like it in the near future.

However, his extreme demonstrations often brought his native congregations to tears. Through these dramatic illustrations and sacrifices, the congregation became convinced of his humility and absolute devotion to God, as well as his dedication to bring the Gospel to them. This must be where the preacher got the line "if you can't say amen, say ouch!"

Excerpt from the book: **"Digging the wells of revival" By Lou Engles**

> On November 4, 1775, a group of Indians attacked and killed Father Luis Jayme at the mission in San Diego. The reaction of Father Serra to the news of his comrade's death speaks volumes about the attitudes of the early friars. Far from being disappointed and saddened, Father Serra said, "Thanks be to God; now that the terrain has been watered by blood, the conversion of the San Diego Indians will take place." His words echo the famous words of Tertullian, an early Church father, who said, "The blood of the martyrs is the seed of the Church." Immediately after this massacre, Serra wrote to the Viceroy asking for mercy for the Indians, reminding the Viceroy "that in case the Indians, whether pagans or Christians would kill me, they should be pardoned."
>
> Unfortunately, not all Spaniards who came to the New World shared Father Serra's apostolic view of sacrifice, and not all Spanish influence on California's soil was Godly. Often the missions became outposts of Spanish Imperialism from which the native people were oppressed. The common misconception of the colonial era was that before one could "Christianize" pagans, one had to first "civilize" them. This well-intentioned zeal to produce what was thought to be a superior and Godly culture resulted in a total, and often severe, subjugation of the Indians. Some

Indians genuinely turned to Christ, but many more conversions were the result of coercion. In fact, many native Californians suffered a virtual state of slavery as the padres enforced a Spanish lifestyle with a strict regime. The native peoples also suffered greatly, and their population plummeted drastically during the time of missions and the years immediately following, because of the introduction of European diseases and the interruption of conventional native lifestyles.

California, "The vineyard of the Lord"
Nevertheless, the fact remains that California was founded in Christian missions. This heritage has continued in recent generations, with missions activity from this state being far greater than from most other places in America. Many worldwide ministries have been birthed here. Father Serra's description of California as "the vineyard of the Lord" is likewise a covenantal name, prophesying of the fruitfulness that would spring from this state.

No doubt Serra would surely be defined as an extremist today. But I sincerely believe that his spirit of evangelism and his heart of love for the lost was a forerunner of God's plan for California. Serra had a deep and personal desire for the salvation and well-being of the aboriginal people in California. By all reports he was constantly at odds with the Spanish military leaders for standing for the rights and proper treatment of the Indians. At one point he traveled all the way to Mexico City to petition the Viceroy, the Spanish King's representative, to remove the abusive military leader and to approve his prepared document of what some would call a "Bill of Rights" for the natives. The Viceroy approved both of his requests.

Consequently, through his relentless and many times heroic efforts, the California Missions met with remarkable success. They accomplished the conversions of the majority of the natives on the Pacific coast as far as north as Sonoma.

"catch them in the nets of heaven" — Padre Junipero Serra

The Spanish colonization and the Mexican period
Spanish Rule: 1769 to 1821 ~ Mexican Rule: 1821 to 1846

During the Spanish colonization period of California, three main types of land claims were made by the Spanish crown. Missions were for religious use, Presidios were for military use, and Pueblos were for civilian use.

Land outside of these jurisdictions was granted to individuals by the Spanish and eventually, Mexican governments. These individual land grants were known as "Ranchos, or Spanish Land Grants." Soon the Californios established sprawling Ranchos, or cattle ranches throughout California. Most of the ranchers sold cattle hides, which were called "California bank notes" by the Boston shipping traders. They also sold them tallow and animal fat that was used to make candles and soap. Also exported were wines and citrus fruits.

But, all in all, before the Mexican American War and the discovery of gold, life was relatively quiet and laid back in California. It is estimated that there were less than fifteen thousand non-native people in California then.

"If My People …"

CHAPTER **7**

MEET JEDEDIAH STRONG SMITH GOD'S MOUNTAIN MAN
1799 - 1831

"Jedediah" means "Beloved of Jehovah"[1]

It is said of him that more than any other, "He was the one who 'opened the west.'"[1]

Jedediah Strong Smith

As we study the history of California and see the plan of God for the Golden State begin to unfold, it comes as no surprise that God's first man into the state over land and through the western frontier, was a Bible reading man of prayer with a name that means "Beloved of Jehovah."

Every account I read about "Diah," as his friends called him, makes clear mention of his Christianity. He was not your typical mountain man. Unlike classic mountain men, Jedediah Smith was quiet, unassuming and deeply religious. He was also revered by most in his day as the greatest of the breed. His dream since boyhood in New York State was to see and explore places in the west where no man had ever set foot. He had read everything he could get his hands on about Lewis and Clark, and their trek across the Northwest. On one of his earliest trapping expeditions, in his early twenties, he was assigned to lead a party with renowned men like Jim Bridger, Thomas "Broken Hand" Fitzpatrick, Jim Beckwourth and Mike Fink under him.

Jedediah Smith crossing the Mojave, by Frederick Remington

God sent His man first

Early in his career while still in his late twenties, Smith put his own company together, and then made two major trapping expeditions through California and the west coast. On one expedition in his career he had bagged seven hundred beaver pelts. The first California expedition was in 1826 and 1827 when he was only twenty-seven years old, and the second was in late 1827 and 1828. In the process he was the first white man "by land" to set foot in California. Contrary to the typical mountain man of the day, he was literate in English and Latin, and most importantly, he was a devout Bible reading man of prayer.

God picked a devout believer, with a name that means "Beloved of Jehovah" as His first man to walk and ride the Golden State. As he was exploring almost the entire west, Diah filled his journal describing the wonders of God's creation. When he faced hardship or peril, he looked to God through Scripture and prayer for strength. His best friends were his Bible and his rifle. Smith traveled and prayed his way through California from the Mojave desert to San Diego, then all the way up through the Great Valley and across the mountains to the coast, and to what is now, the Oregon border.

- He was the first white man to enter California by land from the east

- He was the first white man to cross the Sierra Nevada Mountains

- He was the first white man to trace a route from the inland valley through the Humboldt-Trinity Alps range to the Pacific (Smith River)

- He was the first American to travel from the Great Salt Lake to California by two different routes

- He was the first American to cross the southwestern part of the American continent. He then went all the way up through California to Fort Vancouver, Canada.

"Jedediah Strong Smith" was a highly intelligent and adventurous young man with exceptional moral character. Contrary to many in that profession, he was not a flaky deserter of his family or domestic responsibilities. In fact, he was quite the opposite.

One of the main objectives that drove him so passionately through all the hardships he faced, was his desire to send financial support to his aging parents back in New York. The fur business was a flourishing industry and Smith was determined to make enough money to help his family. As often as he could, he sent letters home to his family. In one letter he wrote:

> "It is a long time since I left home and I feel the need of the watch and care of a Christian Church -- you may well suppose that our society is of the roughest kind. Men of good morals seldom enter into business of this kind. I hope you will remember me before the throne of grace."

Another time in a letter he sent $2,200.00 home to his parents. As you can imagine, that was quite a sum of money in those days. He also helped support the care and schooling of his younger siblings.

As I state in the chapter, "The Seed of Original Intent," I sincerely believe God sent a holy man to be the first to travel overland, and enter and walk the land that He would one day use for world-wide revival. It was a rendezvous from heaven. The first overland explorer from America to set foot on California soil was a man of God called "Beloved of Jehovah."[2-7]

"If My People ..."

CHAPTER **8**

THE GOLD ~ HIDDEN IN PLAIN SIGHT
A Supernatural Veil

I have never heard this lectured or preached anywhere, but one of the major miracles of California's history has to be this one ...

God actually blinded the eyes of the people to the gold until He was ready to use it to open California and the west. It was "hidden in plain sight." He literally must have pulled a blind or blanket of passivity over the eyes and awareness of the inhabitants of the land. I say this because there are numerous reports that the Indians and the Spanish inhabitants of Old Californio were well aware of the abundance of gold in the Sierra foothills. Plus there had already been a small discovery near Los Angeles in 1842 that, strangely enough, nobody ever got excited about. The fact is that much of the placer gold, which is the nuggets and gold dust that you pan for in the creeks and rivers, was in plain view. Some reports have said that some of the nuggets were the size of bread loaves and were lying on top of the ground. It is well recorded that the first "forty-eighters and forty-niners" to arrive in the goldfields found easy pickings and many of them struck it rich in a very short time.

We all know that there is something about gold. It makes people go crazy with excitement; when they find it they can't keep their mouths shut. Yet, there was absolutely no fuss about the California gold until the territory was solidly in the hands of America.

So, without a "super-natural hush" how could it have been so quiet and passive? Only God could have kept a lid on that one. At the time, California was part of Mexico. Furthermore, besides America, there was a Spanish presence here, plus a British and Russian presence. France was also flirting with acquiring California. Like the poetic Californio officer, Arce, said, "California is like a pretty girl, everybody wants her." Yet gold was never an international issue and the final acquisition of California by America would be considered by most as a relatively passive and peaceful event with very few shootings and killings.

I will suggest to you, that had gold been "discovered" even a few months before it was, the U.S. acquisition of California would have caused the rivers and mountain streams to have run red with American and Mexican blood.

However, the gold of California lay here in the creeks and rivers in plain sight for thousands of years and man just couldn't see it, until …

"If My People …"

CHAPTER 9

The Conqueror of California
MEET JOHN CHARLES FREMONT
1813 ~ 1890

"Manifest Destiny"

John Charles Fremont, 1852 portrait, by William S. Jewett

THE GREAT PATHFINDER ~ EXPLORER ~ MAN OF GOD

Lt. Col. John Charles Fremont (later promoted to Major General during "The War Between the States") was the main catalyst used by God to secure California as American soil. Called "The Conqueror of California," he was the architect of the Bear Flag Revolt that established California as an independent Republic, and negotiated the Treaty of Campo de Cahuenga and the final surrender of General Andres Pico, the ruling commander of the Mexican forces. He was the first U.S. civilian Governor of California and the first U.S. Senator.

"The Young Eagle of the West"

The early Californios, which were the original Mexican residents, called him "The Young Eagle of the West."

Midge Sherwood's "Fremont: Eagle of the West"

I have studied the history of John Fremont for over 25 years and have read countless accounts of his adventures. However, a short time ago I discovered an excellent reading on him in a recent book by Midge Sherwood, "Fremont: Eagle of the West." It is the latest and best account with the most exhaustive, non-biased research of his explorations, relationship with the Lord and the controversial struggles with his adversaries that I have found. Much of my commentary here comes from this excellent resource.

A spiritual encounter ~ A story before the story

Before we begin Fremont's California story, I want to tell you another story about him and his wife Jessie that defines why I believe God chose him as the catalyst for California.

It was on his fifth expedition when he was exploring for a railroad passage through the Utah Rockies that this encounter takes place. It was late December of 1853 that the story begins. As they ascended through a pass in the Wasatch Range Fremont and his party encountered impassable snows and impossible conditions. Finally, he called a time out and went into council with his Delaware Indian staff. After they scouted the entire area, they said it was impossible to get through. But being the man of resolve and perseverance that he was, he quickly responded, "That's not the point," he replied, "we must cross; the question is, which is the most practicable – and how can we do it?"

This was the courage and determination that had driven him on all of his previous expeditions. It is the spirit behind "Manifest Destiny" that conquered California and opened the west to untold millions. Once he committed to an endeavor, he was never tempted to quit just because it was impossible. Once, at Fort Laramie on his first expedition, when he was told by the highly respected mountain man and guide Jim Bridger, and the friendly Laramie Indians, that to continue was certain ruin because the Sioux and Cheyenne Indians were in an up-roar, Kit Carson, his brave and quite capable guide, began making out his will.[1] He did that before Fremont gave his response because he knew Fremont. To him, the decision "to go or not to go" was already made at the beginning of the expedition.

Now, his present destination, or target, was the new little Mormon settlement of Parowan in the Little Salt Lake Valley just across the mountains. From the time they left Missouri, Parowan would be the first civilization they would experience. With the help of his Jewish friend and expedition photographer, Carvalho, he made his way that night to a high point in the snow and used the stars to take his bearings and determine his position and the direction to travel.

The next day he continued leading his party over mountains and through canyons that were thought to be impossible. Now without shoes some of the men wrapped rawhide around their feet. Fremont wore worn-out stockings and old moccasins. Regardless, freezing cold and half-starved, they pushed on. It was impossible to ride the horses so they had to lead them with each man following the one in front of him. If his calculations on the bearing of Parowan were off by one mile they would face total disaster.

December in the Rocky Mountains is no picnic today, let alone when no man, including Indians, had ever set foot over these mountain passes before. Finally, above the timber line, they made the summit. The entire group was astonished at the physical feat that they had accomplished. Fremont pointed the direction, and after a rest, they began the descent. Finally, after forty days of extreme hardship and near death from cold and starvation, on February 6, 1854, they emerged from the mountains, with what his men credited as supernatural guidance from Fremont. Parowan was right where Fremont said it would be.

Now here is where the story gets good. The Mormons immediately extended great hospitality to Fremont and his party. They fed and lodged all of his men. That night after making the rounds to say "a thankful good night" to his men he retired to his room. There by the log fire "with great relief of mind," he thanked God. It was then that he wished more than anything else he could tell Jessie that he and his party had arrived safely. He prayed fervently for the Lord to tell Jessie that they were indeed safe.

Now, let's switch to Jessie at her home in Washington. Of all their extreme experiences through the years, this time, for the first time, Jessie comes under the spirit of depression. She and John had just lost their little baby girl a month before this expedition, and now for the first time she had a premonition that he was starving to death. She was also pregnant with another child.

> "In midwinter," Jessie wrote later, "I became possessed by the conviction that he was starving; nor could any effort reason this away. No such impression had ever come to me before, although more than once dreadful suffering, and even death from starvation, had befallen his other expeditions."

This time she was unusually depressed, losing sleep and couldn't eat. Then one evening her sister and a cousin dropped by to cheer her up. They had just come from a wedding and they came to give an account of the bride and the festivities.

Jessie Benton Fremont

As they were making themselves comfortable, Jessie stepped into the next room to get some wood for the fireplace. When she knelt down to pick up a log, "a hand rested lightly on her shoulder."

Then she heard John's voice, "pleased and laughing," whisper her name!

"There was no sound beyond the quick-whispered name - no presence, only the touch and that was all," Jessie recorded later. When she returned to her sister and her cousin, before she said a word, her sister let out a cry and fell out on the floor. Her cousin then saw her and let out a startled cry, "What is it – what have you seen?" When she replied that John had touched her shoulder and spoke to her, her sister, usually calm and "steady nerved," started screaming, thinking she had at last lost her mind and had a nervous break down.

MEET JOHN CHARLES FREMONT

But Jessie was now calm and totally set free from depression. She had heard from heaven. God had answered John's "effectual fervent prayer" and touched her heart. Although it would be some time before she could confirm it, she was at peace in her heart that her husband was "now safe and light of heart." With the depression stronghold broken, for the first time, she slept well that night.

Later when she and John compared notes they were both astonished to confirm that at the precise moment he prayed that prayer in the little house in the wilderness of Parowan, Jessie had that encounter with the Lord and was totally set free!

So, without a doubt, the great pathfinder and conqueror of California, and his wife, were committed Christians. They were totally devoted to the Lord and they prayed prayers that moved God.[2]

The Main Trail

Now back to the main trail. Born in Savannah, Georgia in 1813, John C. Fremont was educated at College of Charleston where his teachers described his ability to learn as "phenomenal" and "amazing." One instructor, Dr. Roberton, a graduate of Edinburgh University, cited Fremont as a "genius."[3]

In 1838, he was appointed a Second Lieutenant in the Army Corps of Topographical Engineers. In 1841, he married Jessie Benton the daughter of Thomas Hart Benton, the very influential senior senator from Missouri. That marriage appears to have been made in heaven and very much a part of California's history and western America's "Manifest Destiny."

Raised in church by his widowed mother, young John had a heart for God and it manifested in many ways through the years and expeditions to come. Seeing his potential for spiritual things, his bishop suggested that he be trained for the ministry. He gave it great consideration before he ultimately chose science and engineering, which we now know was God's plan for his life.[4]

Fremont was totally devoted to Bible reading and memorized up to three hundred verses a day. He continued his Bible studies throughout his career as an explorer. According to Solomon Nunes Carvalho, Fremont's Jewish artist, photographer and daguerreotypist for the fifth expedition, who was educated by leaders of the Jewish Reform movement, Fremont displayed "supernatural powers" to guide his men through some of the impossible situations that they encountered. His favorite hymn was appropriately, "Lead Kindly Light."[5]

California is destined to be a world leader in the things of God. So, it is no surprise that God hand-picks His own to lead the way and establish the land for His purpose.

"Manifest Destiny"
From Sea to Shining Sea ~ The Will of God

The term "Manifest Destiny" has its roots in the westward expansion "cause" in Congress. The original architect of the movement, although he didn't coin the term, is credited to Thomas Jefferson, who was convinced of the importance of the concept after the success of The Louisiana Purchase. The adherents to that doctrine, "the expansionists," sincerely believed that it was "God's will" that the North American continent, from the east coast to the west coast, should belong to the citizens of the United States, and that getting those lands was the country's "Manifest Destiny."

Senator Benton, also known as "Old Bullion," for his doctrine of the gold standard, was the powerful champion of the westward expansionist movement in Congress. It is said that his fervor for the movement began many years before in a private meeting with Thomas Jefferson. It was Benton that pushed appropriations through Congress for surveys of the Oregon Trail in 1842, the Oregon Territory in 1844, the Great Basin, and Sierra Mountains to California in 1845.

Senator Thomas Hart Benton ~ Old Bullion

Consequently, through his power and influence, Benton got Fremont the leadership of those expeditions. It should also be noted that Jessie was a prolific writer. Fremont was a brilliant explorer and educated scientist and engineer and he kept detailed reports of his explorations. Jessie would then write articles from his stories and the reports, and they were published nationally. Consequently, Fremont literally became an international legend in his own time. His name became a household word on two continents, America and Europe. This in turn helped Benton get support for the expansion movement.

There is another prophetic ring here in Benton's nickname "Old Bullion." As one of the key players in the acquisition of California, now known as The Golden State, and the ensuing gold rush, it is interesting that he was in essence called

MEET JOHN CHARLES FREMONT

"Old Gold." In fact, today, just ten minutes north of the town of Mariposa, right on Highway 49 which runs through the heart of the Mother Lode, is the old gold mining town of Mount Bullion. It was the town built for the Princeton Mine which was the most successful mine in the Mariposa Mining District.

Many people mistakenly assume that the name Bullion given to the town was derived from the gold bullion, but that is not exactly the case. Jumping a little ahead of the story here, just before gold was discovered the Fremonts wound up owning an old Spanish Land Grant called "Rancho de Las Mariposas." It was a forty-four thousand acre tract that, to everyone's surprise, included the southern portion of the main gold vein called the California Mother Lode. John and Jessie eventually moved there and began mining the area. It was then that they built Mariposa. They also built and named the town of Mount Bullion in honor of her dad by using his nickname.

Now, back to this marriage and family relationship that I believe was dove-tailed for a master plan. I don't think it is a stretch to acknowledge that this family trio has the hand of God written all over it. I believe it is one of those coincidences that people tend to overlook. The Fremont/Benton relationship was clearly part of God's plan for America. God used them in a big and effective way.

Fremont and The Bear Flag Revolt

"I saw the way clear before me. War with Mexico was inevitable; and a grand opportunity now presented itself to realize the farsighted views of Senator Benton, and make the Pacific Ocean the western boundary of the United States."
John C. Fremont

The Bear Flag Revolt

Now to, "the rest of the story," as Paul Harvey would say. It was on Fremont's third expedition that began in 1845, with Kit Carson as his guide that "Manifest Destiny" kicked into high gear. Under the disguise of another mapping and exploration venture Fremont was somewhat secretly commissioned by an elite Washington group including Senator Benton, President Polk and other expansionist members of congress, to initiate a revolt to acquire California from Mexico.

It was on that expedition that The Bear Flag Revolt was initiated. Fremont was the main catalyst or architect of the movement. I am admittedly making a longer story very brief but through some various maneuvers and a secret Washington arrangement with the Navy Commodore (first Sloat then Stockton) who was anchored and headquartered in Monterey, the plan succeeded.

On June 14, 1846, Fremont sent a small rough-looking band of militia from his camp in the Sacramento Valley to the home and expansive rancho of the Mexican military leader of northern California, Comandante Mariano Vallejo at Sonoma. In an almost humorous encounter Vallejo, who was actually secretly in favor of the succession of California to the United States, invited the invaders in to sit down and have a glass of wine and enjoy a bit of camaraderie … an invitation which they politely accepted. In fact they were so polite and respectful of the hospitality that in a short while several of them could barely walk. At that table in his parlor Vallejo peacefully surrendered his military garrison to this unlikely group of trappers and ranchers dressed in coonskin caps, buckskin trousers and greasy shirts. But to his surprise, by Fremont's orders, he was then put under arrest and taken to Fremont who had by this time moved to Sutter's Fort.

Now, with the departure of Vallejo from Sonoma, The California Republic was born. It was probably at dawn the following day of June 15 that the Bear Flag was raised in Sonoma. Following this, Fremont secured Sutter's Fort's surrender and then with the collaboration of the Navy, and a small a skirmish or two, they secured all of northern California.

The Golden Gate ~ Prophetic Act
On July 1 of 1846 John Fremont and his band of ten men, including Kit Carson, crossed San Francisco Bay from San Rafael and went to the old Spanish Presidio at Fort Point. There, as a triumphant and conquering gesture, he ceremoniously spiked the old obsolete Spanish cannons that overlooked the entrance to San Francisco Bay from the Pacific Ocean. At the same time he renamed the straight where the famous bridge now spans to "The Golden Gate." In his memoirs, he later wrote, "To this gate I gave the name of 'Chrysopylae,' or 'Golden Gate.'

Up until this time it was called "Boca del Puerto de San Francisco," or in English, "Mouth of the Port of San Francisco."

This is another point that I have never heard lectured or preached. Folks, "The Golden Gate" is literally, and metaphorically, the main entrance to California. Indeed, it represents the main western entrance to The United States of America. <u>This is a year and a half 'before' gold is discovered</u> in the hills to the east. This is where the heavy traffic of ships loaded with people and supplies are soon to be passing, going to and from the goldfields of the newly acquired California. Gold seekers and people looking for a new life will be going in through "the Gate," and ships laden with gold will be sailing out of "the Gate" carrying tons of gold around the world and dramatically affecting the world's economy.

It is of no coincidence that, at this particular time in history, God was literally changing the name of the entrance to California at the very time He was establishing the land for His Glory. Here through Fremont and his little band of men, God was literally and prophetically opening the gate to California.

De-commissioning those cannons is similar to a new Godly King of Israel pulling down the groves, and tearing down the altars of pagan worship. Remember, Fremont and his "Manifest Destiny" backers in Washington truly believe that it is God's will for America to prevail "from Sea to Shining Sea."

GOD, GOLD & GLORY! ~ 2

Looking past the gold rush we will see that **God** had big things in mind for the Golden State. As we are revealing in the pages of this book, He was destined to impact the nations with the "Good News of Jesus Christ and a fresh outpouring of the Holy Spirit" like no place on earth had ever done before. For example, a mere sixty years from this date of Fremont's ceremonial act; The Lord's real **Gold**, His Spirit, was being poured out to the nations from The Golden State through the mighty 1906 Azusa Street Revival. And that is only the beginning of the story. California was established for His **Glory!**

So, the timing of this name change of such a strategic place should not be surprising to students of the Bible who have a basic understanding of how God works. Historically God has established a pattern of changing the names of places or people when He is fixing to do something big. God, through man, speaks or prophesies things into being. These name changes initiate a prophetic proclamation of the coming manifestation. Like Abram to Abraham, "a father of multitudes," or Jacob to Israel, "the name of His nation," or Simon to Peter, "a rock," or Jerusalem, "City of Peace," just to name a few.

So, in the middle of the summer of 1846, during the war with Mexico to conquer California, and just before the impending Gold Rush that literally opened the west, that very strategic harbor entrance to California became The Golden Gate.

Just in time ~ The British are coming!

Then a few days later on July 7, 1846, a Captain of the American Navy went ashore in Monterey with 250 Marines. With little Mexican military resistance, he led his men to the Customs House and read aloud the declaration that California now belonged to the United States. The marines gave loud cheers and the ships in the harbor followed with a twenty-one-gun salute.

All this was just in time. Remember, saints, God is never late! Contrary to what we think sometimes, He is always on time. The English warship, H.M.S. Collingwood, the Flagship of the British fleet, the largest ever sent into the Pacific, which had been playing hide-and-seek in Mexican waters, had just rounded the point. As the story goes, when the British Admiral Seymour saw the United States warships in the harbor and the American Flag flying over Monterey, "he flung his hat to the deck and stomped his foot in rage!" [6]

Then just two days later on July 9, 1846, by direction of the Navy Commodore, Commander Montgomery took seventy men ashore at the tiny pueblo of Yerba Buena (now called San Francisco), marched them to the public square and read the proclamation and raised a second American flag.

Thus, the 25 day legacy of The California Republic was already over, and "Manifest Destiny" for America was already nearing fulfillment.

Now after several thousand years of belonging to the Indians, two hundred and seventy-nine years as a province of Spain, twenty-five years as a Mexican province, and twenty-five days as The California Republic, California had now become American soil. Now there was only one maneuver left to secure California once and for all. Two forces remained to oppose the Americans, General Castro and Governor Pio Pico to the south.

Making another story very short, Fremont and Navy Commodore R.F Stockton sailed south to encounter any remaining adversary and end the conflict. When news of this coming invasion reached Pico and Castro they both fled south to Mexico. Consequently Fremont and Stockton marched into Los Angeles and took possession. They then sent Kit Carson back east to Washington to inform President Polk that California was now secured under the American flag. At that point they then left Captain Archibald Gillespie and fifty soldiers in charge and returned to Monterey.

However, the conquest was not quite over. Gillespie tried to be too strict with the Californios and they drove him out of Los Angeles. A number of the southern Californios rose up to fight for their land. Now General Andreas Pico, the cousin of Governor Pio Pico, was in charge of the small Californio "make-shift" but witty and well-mounted army. Commodore Stockton then sent reinforcements to help Gillespie but the Americans were defeated in a battle at Dominguez Ranch.

Stockton then sailed to San Diego and marched north toward Los Angeles. Fremont formed the California Battalion, an imposing force including his fierce fighting Delaware Indians, a company of Marines, mountain men, and sharpshooters, and rode south along the coast. Fremont's California Battalion was over four hundred strong.

At the same time U.S. Army General Steven Watts Kearny with three hundred soldiers, not knowing exactly what was happening in the acquisition, had entered the southeastern corner of California. He had been told by Kit Carson who met him on his way east that California had been secured. Kearny forced Carson to return to California with him. He was at first unaware that there was a revolt taking place. A short while later his unit was soundly defeated by Mexican General Pico in the Battle of San Pasqual, which is near present day Escondido. As it turns out, that defeat was the worse spanking the Americans took in the entire California crusade. The losses were significant and Kearny himself was wounded in the battle.

He was again outmaneuvered by the Californios at San Bernardino ranch. Finally, after joining forces with Stockton they won the Battle of San Gabriel and they prevailed in another skirmish with the Californios just south of Los Angeles. On January 10 they raised the American Flag in the plaza at Los Angeles.

Meanwhile, Fremont was engaged with Californio General Pico at Campo de Cahuenga which is in present day North Hollywood just north of Los Angeles. It seems that General Pico, after seeing Fremont's California Battalion, realized that victory was hopeless and he had no stomach to surrender to either Stockton or Kearny. However, Fremont had previously created much good will with the Californios and was favored over Stockton and Kearny. So Fremont had the famous "Treaty of Campo de Cahuenga" drafted. It was actually drafted by Captain José Antonio Ezequiel Carrillo, a Californio rancher, officer, and politician. It was drafted in English and Spanish and it granted Pico a friendly and generous peace. The treaty, signed by Fremont and Pico, allowed the Californios to return to their homes with honor and dignity. It also granted surrendering Californios all the rights enjoyed by Americans. The entire encounter between Pico and Fremont took place without either side firing a shot.

Now, here is one for you ladies ~ Meet Donna Bernard Ruiz
During our research for this book Grace and I visited the historic park at Campo de Cahuenga, which is now across the street from Studio City and the NBC building in North Hollywood. The park is a historic museum located on the grounds of the pueblo where Fremont and Pico signed the treaty. The day we were there the facility was closed to the public and although no work was going on at the time, it was in the process of restoration.

However, as it happened, a small group of officials were there for just a few minutes discussing the renovation. I was able to slip through a partially open gate while Grace was parking the car. They were actually just leaving and were going to lock the gate. When they saw me I was sure I was going to get the left foot of fellowship. However, when I shared with them a bit about this book they were very receptive. One of the group members was Guy McCreary, Chairman of the Board of the Memorial Historical Association. Guy graciously stayed behind and gave us a quick private narrated tour of the grounds and we even traded Fremont stories. It was a divine appointment. We learned more, and made better contact at the closed facility than we would have had it been open to the public. In addition, before we left, Guy showed us a small memorial plaque that was in the center of the grounds. It was a memorial to Donna Bernard Ruiz.

As the history goes, when Fremont and his battalion were on their way south but still in the Santa Barbara area, he was convinced by Californio General Don Jesus Pico, another cousin to Pio and Andreas Pico, to talk to Donna Bernard Ruiz. Pico told Fremont that Senora Ruiz was very well connected with the families and the social mind set and spirit of the region. She could help him draft a treaty that would best benefit both sides, and would treat the Californios with integrity and honor. Historians say that Fremont visited her Hacienda but expected a short half hour or so meeting. However after meeting her and perceiving her personal demeanor and substance of character, that meeting lasted several hours. In that meeting she outlined to Fremont many of the central ideas that led to the quick success and permanency of the treaty.

This lady played a key role in the history of this state and yet little is said about her. We couldn't even find her listed in "Google." Had Guy not shown us that little memorial and told us the story I too would have passed her up in the chronicles of this book.

Fremont & his California Battalion

The plaque honoring Donna Ruiz - Campo de Cahuenga Historic Park

Seeds of Equality

As God's man for California, Fremont was a staunch believer in freedom and had no use for slavery. He honored his wife and his mother in a very respectable and Godly way. He also kept Native Americans in his exploratory party at all times and respected their expertise of the land. Fremont went to great lengths to develop and maintain a relationship with the Native Californios, or Mexicans. He also had the deep respect of his men because even in the severest crisis he was always a gentleman and constantly treated them as such.

Furthermore, it is very interesting that, under his prayerful leadership, the very document that secured California was greatly influenced by a woman. God has a way of evening things up. In the very beginning of California's history as American soil, the seeds of equality were sown. God did the same kind of thing when He put the world-wide revival at Azusa Street under the leadership of an uneducated one-eyed black man named William J. Seymour.

So, concerning Senora Ruiz and the treaty, as is many times the case, the men can fight and shoot and make a lot of noise, but in the end it takes a woman to straighten it all out. Can I get an amen, Ladies?

Conquest complete once and for all

So, with the treaty written and signed, on January 14, 1847 Fremont marched his California Battalion through the Cahuenga Pass to Los Angeles. He entered it four days after its surrender to Navy Commodore Stockton. The conquest of California was now complete. Fremont presented the treaty to Stockton, who immediately approved it.

In a little more than six months, in a combined effort of Lieutenant Colonel Fremont, with his California Battalion, and the U.S. Navy Commodore, America had seized and pacified the whole area that is, today, the state of California.

To Fremont's credit, the Treaty of Campo de Cahuenga brought peace with honor, allowing both nationalities in California to calmly assimilate into the United States.

One year later the Treaty of Campo de Cahuenga was consolidated into the final treaty of Guadalupe Hidalgo of February 2, 1848, between the United States and Mexico. Now all disputes between America and Mexico were settled and laid to rest. California was now America!

Campo de Cahuenga to Azusa Street ~ 10 miles and 60 years

It is more than interesting that the location of the signing of the treaty at Campo de Cahuenga was less than 10 miles from the location of Azusa Street in Los Angeles. Little did those players know that in a mere 59 to 60 years, in that very vicinity, God would change the world spiritually and launch latter-day Pentecost.

Campo de Cahuenga Historic park, Now North Hollywood

THERE IS MUCH MORE TO THE FREMONT STORY

Fremont was a man that did the impossible on a regular basis. When he committed to an endeavor he didn't let negative circumstances dictate whether he continued on or not. Those things had already been decided. Among other things, on separate expeditions, he crossed both the Wasatch Mountain Range in Utah, and the High Sierras in California (from east to west) in the dead of winter. Even the Indians told him it was impossible. Kit Carson and other noted mountain men were constantly amazed at the incredible things they accomplished under his leadership that no human had ever done before.

⤺ GOD, GOLD & GLORY!

A quote from Kit Carson

Kit Carson

"I was with Frémont from 1842 to 1847. The hardships through which we passed I find it impossible to describe, and the credit which he deserves I am incapable of doing him justice in writing. But his services to his country have been left to the judgment of impartial freemen, and all agree in saying that his services were great and have redounded to his honor and that of his country. I can never forget his treatment of me while in his employ and how cheerfully he suffered with his men when undergoing the severest of hardships. His perseverance and willingness to participate in all that was undertaken, no matter whether the duty was rough or easy, is the main cause of his success. And I say without fear of contradiction, that none but him could have surmounted and succeeded through as many difficult services, as his was." Col. Cristopher Carson, 1856 [7]

It would be impossible in a section of this book to tell all of the incredible stories of Fremont and his five expeditions. His heroic feats of courage and perseverance in fierce and very dangerous conditions would take a large volume by itself. He and Jessie were very much in love with each other and they endured many months and years of loneliness, and personal self denial and comfort. John suffered deep snows, Indian attacks, frost-bite, starvation, days without water, and exhaustion many times. There was also an unfortunate court martial instigated by a very jealous and resentful General Kearney.

As stated at the beginning of this chapter, Fremont went on to be the Governor and then Senator of California. In 1856 he was the Republican nominee for President of the United States. He was first offered the Democratic ticket for President, which was considered a shoo-in, but he would have had to compromise his anti-slavery principles and some other political ethics, so he and Jessie declined the offer.

His name was a household word on two continents (America and Europe) and today his name is found everywhere you go, especially in the west. There is barely a town that doesn't have a Fremont Street or boulevard. Hospitals and schools are named after him. The city of Fremont, California is named for him as are cities in several other states, even as far east as New Hampshire. Two mountains, a river and a bridge are also named after him. His name literally indicates freedom.

I believe that God raises up men and women at particular times in history to accomplish His will in the earth. Abraham, Moses, Deborah, Esther and David were such vessels. John Winthrop, George Washington, Abraham Lincoln and Ronald Reagan would also qualify here. In that same spirit, I think it is no stretch at all to say that John Charles Fremont was God's man of the hour for the "Manifest Destiny" of California.

At one point in Monterey right after they had raised the American Flag there, and in San Francisco and Sonoma, Fremont had a reflective moment as quoted from Midge Sherwood's book, Fremont: The Eagle of the West:

> As Fremont watched from the Point of Pines (now Point Pinos in Pacific Grove) he suddenly caught sight of the banner on the American Flagship, Savannah. He mused that as Savannah was his birthplace, the Savannah of the seas presided over the birth of California.
>
> A coincidence? Perhaps. But still it seemed to Fremont, in this solitary moment alone with God, that it confirmed his destiny.
>
> Fremont would remember the entire California adventure as a grand chessboard. The players were great military men, dedicated statesmen and women, and he was 'but a pawn.' And like a pawn, I had been pushed forward at the opening of the game."

However, history would record it differently: The Queen had fallen to the courageous game plan of "a pawn."[8]

It was said in his day by people in Washington that "the Story of Fremont is the story of California." But for the sake of staying on the subject of California we

◄ GOD, GOLD & GLORY!

will continue that history at this point.

This painting (circa 1872) by John Gast, called "American Progress," is an allegorical representation of "Manifest Destiny."

This painting (circa 1872) by John Gast, called "American Progress," is an allegorical representation of "Manifest Destiny." Here, Columbia, intended as an angelic personification of the spirit of America, leads civilization westward with American settlers, stringing telegraph wire as she travels. She holds a book, which can be interpreted as the Bible or a schoolbook, depending upon ones personal view. Notice the darkness in front of her as she brings the light of America westward. The different economic activities of the pioneers are highlighted, and especially the changing forms of transportation. Before her all wildness flees.

Although the principle began with George Washington and Thomas Jefferson, and as far back as the pilgrims, it was journalist John L. O'Sullivan in 1845 who is first credited with the first usage of the phrase "Manifest Destiny." He, like the forefathers, believed that Providence (God's divine plan) had given the United States a mission to spread republican democracy ("the great experiment of liberty") throughout North America.[9]

"If My People ..."

CHAPTER **10**

EUREKA!
NOW THE BLINDS ARE REMOVED & GOLD IS "DISCOVERED!"

"Eureka," the California state motto, means "I have found it." On January 24, 1848, James Marshall "discovered" gold at Sutter's Mill. Again, it had been obvious to the inhabitants of the land all along. The gold had been rumored, written about and talked about, but now it is "discovered."

This has to be a move of God because it is beyond one's capability to calculate the odds of the timing. It reminds me of Elisha when he is leading the Syrian Army around blind until he has them right where he wants them, and then the Lord opens their eyes.

"And it came to pass, when they were come to Samaria, that Elisha said, Lord, open the eyes of these men, that they may see. And the Lord opened their eyes, and they saw." (2 Kings 6:20)

California as a piece of real estate is as old as any place on earth. The gold had been there in plain sight throughout the ages. Normally I don't like referring to an act of God as "divine providence." It seems to be too impersonal by implicating that something happened by some deity somewhere for some kind of mysterious master plan. But if the term ever applied to anything in a revelatory way I believe it could apply here. By "divine providence," which by my application, is the Lord's direct and on-purpose plan for America, man could not see or get excited about the gold until God said so. It was only when He was ready that He removed the veil. It gives the second half of Isaiah 22:22 fresh meaning, *"... so He shall open and none shall shut; and He shall shut and none shall open."*

> "It was a clear cold morning I shall never forget," wrote James Marshall in his diary on January 24, 1848. "My eye was caught with the glimpse of something shining in the bottom of the ditch. I reached my hand down and picked it up; it made my heart thump, for I was certain it was gold. Then I saw another piece. Putting one of the pieces on a hard river stone, I took another and commenced hammering. It was soft and didn't break; it therefore must be gold."[1]

With these words, James Marshall recorded his discovery of the substance that would change California forever. Now practically overnight California would transform from a sleepy territory into the fastest-growing state in the rapidly expanding United States of America. Within months of Marshall's discovery, word had spread that there was gold throughout the streams and hills of north central California. It wasn't long until thousands of gold-hungry prospectors were pouring in from all over the world in what is now known as "The Great California Gold Rush."

One account said "Gold seemed to be everywhere, lodged among the rocks, glittering in sand bars, swirling in pools and eddies." "My little girls can make from 5 to 25 dollars per day washing gold in pans" a miner wrote home to Missouri. In those days, in America, a man worked long hours for a dollar to a dollar and a half a day.

Lieutenant William Tecumseh Sherman, accompanied by Colonel R.B. Mason, the military governor of California, took an official tour of the goldfields and they were stunned by what they saw. "I have no hesitation now" Mason wrote, "in saying there is more gold in the country drained by the Sacramento and San Joaquin rivers than will pay for the war with Mexico ten times over."

There were so many reports of gold strikes that the teachers, merchants, doctors, lawyers, sailors and sea captains all abandoned their posts and left for the goldfields. When the news reached President Polk in Washington he told congress,

> "The abundance of gold in that territory (California) are of such extraordinary character as would scarcely command belief were they not corroborated by authentic reports of officers in public service."

Thomas O. Larkin, the American Consul to Mexico, wrote:

> "Everyone had gold or yellow fever. Nine-tenths of every storekeeper, mechanic and day laborer leave for Sacramento."[2]

A prophetic Don ~ Father knows best

However, it was Don Luís María Peralta who spoke the words of spiritual revelation to his family. At ninety years old, Don Luis was a Californio rancher and had been a soldier in the Spanish King's Army before the Mexican period. Throughout the California acquisition he had been allowed to keep ownership of his huge land grant, "Rancho San Antonio." It was an area that now includes much of the east bay and the cities of Berkeley, Oakland and Alameda.

When everyone was succumbing to the fever and running off to the goldfields he said,

> "My sons, God has given this gold to the Americans. Had He desired us to have it, He would have given it to us ere now. Therefore go not after it, but let others go. Plant your lands, and reap; these be your best gold fields, for all must eat while they live."[3]

The family honored the words spoken by the wise father and remained on the land and worked it. Within a year the old gentlemen's prophetic words manifested true. Their food and herds of cattle were more valuable than gold as California was instantly flooded with tens of thousands of people.

"If My People ..."

CHAPTER 11

THE WORLD RUSHED IN ~ THE 49'ers

The California gold rush was the largest migration of people in the entire history of America. Some accounts say over three hundred thousand, and other reports say over a half million adventurers made their way to California.

Today when you hear somebody say "the '49ers" you think of the National Football League and the San Francisco football team (although I'm a dyed-in-the-wool Dallas Cowboys fan). But that football team was named after the real '49ers.

Marshall discovered the gold at Sutter's Mill in January of 1848, but due to the antiquated, or should I say, non-existent, communication and transportation systems of the time it was late in the year before the news reached the east coast. There was, however, a relatively small rush of several thousand people to the goldfields in '48 by the people in the area and ships that were already in the Pacific. However, when the news hit the newspapers in the east and when President Polk officially announced it to Congress in late '48, the '49er Gold Rush was on.

By the time 1849 arrived, the news was around the world .. Gold! Gold! Gold in California! The great migration was under way. Although the rush began in 1849, it was actually late in the year before most of the people began arriving. Whether they traveled by land or sea the journey was extremely arduous and it took months to get there.

But be assured, to use the term "rush" is quite appropriate here. By 1850, California's American and European population had increased tenfold. San Francisco alone grew from a sleepy village of less than five hundred to a bustling city of thirty-five thousand people. Ships that docked in San Francisco Bay at the height of the fever risked losing their entire crews to the goldfields. The state's non-Indian population increased from about fourteen thousand before the discovery to nearly a quarter million by 1852. Although most of the "forty-niners" were from the United States, and all states were represented, this migration was also a global event, drawing gold seekers from the islands of the sea, east Asia, Chile, Mexico, and western Europe. For the United States it was the largest mass migration to date, flooding the previously lightly traveled trails to the West Coast. A fair percentage of the nation's population moved to California in just a few years. One report I read said there were over seven hundred ships anchored and rotting in San Francisco Bay. Many of the ships were actually salvaged for their lumber and materials. They used the cannons and hardware in the foundries and blacksmith shops and melted them down for construction and mining equipment.

Gold Rush ships in San Francisco ~ Many were abandoned

Here is an excerpt from an article I read ~ The California Dream

Between 1847 and 1870, the population of San Francisco increased from 500 to 150,000. The Gold Rush wealth and population increase led to significantly improved transportation between California and the East Coast. The Panama Railway, spanning the Isthmus of Panama, was finished in 1855. Steamships, including those owned by the Pacific Mail Steamship Company, began regular service from San Francisco to Panama, where passengers, goods and mail would take the train across the Isthmus and board steamships headed to the East Coast. One ill-fated journey, that of the S.S. *Central America*, ended in disaster as the ship sank in a hurricane off the coast of the Carolinas in 1857, with an estimated three tons of California gold aboard.

Fair weather on the deck of a clipper-ship carrying gold seekers to California

The journey to California ~ Emigrants crossing "The Rocky Mountains"

Within a few years after the end of the Gold Rush, in 1863, the groundbreaking ceremony for the western leg of the First Transcontinental Railroad was held in Sacramento. The line's completion, some six years later, financed in part with Gold Rush money, united California with the central and eastern United States. Travel that had taken weeks or even months could now be accomplished in days.

The Gold Rush stimulated economies around the world as well. Farmers in Chile, Australia, and Hawaii found a huge new market for their food; British manufactured goods were in high demand; clothing and even pre-fabricated houses arrived from China. The return of large amounts of California gold to pay for these goods raised prices and stimulated investment and the creation of jobs around the world. Australian prospector, Edward Hargraves, noting similarities between the geography of California and his home, returned to Australia to discover gold and spark the Australian gold rushes.

California's name became indelibly connected with the Gold Rush, and as a result, was connected with what became known as the "California Dream." California was perceived as a place of new beginnings, where hard work and good luck, could reward great wealth. Historian H. W. Brands noted that in the years after the Gold Rush, the California Dream spread to the rest of the United States and became part of the new "American Dream."[1]

Instant statehood & multi-million dollar economy
True to the spirit of California, things were happening quickly. In 1850, California was admitted to statehood as the 31st state. In less than four years, it transformed from an unpopulated Mexican territory, that was thought to be too far away and too hard to get to, into a prosperous and fast-growing state. In fact, I believe it is safe to say that because of the gold, in its first year as a state, California's GDP (Gross Domestic Product) was the largest in the nation. That's my guess, without researching all of the states GDP revenues for 1850.

According to the California Division of Mines & Geology, Bulletin 193, over 106 million ounces of gold was mined in California by the mid 1960's. That would translate to over 100 billion dollars at today's gold prices. However, when I talked to the managing ranger at the California State Mining and Mineral Museum in Mariposa, he said no one knows for sure how much gold really came out of California, because no one was recording all of it. Most people just took their gold, and that was it. So the CDMG figure is just what they know about. All we know is that the gold that was recorded amounted to many multi-millions of dollars. And that was when gold only brought twenty dollars an ounce. So, millions of dollars was an astronomical number in relation to the economy of the time, especially when you consider that today, as of this writing, gold is selling at closer to a thousand dollars (over 50 times the 1850 price) per ounce.

During the Gold Rush much of the gold was sent back east and to other nations, but a good portion also stayed in California. San Francisco and Sacramento were now prospering cities. The California gold fields established San Francisco's financial district as the Wall Street of the west. Many prominent international banks, including Bank of America and Wells Fargo, were established there during the Gold Rush.

Although the Gold Rush was relatively short-lived, its lasting effects are undeniable. It literally crushed the anti-expansionist mindset and silenced them forever. California and the entire west coast was now on the map and booming. More towns and cities sprang up all over.

Unfortunately, however, many of the gold seekers arrived too late for the quick and easy riches that they dreamed of. Some of them returned home broke and disillusioned. Because of the hundreds of thousands of miners which were working every stream and looking under every rock, most of the placer or surface gold was pretty well removed by the mid-1850s. However, many of the adventurers found the region quite livable and stayed and settled in and sent down roots. The climate was temperate and the soil was fertile. It was a great place to start a whole new life.

In addition, many made the journey to the land of opportunity never intending to mine for gold, but to establish businesses, farms and ranches in what was now a fast-growing economy and a land of promise. Not only did the new population create a market for business, but millions of dollars of gold were still being pumped into the economy by the established gold mining companies, which continued for many years.

California's gold and the Civil War
In the first years of "The War Between the States" President Lincoln appointed John C. Fremont as Major General and placed him in command of the Department of the West, based in St. Louis, Missouri. Because of the main war effort, the assignment came, however, without enough money to properly supply and manage the command. Consequently, Fremont had his own gold shipped in from his Mariposa mines and personally helped finance the U.S Military's Department of the West.

Untold millions dollars of California's gold also supported the Union Army in general.

> "I do not know what we would do in this great national emergency were it not for the gold sent from California," Gen. Ulysses S. Grant once wrote.

"If My People ..."

CHAPTER **12**

THE GOLD IS STILL HERE

Although it is a mere shadow of its former glory days there is still a bit of mining activity going on here in gold country today. The streams and rivers still yield "color" to the ones that are willing to work for it. It is common to pan a local stream and get "color," (gold dust or nuggets) in your pan, particularly after heavy rains wash new material down. It just takes a lot of work. Nonetheless, frequently there are still good veins found from time to time.

It runs in the family
My son-in-law, Trent Davis, is a professional fourth generation miner. He has several claims here in the Mariposa area. He works them when he can, that is when he is not working for large mining companies elsewhere, and he frequently finds gold. A couple of years ago he made me a handsome bolo tie, and Grace a beautiful broach from large quarter sized nuggets from one of his diggings. I wear and show off my bolo tie (and brag about my family) a lot when I preach around the world.

It is common knowledge here in gold country, but some of you readers might find it interesting to know that the professional miners and geologists tell us that "between eighty and ninety percent of the gold is still in the ground." In many places they know right where it is, and how it assays out at ounces per ton of ore. The problem is that at its present price, and strict environmental laws, much of it is too expensive to mine. Many miners are holding their claims waiting for the price of gold to go up. If it ever hits several thousand dollars an ounce like some predict there will be another gold rush in California.

In fact, Trent recently told me that some experts speak of three different areas in the Mother Lode with over a million ounces each. One of those areas is less than 10 miles from our town of Mariposa.

Billions to trillions still here

Just using some round numbers for an estimation of the value of gold still in the ground in California, let's do some figuring. Starting with the 106 million recorded ounces mined by the 1960s, let's guess that between the gold mined in the forty years since, and the gold that wasn't recorded in the first place, that 130 million ounces has come out of California. I am sure it is much more but let's just be extra conservative and use that figure.

So now, if 130 million ounces is approximately fifteen percent of the total gold in the ground in the first place, then we can estimate that there were at least 870 million ounces of gold in California. Eighty-five percent of that would be approximately 740 million ounces still here. At $1,000 per ounce that would mean that 740 billion dollars worth of gold is still here. However if gold goes to $2,000 to $3,000 an ounce like many predict, that number goes into the trillions.

"The gold is Mine says the Lord!"

It is just possible that God has reserved the best for last.

" … and I will fill this house with glory, saith the LORD of hosts. The silver is mine, and the gold is mine, saith the LORD of hosts. The glory of this latter house shall be greater than of the former, saith the LORD of hosts …" (Haggai 2:7-9)

So, the long and the short of it is;

In the true spirit of America, California was claimed and Americanized by a Christian government for the purpose of expanding a Godly nation to the Pacific Ocean. Fremont and the founding fathers did not initially come for the gold or furs or earthly treasures, as had the earlier explorers.

The expansion was in keeping with the heart of the original Pilgrims who settled in Massachusetts a little over two hundred and twenty years before. So, as I wrote in a previous chapter, the words of John Winthrop in his sermon "A Model of Christian Charity," where he speaks of America as, "A City Upon a Hill," rang as clear for California as they did for that first tiny little colony in 1630.

God, Gold & Glory! 3

As we are discovering in the pages of this book, God had an awesome plan to use California as a place of uncommon spiritual "export" to the nations. Its part as a major player on the world scene was just around the corner. **God** obviously used the **Gold,** and "the gold rush," for His own timing, and to explode California and the American west into its "Manifest Destiny" for His **Glory**.

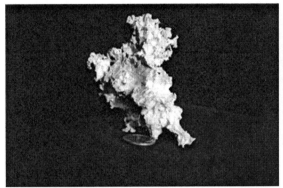

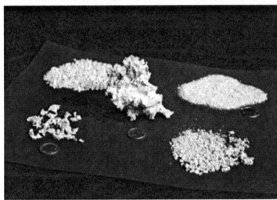

"These gold specimens were recently mined by my son-in-law, Trent Davis, in one of the local Mariposa mines. Dimes are shown for size reference."

"If My People ..."

CHAPTER **13**

The Prophetic Symbolism of ...
YOSEMITE'S FAMOUS FIREFALLS
1871-1968 ~ For almost 100 years

In 1997, during one of our "Feast of Fire Revival" meetings (which you will read about in a later chapter) we were holding in one of the central California cities, a man came up to the platform and reminded me of the Yosemite Firefalls. I had witnessed the Firefalls several times back in the fifties when our family would camp there during the summer months. So when he mentioned the event I was well aware of what he was talking about. He said that public television had just aired a documentary on the Yosemite Firefalls. He told me that one of the old-timers interviewed in the program testified of how spiritual the event was. That got my attention because I know how important prophetic symbolism is to the Lord.

Many may remember the famous Firefalls in Yosemite National Park. This, we feel, has strong prophetic significance. Yosemite Valley, and all of its wonders, is in the gold rush Mother Lode county of Mariposa, Ca. With the advent of The Azusa Street Revival in Los Angeles in 1906, and with the subsequent prophetic words in recent years that California will be a significant factor in the coming move of God, many of us believe that the Yosemite Firefalls were much more than just a major international tourist attraction. Additionally, in 1997, as mentioned above and described in chapter 21, there was a regional (5 counties) outpouring called "The Feast of Fire Revival" that began in Mariposa, which is home to Yosemite.

THE FIRE FALLS
From 1871 to 1968, thousands of people of many tongues from around the globe would line the meadows and roads every summer evening to watch the spectacular event of fire falling more than 3,000 feet from Glacier Point to the

Yosemite Firefalls

valley floor. In fact, many came to Yosemite just to experience the "Firefalls." It became so popular that more people were coming to the park for the Firefalls than for the splendor of Yosemite itself. Its incredible popularity actually became its demise. By the mid-twentieth century Yosemite became consistently crowded with millions of visitors annually. Today approximately four million people visit the park each year. Consequently, in 1968 the National Park Service decided to discontinue the Firefalls to help relieve congestion in the park.

However, for almost one hundred years, every summer, at exactly 9 p.m. a man would stand at Camp Curry below and shout to the man at Glacier Point 3,000 feet above, **"Let the fire fall."** At that instant, the man tending the fire at Glacier Point would shout his answer down, **"The fire is falling."** In a systematic rhythm they would immediately begin pushing the burning, glowing coals and fire over the cliff. It was a spectacular display of falling, descending fire! In the black of night the observer would see a steady stream of brilliant, flowing, glowing fire cascading 3,000 feet down the sheer wall of Glacier Point. This magnificent event would last for several minutes as the people from the nations stood and observed in awe.

" … I saw in the night visions … the Ancient of Days … His throne was like the fiery flame, its wheels were burning fire. A stream of fire came forth from before Him; a thousand thousands ministered to Him, and ten thousand times ten thousand rose up and stood before Him … " (Daniel 7:7-10, The Amplified Bible)

The Firefalls ~ A spiritual experience

In that *TV documentary interview one of the 'old timers,' that called the fire down, emotionally said, "We always thought it was like a spiritual thing, like a church experience." With his voice breaking, he said "people were deeply touched. Each night when the event ended there would be deep silence, or almost reverence." He said "people would be weeping everywhere. Then, after a minute or so, hesitantly, someone would break the silence with a weak applause. The applause would then escalate into a roar." It was an awesome event, a momentous occasion. Everyone was blessed, the rich and famous as well as the more common folks. All races and colors of people from all over the world were somehow deeply touched by the Firefalls. The old timer said "it riveted the people together." Doesn't that have a prophetic ring to it? Maybe it is more prophetic than even the participants could have believed.

It is said that when the apostle and healing evangelist Smith Wigglesworth from

England witnessed the event he was so moved he let out a loud bellow when it was over.

It is no coincidence that man had been calling, "Let the fire fall," and hearing from above, "The fire is falling," for almost a hundred years right here in the Mother Lode gold country, which is the heart of the Golden State.

Fire on Azusa Street
It is even more interesting that this prophetic act took place for 35 years in California before the Azusa Street Revival hit in Los Angeles in 1906. That revival became known as "Fire on Azusa Street," the latter-day Pentecost to the world. Reports in books and articles about Azusa Street tell us that people witnessed flames as high as fifty feet going up from the old building that were meeting flames coming down from the heavens. The fire department showed up on several occasions. But to everyone's amazement the building was not burning. God literally sent the "Fire of Pentecost" ~ "*cloven tongues like as of fire*" ~ to Azusa Street.

From California's Azusa Street, the fires of Pentecost spread around the world practically overnight. We talk more about the mighty Azusa Street Revival and the incredible reports of fire going up from the building to meet the fire coming down from heaven in a later chapter in this book.

It appears the old-timer in the documentary was right. It is a strong prophetic picture of the cry of the heart of the church right now ~ "Lord, let the fire fall!" ~ and HIS answer, coming from HIS heart of compassion, is ~ "The fire is falling!"

It is the encouragement of this writer that the fire is here already, yet it is about to come in a much stronger outpouring once more to California, as well as the nations. Let's all join in agreement, and let our hearts cry aloud for a "visitation of the Holy Spirit" that becomes a "habitation."

Yosemite ~ The World's Highest Concentration of High Waterfalls
It is interesting to note that Yosemite has the distinction of having more high waterfalls than anywhere in the world. There are numerous waterfalls pouring into Yosemite Valley, some of them falling over three thousand feet. During the spring and summer months the roar and thunder of the falls is heard everywhere in the valley.

Headwaters of the "River of Mercy"
Those waterfalls pouring into Yosemite Valley are the headwaters of the Merced River. The main stream begins high above the valley floor. That stream and all the others pouring into Yosemite Valley are the head waters of the Merced River. Merced means Mercy in Spanish.

So, the Merced River is born in Mariposa "The Mother of Counties." It is "The River of Mercy" and it is flowing from the heart of California.

In other words, God had man standing on the Yosemite Valley floor, in the midst of the world's highest concentration of high waterfalls, on the bank of the "River of Mercy," in the heart of the Golden State, doing a prophetic call for an outpouring from heaven.

God's Own Fire Falls
So, now the Firefalls are gone forever, right? Well, not so quick! I've got good news. God has the last word. A short distance from Glacier Point, very near El Capitan, there is a beautiful seasonal waterfall called Horsetail Falls. It is very interesting to note that in late February and early March there is a natural event that takes place that defies imagination. During these few weeks, when the sun is setting, the sun's rays hit the waterfall in such a way that Horsetail Falls literally looks like liquid fire falling more than 3,000 feet. It is one of the most beautiful and spectacular sites you will ever see. Photographers and enthusiasts come from far and wide to see and photograph this unusual event. It is awesome, it is natural, and it is going to happen until Jesus returns!

God still has a Firefalls happening every year in the heart of California!

So folks, we've got a world to save, so let's all say it together!

"Lord, let the Fire Fall!"
And His answer, coming from His heart of compassion, is ….

"If My People …"

* Huell Howser's video, "California's Gold" ~ # 706 Yosemite Firefall

CHAPTER 14

CALIFORNIA'S APOSTOLIC MANTLE
"The Spiritual Mother Lode"

A brief overview of international ministries launched from California

As that vision showed me that night back in 2000, there is an apostolic (sending out or exporting) mantle on California. Some things are birthed here and some are birthed elsewhere, but when God gets it to California, He puts wings to it and broadcasts it to the world.

In the natural or secular sense

In the very beginning of its history California was shipping untold millions of dollars in gold out of San Francisco Bay to the East Coast and to nations around the world. The wealth of California from its infancy was literally changing those economies.

In 2007 California exported more than 142 billion of dollars of produce and goods from its shores and across its borders.

California is the nation's number one exporter of ...

- √ Computers
- √ Electronic products
- √ Food and kindred products[1]

Hollywood is the world's number one media exporter of movies and television entertainment.

As California is in the natural, so it is even more in spiritual things

Azusa Street Revival ~ 1906

The mighty Baptism in the Holy Ghost with the evidence of speaking in other tongues did not begin in California. Its "Latter-day" beginning was in Topeka, Kansas in 1901 under the teaching of Charles Parham. But when Daddy Seymour took Parham's teaching in Houston, Texas, and began teaching it in Los Angeles, it exploded into a worldwide revival. It was the "Latter-day Pentecost" to the world. Preachers and missionaries came from the nations and received the impartation and took it back and released it in their homelands. Consequently, Pentecostal fires ignited all over the world from Azusa Street. Every Pentecostal or Charismatic organization in the world has roots that go back to that mighty outpouring. See chapter 15 of this book for more history on the Azusa Street Revival.

Church of God in Christ ~ 1907

The Church of God in Christ was originally of Baptist background. However today it is the largest African Pentecostal church in the world and the largest Pentecostal organization in the U.S. Its history is directly connected to the Azusa Street Revival. Please see chapter 16 for more on the story.

The Assemblies of God ~ 1914

The Assemblies of God were birthed from the Church of God in Christ. Originally there was a spirit of unity between the races in the COGIC; however, the launching of the denomination was influenced by the pressure of the Jim Crow laws which were forcing the segregation issue.

When the historical conference that launched the AOG move took place at Hot Springs, Arkansas in April of 1914, Bishop Mason, overseer of COGIC, attended the event and gave the endeavor his blessing.

Today the Assemblies of God is the largest Pentecostal organization in the world. They have a presence in one hundred and ten countries and a membership of close to sixty million people.[2]

You will read in the upcoming chapter on the Azusa Street Revival that two young men, C.W. Ward & Ralph Riggs, who were active participants in the revival, were later some of the early fathers of the Assemblies of God. On the historical page of the AOG web site I found these statements:

> "One of the focal points of the emerging Pentecostal movement was known as the Azusa Street revival (1906-09)."

"…. The revival soon became a local sensation, then attracted thousands of curiosity seekers and pilgrims from around the world."

"… the revival at Azusa Street catapulted Pentecostalism before a worldwide audience."[3]

Aimee Semple McPherson and the Foursquare Church ~ 1918

Although Aimee had already gained a bit of notoriety, it was when she moved to California that her ministry really excelled. In 1923 she built Angeles Temple in Los Angeles, and in 1927 she started the International Church of the Foursquare Gospel. The church today has over eight million members and nearly sixty thousand congregations in a hundred and forty-four countries. See chapter 17 of this book for more history on Aimee and the Foursquare Church.

Dr. Charles Price ~ 1921

Dr. Charles Price was one of God's generals of healing in the 1920's through the 40's. He was born in England and arrived in Lodi, California via Canada. Upon his arrival in California he was, by his own testimony, a "spiritually blind" pastor, "leading his people into a ditch." It was in an Aimee Semple McPherson meeting in San Jose, California, that he received the mighty Baptism in the Holy Ghost, and an international healing and revival ministry was launched.

Dr. Price was pastoring in Lodi, California when the Holy Spirit changed his life forever. He too received the left foot of fellowship from his denomination and left the Congregationalists to begin Lodi Bethel Temple.

Soon he began holding huge crusades throughout the northwest and around the world. Everywhere he went he saw miraculous healings in his meetings and thousands came to Christ. As a prolific writer he wrote several popular Spirit-filled books and published the "Golden Grain Magazine," which included many testimonies of healings and miracles. He also used radio extensively, preaching frequently from Los Angeles when he was not on the road. Dr. Price's ministry saw tens of thousands of souls saved and many bodies healed in nations around the world.[4]

The Henrietta Mears Factor ~ 1928

Henrietta Mears was a powerful influence in many people's lives. Her ministry was used powerfully by God to touch many people who were to become world changers for the Kingdom. She was on pastoral staff at Hollywood Presbyterian

Church from 1928 until her death in 1963. Miss Mears was a deciding influence in the lives of Dr. Bill Bright, and Dr. Billy Graham. She led Bright to the Lord, and she convinced Graham of the inerrancy of the Bible.

Miss Mears also founded and operated Gospel Light Publishing House, and she authored many Christian education publications. In addition she had a powerful ministry to many Hollywood movie stars, for whom she held numerous Bible studies and home group meetings.[5] What's more she owned and operated Forest Home, a Christian camp in the Big Bear area of the San Bernardino Mountains.

West Angeles Church Of God in Christ ~ 1943

Founded in 1943, West Angeles Church in Los Angeles began its phenomenal growth in 1969 when Charles E. Blake accepted the pastorate. Currently, West Angeles Church of God in Christ exceeds 24,000 members. The church has been recognized as one of the fastest growing churches in the nation, with extensive ministry and outreach services including television and radio broadcasts.

Dr. Blake is also the current presiding bishop and Chief Apostle of the entire international denomination.[6]

Franklin Hall ~ "Atomic Power with God through Fasting and Prayer" ~ 1946

Is it possible that what God was doing in California in the 1940's was directly related to God's plan of Israel becoming a nation in 1948?

A quote from a Lou Engle (TheCall) email:

In 1946, Franklin Hall launched a fasting and prayer movement out of San Diego with a book called "Atomic Power with God through Fasting and Prayer." Thousands were stirred to enter into extended consecration fasts. Shortly thereafter, the great healing revival broke out in 1947, followed by the campus revivals and the Hollywood revivals of 1948. In that very same year across the globe in the heart of the Middle East, by God's divine mandate, Israel was again called a nation.

Could it be that there was a connection between what God was doing in California and the orchestrating of His divine purposes in the creation of the nation of Israel? Is it possible that the outpouring of God's presence and the igniting of prayer in California were in reality connected with God's heart to birth an entire nation? I believe that it was a global Joel 2 moment—that after the fast, God restored the land and poured out His Spirit on all flesh, just as He promised He would in scripture.[7]

Dr. Billy Graham ~ 1949

Billy Graham is the most famous evangelist in history, who has preached to more people than anybody in history. He began his ministry in the east. However he was, for all practical purposes, an unknown evangelist until he came to California for a crusade in 1949.

But his "California Contribution" history precedes even that.

> **The Decision:** It was in the southern California area of Big Bear, with the help of Henrietta Mears at her Christian camp, Forest Home Ministries, in the early 40's, that Billy made the decision that the Bible was the infallible Word of God. A simple memorial there still marks the site of Graham's decision.[8]

> **The Modesto Manifesto:** In 1948, in a Modesto, California motel, Billy Graham, along with his associates (whom he called "the Team,") created what one of them called "The Modesto Manifesto." They decided among themselves to avoid certain problems that gave evangelists a bad name. The first item on the list was the matter of money, to which Graham was sensitive, because of the practices of some unscrupulous evangelists. The "Manifesto" proceeded to note the dangers of sexual immorality, criticism of local churches, and exaggerated publicity.[9]

> **"Puff Graham:"** Now here is the big "California Contribution:" In 1949 when he was still an unknown evangelist Billy was in Los Angeles conducting poorly attended tent meetings for a crusade that he planned to hold for three weeks. It was during those meetings that he caught the interest of newspaper mogul William Randolph Hearst. Hearst wrote two words, "Puff Graham" on a piece of paper and had it telegraphed to his editors. The editors did just that. They promoted Billy Graham in Hearst newspapers, magazines, movies, and newsreels. His planned three-week crusade extended five more weeks to a total eight weeks. Within two months, he was preaching to crowds of 350,000.

The 1949 Los Angeles revival is considered to be the time when Billy Graham became a national religious figure.

Full Gospel Business Men's Fellowship International ~ 1951

Founded in Los Angeles in 1951 by Demos Shakarian, the FGBMF now has chapters in a hundred and sixty countries around the world. There are many thousands of chapters of men meeting and ministering to one another. It is the largest network of Christian businessmen in the world.

Dr. Bill Bright and Campus Crusade for Christ ~ 1951

Campus Crusade for Christ is based in Florida, but its beginning in 1951 and for a few years thereafter was in California. Bill Bright and his wife lived with Henrietta Mears for eleven years. She was his personal mentor and the one who led him to the Lord. The Brights used her home near UCLA in Los Angeles as the center for launching Campus Crusade for Christ.[10]

> **The Four Spiritual Laws**, which he wrote while he and his wife were living with Miss Mears, is likely the most widely distributed religious booklet in history, with approximately 2.5 billion printed to date.

> **Campus Crusade for Christ** is an interdenominational Christian organization that promotes evangelism and discipleship in more than 190 countries around the world. In 1996, USA Today called Campus Crusade the largest evangelical organization in the United States. Today, the organization employs over 25,000 full-time missionaries and has trained 225,000 volunteers around the world.

> **The Jesus Film Project,** which is Dr. Bright's vision, and produced in California, has been translated into 1,006 languages and the film has shown in 228 nations. With an audience in excess of 6 billion people. The Jesus Film is the most widely translated and most-watched film ever produced.

In 1995, Campus Crusade for Christ was named the largest religious charity in the United States by U.S. News and World Report.[11]

Crystal Cathedral ~ The Hour Of Power ~ Robert Schuller ~ 1955

The Crystal Cathedral was first known as Garden Grove Community Church. It was founded in 1955 by Robert H. Schuller. Its first services were held in the Orange Drive-In Theatre. In 1980, it moved into the present all-glass "southern California landmark" building that is so well known to the world today.[12]

"The Hour of Power" is the television broadcast of their services. With an estimated average of 20 million viewers, it is said to be the most-watched Christian program in the world.

Youth With A Mission ~ YWAM ~ Loren Cunningham ~ 1960

Loren Cunningham, a young Assembly of God college man, founded **Youth With A Mission** in 1960 in his parent's California home. He subsequently incorporated the ministry in 1961.[13] Today the ministry has offices all over the world but the office of the international president, John Dawson, is in Ventura, California.[14]

> **From the YWAM website:**
> **Youth With A Mission** is an international movement of Christians from many denominations dedicated to serving Jesus throughout the world. Also known as YWAM (pronounced "WYE-wam"), our calling is to know God and to make Him known. Back when we began in 1960, our main focus was to get youth into short-term mission work and to give them opportunities to reach out in Jesus' name.
>
> Today, we still focus on youth, and we also involve people of almost every age (even many people who choose to spend their "retirement" in active service). Our many ministries fit into three main categories: evangelism, training and mercy ministry.
>
> We are currently operating in more than 1000 locations in over 149 countries, with a staff of nearly 16,000.[15]

Today YWAM is one of the largest Christian charitable movements in the world.[16]

Chuck Smith and Calvary Chapel ~ 1965

The story of Chuck Smith and Calvary Chapel begins in 1965. In the days of the Jesus movement, Chuck made room in his heart and his home for a generation of hippies and surfers. In 1968 he brought in a charismatic young convert, Lonnie Frisbee, an 18 year-old hippie from the Jesus Movement, who teamed with his youth leader John Higgins. They went into the streets and community, with outreaches on the beaches and baptisms in the Pacific Ocean. With a more contemporary Christian music, they "bridged the generation gap." Now, as of 2006, 35,000 people attend that church in Costa Mesa, California, and over 1,000 churches have branched out from it.

Both the Calvary and the Vineyard movements, along with the Jesus movement, begin as one amazing story. For more on these stories of Chuck Smith, The Jesus Movement, Lonnie Frisbee and John Wimber, please see chapter 18.

The Jesus Movement ~ 1967

According to my research, the terms *Jesus movement* and *Jesus people* were coined by Duane Pederson in his writings for the movement's own press, "The Hollywood Free Paper." The beginning of the movement is probably best marked with two endeavors: Arthur Blessit opening "His Place" night club and coffee house on Sunset Strip, and the opening of a small storefront evangelical mission called "The Living Room" in San Francisco's Haight-Ashbury district. The movement was directly related to the hippie generation. Although it began in California, like the hippie culture did, it quickly spread around the nation and across the seas. While it was a fairly short-lived movement its lasting effects on church culture and a more contemporary music are still with us today.

For more on the Jesus movement story see Chapter 18.

Church On The Way ~ Jack Hayford ~ 1969

In 1969 Jack Hayford accepted the pastorate of the First Foursquare Church of Van Nuys. The original church was chartered in 1951. At the time Hayford took the church, it had eighteen members. Now it is called "Church on the Way," and under his leadership it has grown to one of the largest churches in California with a congregation of fourteen thousand five hundred souls. Today it has three campuses in the North Los Angeles area. Many well known people, including Hollywood movie stars, are a part of its thriving congregation. Hayford pastored the church for thirty years and stepped down in 1999. The present pastor is Jim Tolle.

Jack Hayford continues as the president of the International Church of the Foursquare Gospel, an office which he has held since 2004. He has authored over 40 books and is the General Editor of the "Spirit-Filled Life" publications produced by Thomas Nelson Publishers. He has composed over 500 hymns, songs, and choruses, the most noted of which is the classic "Majesty."

TBN ~ 1973

Trinity Broadcasting Network is the world's largest religious network and America's most watched faith channel. Founded in 1973 in southern California by Paul and Jan Crouch, TBN now broadcasts the Word of God all around the world.

From the TBN website:
"TBN is now the world's largest Christian television network. Across America and around the world TBN is carried by TV stations and cable systems to millions of homes. As a matter of fact, TBN is featured on over 5,000 television stations, 33 satellites, the Internet and thousands of cable systems around the world. And the number continues to grow!"

Crenshaw Christian Center ~ Ever Increasing Faith Ministries ~ Fred Price ~ 1973

Crenshaw Christian Center, now 22,000 members strong, was founded by Dr. Fred Price in 1973. Its campus today is the old Pepperdine University Campus in Los Angeles. The Faith Dome is a modern 10,000 seat sanctuary that Price built on the campus.

Dr. Price is one of the first African-American ministers to have a mega-church and an evangelical broadcast on television. His broadcast "Ever Increasing Faith Ministries" reaches over 15 million households each week across the nation and internationally.

The Vineyard Movement ~ 1974 & 1982

According to Chuck Girard, the Christian musician and song writer, when he was ministering in our church last year, the first Vineyard church began at a Bible study in his home in 1974. The founder then was Kenn Gulliksen who was affiliated with Calvary Chapel. In 1982 John Wimber, who was pastoring a Calvary Chapel in Yorba Linda, California, became less in agreement with that movement and their view of the power of the Holy Spirit. He eventually left Calvary to become the leader of the small number of Vineyard churches that Gullikson had founded. It was then that the Vineyard movement was born. Again, both the Calvary and the Vineyard movements, along with the Jesus movement, begin as one amazing story. For more on these stories of Chuck Smith, The Jesus Movement, Lonnie Frisbee and John Wimber please see chapter 18.

Dr. Ralph D. Winter ~ U.S. Center for World Mission ~ 1976

Founded by Dr. Winter, The United States Center for World Mission is a ministry where mission agencies work together to strategize, research and promote ideas that will help to complete the unfinished task of reaching every people group with the Gospel. It has been described as a missions think tank or "missions Pentagon."[17]

Billy Graham once wrote: "Ralph Winter has not only helped promote evangelism among many mission boards around the world, but by his research, training and publishing he has accelerated world evangelization." Dr. Ray Tallman, shortly after Winter's death, described him as "perhaps the most influential person in missions of the last 50 years and has influenced missions globally more than anyone I can think of."[18]

Dr. James Dobson ~ Focus on the Family ~ 1977

Dr. James Dobson birthed the ministry, Focus on the Family, in Pomona, California in 1977. The ministry, mostly through its popular radio talk show broadcast, reaches more than 220 million people in 155 nations. The ministry is now based in Colorado Springs, Colorado, but its first 15 years of operations were in California.

TheCall ~ A Global Prayer Endeavor ~ 2000

Birthed in California, TheCall is a global vision for prayer and fasting that God imparted to Lou Engle. It is probably the most intense and effective "spirit-filled" national and international call to prayer in the world. Lou has obediently taken TheCall to cities around the country, including Washington D.C., and gathered the people for fervent prayer. He has also taken it to the nations.

When I picture it in my mind I can envision Lou cupping his hands to his mouth and calling out. Remember the story of the Firefalls. He reminds me of the man at Camp Curry calling the fire down. The nations and many tongues were always gathered as the caller called the fire down. I sincerely believe that The Firefalls, Azusa Street and TheCall have a divine connection.

From TheCall Web Site ~ 2009

Hollywood Presbyterian Church - 1923

"Follow with Lou a journey into the history of **TheCall** and the prayer movement that **started in California**. Pray along with TheCall Team to re-dig the wells of revival in these geographical areas."

"Lou and TheCall family talk with Pastor Christian from Hollywood Presbyterian Church to hear his personal testimony in being apprehended by the Holy Spirit. Lou and Christian tell of like dreams of Hollywood turning into "Holywood". Join with Lou and Theresa Engle on location at **Hollywood Presbyterian Church, where Billy Graham, Bill Bright, Henrietta Mears, and Jill Austin started their**

ministries." …. "This was a training ground for over 400 evangelists during the last 150 years."[19]

Saddleback Church ~ Rick Warren ~ The Purpose Driven Life ~ 2002

Saddleback Church in Lake Forest, California was pioneered by Pastor Rick Warren in 1980. The church is Southern Baptist and has a weekly attendance of about twenty thousand people. Rick Warren is best known for his very popular books, "The Purpose Driven Church" and his devotional book, number one New York Times best seller, "The Purpose Driven Life." According to the Wikipedia web site, "The Purpose Driven Life" had sold thirty million copies by 2006.

Pastor Warren's "Forty Days of Purpose" bible study program, based on the book, "The Purpose Driven Life," has been used by thousands of congregations world-wide.

In 2005 George Barna conducted a survey of American pastors who voted the two books as the most influential in their lives.[20]

Another report said that over 400,000 pastors attend his "purpose-driven" church seminars.[21]

In August of 2008 Pastor Warren hosted "The Civil Forum on the Presidency," with U.S. presidential candidates John McCain and Barack Obama, in the sanctuary of Saddleback Church.

In summary to this chapter

Jesus said " … *for the tree is known by his fruit.*" Matt. 12:33

"If My People …"

CHAPTER **15**

FIRE ON AZUSA STREET
Latter-day Pentecost to the World

A dramatization of the Bonnie Brae House and Azusa Street Mission
Artist; Robert E. Hunt, used with permission. Postcards and prints available at
www.foursquaremissionspress.com

A to Z USA

The story in the chapter you are about to read confirms without a doubt that God had uncommon things in mind for the "Golden State." A mere sixty years from a remote Mexican territory, as He did with the natural Gold Rush, God did it with a spiritual Gold Rush. Through the Azusa Street Revival God explodes California into world leadership with the fresh wind of "Pentecost." The mighty Azusa Street Revival was a key component of "The California Contribution" to the world.

"And when the day of Pentecost was fully come, they were all with one accord in one place. And suddenly there came a sound from heaven as of a rushing mighty wind, and it filled all the house where they were sitting. And there appeared unto *them cloven tongues like as of fire, and it sat upon each of them. And they were all filled with the Holy Ghost, and began to speak with other tongues, as the Spirit gave them utterance."* (Acts 2:1-4)

"But Peter, standing up with the eleven, lifted up his voice, and said unto them, Ye men of Judaea, and all ye that dwell at Jerusalem, be this known unto you, and hearken to my words: For these are not drunken, as ye suppose, seeing it is but the third hour of the day. But this is that which was spoken by the prophet Joel; And it shall come to pass in the last days, saith God, I will pour out of my Spirit upon all flesh: and your sons and your daughters shall prophesy, and your young men shall see visions, and your old men shall dream dreams: And on my servants and on my handmaidens I will pour out in those days of my Spirit; and they shall prophesy: And I will shew wonders in heaven above, and signs in the earth beneath ..." (Acts 2:14-19)

Please understand that when I refer to a Pentecostal movement or outpouring in this book, I am not referring to a man-made religion or denomination. I am referring specifically to church according to Acts chapter 2 and the rest of the book of Acts.

The 1906 Azusa Street Revival is probably the mightiest move of God since the Book of Acts. It is also incontestable evidence that God indeed had a special plan for California in its very young age. Ordinarily when we read about this revival we get some very interesting information, but many times it is usually coming from one particular perspective of its history.

However, as is frequently the case in most revivals, God was laying the groundwork and well-springing several different streams of "living water" for this mighty outpouring years before it happened. My intent, with a touch of brevity, is to illustrate each tributary and then merge the confluence together for the main river of God, which outpoured in Los Angeles a little over a hundred years ago.

"There is a river, the streams whereof shall make glad the city of God, the holy place of the tabernacles of the most High." (Psalm 46:4)

Azusa stands alone

As a revivalist to my bones, and also a bit of a history buff, I have studied many of the revivals of the past: the Great Awakenings in early America, Charles Finney in the pre-Civil War years, the Welsh Revival in 1904, the Hebrides Revival in the Late 40's, the Argentina Revival of the 80's, and The Toronto Blessing and the Pensacola Outpouring, both in the mid-90's, and the list goes on. Each and every one of them is an amazing story and is full of inspiration. The power of God fell, sinners were saved by the droves and lives were changed, as the Lord romanced His people. In most cases, communities and even nations were profoundly affected. Every time I read about any of them my heart cries, "Lord, do it again!"

Where Azusa differs from these revivals is the phenomenal results of spawning the greatest move of God in history. It birthed the Pentecostal and Charismatic movement into the earth. Azusa itself only lasted about three-and-a-half years before it started to wane, but it ignited and exploded Pentecost into the world in the process. More than any other revival before it, the effects of Azusa are alive and well, and advancing through the earth today. Indeed, the Pentecostal and Charismatic movements are the fastest growing movements in Christianity worldwide. As a direct result of that move people are entering the Kingdom of God by the mass every day. One report I read said that four-fifths of the worlds Christians are now Pentecostal or Charismatic. That all ignited at Azusa.[1]

"Blessed Miracle"

> "...the very name Azusa was derived from an Indian word that means 'blessed miracle.' This was first noted by Father Juan Crespi in 1769 ... At the time, Azusa referred to the site of an old Indian village ... in the San Gabriel Canyon. There, a young Indian girl named Coma Lee used to pray and fast for the healing of her people. ... After she prayed for a chief who was wonderfully healed, he gave her the name Azusa to commemorate his miracle of healing. For many years, Azusa continued her healing ministry while her fame spread all over southern California. During that time whenever there was suffering, people said, 'Go to Azusa and be healed ... go to Azusa.'"[2]

Charles Parham ~ Topeka, Kansas

Let us start the story of the Azusa Street Revival in Topeka, Kansas in 1900. Charles Parham, known as "the Father of Pentecost," was ministering the baptism in the Holy Ghost at his Bible school, Stones Folly. It was New Year's Eve when a student by the name of Agnes Ozman asked him to lay hands on her for the baptism of the Holy Spirit. Miss Ozman was dramatically touched and began speaking in tongues. Within the first few days of 1901 others were also receiving the blessing. Soon it was in the newspapers and being discussed all around. For the next few years Parham wrote, studied, traveled, preached, and taught about the Holy Ghost experience.

Daddy Seymour ~ Houston, Texas

In the winter of 1905 Parham opened a Bible school in Houston, Texas. It was in that school that William J. Seymour, affectionately known later as "Daddy" Seymour, the "Father of the Azusa Street Revival," attended and received the teaching of the doctrine of the baptism in the Holy Ghost, with the evidence of speaking in other tongues.

Now, let's back up to 1904 and discover some things taking place two years before the fire of God fell at Azusa Street. Then we will get back to the story of Daddy Seymour.

They Told Me Their Stories ~ The Pisgah House

As part of the research for this book, Grace and I were blessed to spend the better part of an afternoon, and the following morning, with Tommy Welchel.

Daddy Seymour
Courtesy "Flower Pentecostal Heritage Center"

Tommy, who now lives back in his home state of Oklahoma, recently wrote the book "They Told Me Their Stories." He was visiting and ministering in L.A. when we were able to fellowship with him. We first saw him and heard about his book while watching the Sid Roth, "It's Supernatural" show, on Trinity Broadcasting Network.

As a teenager back in the sixties, Tommy spent several years at the Pisgah House, which was a kind of old mission home where many of the old saints from Azusa Street eventually retired. Pisgah is in Highland Park which is between Los Angeles and Pasadena. Now, with Tommy's book, we are finding out that Pisgah's history is very much a part of the Azusa story. With Tommy as our guide, we actually visited the old grounds there and the church on the grounds that he and the Azusa saints attended in those days. In the old church, with the present Pastor and his wife, Steve and Tina Gunn joining us, Tommy told us many of the stories and miracles that he experienced there with those "post revival" saints.

Henry & Grace with Tommy Welchel in front of the Pisgah Church

Over the years, I have read a lot about the Azusa Street Revival, but between Tommy's personal stories and his book I have recently learned some interesting facts that I didn't know. Now, with his blessing, I am including some of our newly acquired knowledge in this book.

You see, while he lived at Pisgah, Tommy spent many hours at the feet of Azusa Street saints who were the younger of the participants in the revival. Over and over they told him their stories. Then one day Tommy received a prophetic word.

Jean Darnell, who had taken over the pastorate of Angeles Temple after Aimee Semple McPherson died, called him over to her one day and said:

> "Brother Tommy, come over here, I have a word from the Lord for you. The Lord is showing me that all these stories that the Azusa Street saints

are telling you, and you have been learning and memorizing, will some day be put into a book."

Well, with help from his church in Oklahoma, Tommy indeed wrote the book, and just in time for the one-hundred-year Azusa Street Revival Centennial in 2006.

The Pisgah House was founded by Dr. Yoakum who, in 1895, when a local pastor prayed for him, received a miracle healing from a bad horse-drawn buggy accident. From that time on he gave his life to God and opened the Pisgah House for the less fortunate. During the Azusa Street Revival Pisgah hosted many of the followers of the outpouring. Dr. Yoakum also conducted frequent prayer meetings and Bible studies there.

In 1903, a young man named Brother Lankford was led of the Lord to leave Highland Park to go to Topeka, Kansas, to learn of the mighty baptism of the Holy Ghost. In 1904 he returned to California and introduced the teaching to Dr. Yoakum. After embracing the teaching and receiving "the baptism" himself, Dr. Yoakum began teaching it at Pisgah.

Sister Carney
It was in those meetings in 1904 at Pisgah that Sister Carney, a fifteen year old who was already married, attended those meetings. Being very hungry for God she was one of the first ones to receive "the baptism" under Yoakum's teaching. With this new and exciting experience from heaven, and with a fire in her bones, Sister Carney went to the First Baptist Church in Pasadena and began ministering it to her friends. But by 1906 she and her friends had received "the left foot of fellowship" from the church because of this move of God. The mighty baptism in the Holy Ghost didn't fit Baptist doctrine. That little group didn't know it at the time, but God was setting the stage for something big!

Now in 1906, with a fire burning in them that something was brewing in the Spirit for Los Angeles, those young ladies met in one of their member's apartments for several months for fervent prayer. Little did they know how God was about to use them in the awesome outpouring that was just about to come.

In the years that Tommy knew Sister Carney, which was the early 1960s, she was in her mid-seventies. Her active participation in the revival, and her later relationship with Tommy, with her first-hand stories to him, are an invaluable addition to the story of Azusa Street.

Frank Bartleman

Frank Bartleman was known as "the architect for the Azusa Street Revival." He was a pastor, traveling evangelist and a journalist from Pennsylvania with a cry in his heart for revival. He came to California with his family in 1904. "I had felt strangely drawn to this city for some time," he wrote.[3] Bartleman is the one that cried, "Give me revival, or I'll die."

In early 1905, just a few weeks after their arrival in Los Angeles, at just three years old, their little girl Esther passed away. It broke his heart and grief was the issue of the hour. But what the enemy meant for devastation God turned it for His Glory.

As the atmosphere of revival began to move into the area, Bartleman wrote,

Frank Bartleman, Courtesy "Flower Pentecostal Heritage Center"

> For many years have been prepared for just this present time ... My own awakening, or reawakening to this plan, was brought about through the loss of my little girl .... So God could only speak to me His thought by driving me in desperation of need of Him to know what meaneth this. And then He told me. But my little treasure, my heart's love was gone. She was the price. She had done her work up early and gone home in the morning. A little "morning glory."[4]

Revival never comes cheap. There is always a price to pay. With his big heart breaking Frank Bartleman knelt by the body of his little "morning glory" and committed his life totally to God's purpose.

> Beside that little coffin, with heart bleeding, I pledged my life anew for

> God's service. In the presence of death, how real eternal issues become. I promised the rest of my life should be spent wholly for Him. He made a fresh covenant with me. I begged Him to open a door of service quickly, so that I might not find time for sorrow.[5]

God answered his prayer. Within a week he began preaching twice a week for a month at the Peniel Mission in Pasadena. Souls were saved and a number of young men received the call during those meetings. That was just the beginning as he ministered and preached in groups and churches all around southern California that an outpouring was coming. He said God spoke the word "Pentecost" to him and to "work quickly; I come quickly."[6]

On about the first of May 1905, Bartleman connected with the Lake Avenue Methodist Episcopal Church in Pasadena, which had just moved into a powerful revival. Some of the young men from his Peniel Mission meetings were there and had gotten under the burden for revival. It spread through the congregation. On one particular night, nearly every lost soul got saved. In a two-week period two hundred souls knelt at the altar to seek the Lord. The whole city became stirred and helpers came from all directions. The saints were encouraged and began to cry "Pasadena for God!"

At this point Bartleman began to claim the whole state of California for God. "Pentecost" was the thought that was laid on his heart.[7]

> The ministry of intercession was the most real and tremendous. I was in pain, as a woman, to be delivered. It seemed my mind could be sapped of its very blood through the tremendous concern, solicitude and agony of those fifteen months of solid prayer prior to the final "outpouring" in the spring of 1906.[8]

Uncommon moves of God and smaller revivals were happening all around as the expectation increased. People were praying and Bartleman was fanning the fire with his preaching, encouraging, and Pentecostal articles, and passing out tens of thousands of his own tracts. With an obsession, he moved all over the region preaching repentance and prayer. He had a "prophetic" fire in his belly for the impending move of God. He also wrote personal letters to spiritual leaders all over the country to pray for revival.[9] Bartleman literally gave himself to the birth of revival in southern California.

The spirit of intercession sent to California

It is no stretch to say that God sent this instrument of revival to the Golden State to prepare the way, and cleanse the air, and fan the fire for His purpose. Bartleman was indeed the embodiment of the spirit of intercession sent to California. Uncommon prayer always precedes revival. John Wesley said, "Everything by prayer, nothing without it."[10] I have always told my congregation, "When God is fixin' to do something, He always gets His people a-prayin."

Due to Bartleman's intercessions, writings and other influences, there was so much excitement and expectation that a big revival was about to break out that people moved from out of state and foreign countries to southern California in order to be a part.[11]

The Welsh Revival had started in late 1904, but the news of it had not reached Bartleman at this point. A sovereign move of God was already brewing.[12] Nevertheless, when he did hear about the Welsh Revival, he was greatly inspired and wrote Evan Roberts for prayer and revival instructions three times. Roberts responded with encouragement and prayer for California each time.

Pastor Joseph Smale

Frank Bartleman calls Pastor Joseph Smale the Moses of the Azusa Street Revival. Smale was the pastor of the First Baptist Church of Los Angeles. In 1905 he traveled to Wales and connected with Evan Roberts. He was hungry for what was happening in Wales to happen in Los Angeles. Upon his return to Los Angeles he established daily prayer meetings and nightly revival meetings. He had brought an impartation back from Evan Roberts and he testified of the wondrous things he witnessed in Wales. His ministry and vision of revival was anointed and it ignited hearts for the same. Bartleman visited those meetings and found a favorable spirit there. He then began writing articles in papers and magazines about the move of God in Smale's church.

God was moving powerfully and for fifteen weeks they held services every night. Unfortunately the church leaders did not have the same passion as the pastor. They issued him an ultimatum, stop the revival or leave. To his credit Smale chose the latter.

In order to maintain the fire in his heart, in late 1905 Smale started The New Testament Church. Many of the revival saints from the old church followed him. Bartleman also joined the new work and helped fan the fires there with his writings and personal contacts. Smale preached and prophesied that a mighty move of God was coming very soon. The meetings were powerful and God was moving. People were getting saved and the fire of God was emanating from the church. But unfortunately his new church began to wane too as it began to structure for more organization, and to be more like a normal church. Nevertheless, in the process of it all Smale played a major part in preparing the entire Los Angeles area for what was just ahead. Like Moses he helped bring the people to "The "Promised Land," but in the end he couldn't cross over.

Now, back to Seymour
William J. Seymour was an uneducated, one-eyed, black man from the southern bayou country of Louisiana. His parents had only been freed from slavery a few years before he was born. The Civil War ended in 1865 and he was born in 1870.

When I grew up in the bayous and swamps of the central west coast of Florida in the 1940's & 50's segregation was still very much alive even then. We had black schools, a colored section of town, and the blacks always rode in the back of the bus. If you went to the department store there were white porcelain water fountains and there were black porcelain water fountains. The same was so with restrooms, there were white restrooms and there were black restrooms. I can remember when a new doctor came to our little back woods town of New Port Richey in the fifties. When he had to go down into the Negro quarters to deliver a baby, he was afraid to go by himself. So, he got my dad to go with him. Dad never did agree with that segregation stuff and had always befriended the Negroes and even played on their baseball teams with them. But that's just the way it was in those days in the south.

So, you can imagine how much worse it was fifty years before that. In Seymour's day the Jim Crow laws had been passed to prohibit all blacks from any social justices at all. Those laws, which were state and local laws, mandated that all public facilities be "Separate but Equal" in status. In most cases in the south, as well as in California, the states also made marriage between blacks and whites illegal.[13] In 1906, there were more lynchings of black men than in any other year of America's history.[14]

I am making this point to stress the significance of what God did to jerk the heads of the religious and pious spirits of this world through the Azusa Outpouring. If you don't understand some of the social circumstances of the times you may miss a key move of God here. A big part of "the California Contribution" is God stressing equality and unity ~ one body, one Spirit. To do this He reached down through the social structures of man to anoint an unpolished black man to lead a world-changing revival. If you think about it, this is God's pattern. Do you remember a fella named Gideon? Or a little shepherd boy taking out a giant and putting the entire enemy army on the run? Or a common family with a donkey, and a baby being born in the feed trough in a barn in a little place called Bethlehem?

Seymour heads north

As a young man of twenty-five, Seymour broke free of his mental bondage and the old slave inferiority complex, and went north. First he went to Indianapolis, then finally to Cincinnati. In his travels he moved through various churches searching for God and growing. He was a devoted follower of John Wesley, who believed in strong prayer, holiness, and divine healing. Wesley also believed there should be no discrimination between the races.

While in Cincinnati Seymour caught the small pox, which was usually fatal in those days. He suffered horribly for three weeks but survived. The disease, however, left him blind in his left eye and he had severe facial scarring. He wore a beard the rest of his life to hide the scars. During this time he had been wrestling with his call to preach and he was convinced that the disease was a result of that resistance. So, he quickly submitted to the plan of God and received his ordination through the Evening Light Saints, a group with whom he was fellowshipping at the time. He then began evangelizing as an itinerant preacher.

Seymour heads back south to Houston

Seymour soon left Cincinnati and moved back south to Texas. Arriving in Houston, he found family, so he based his ministry there.

In 1905, Charles Parham was holding crusades in Houston, preaching the mighty baptism in the Holy Ghost. Seymour had not yet met or heard the teachings of Parham. After the crusades Parham asked Mrs. Lucy Farrow, the pastor of a small Holiness Church in Houston, to accompany his family back to Topeka, Kansas where they lived. Parham offered her the position of governess for his family while they temporarily returned home. When she accepted Parham's offer she asked Seymour to pastor her church until she returned. He agreed to the arrangement and saw after her congregation until she returned two months later.

When Mrs. Farrow did return home, she shared with Seymour about her awesome experiences with the Parham family, none the least of which was her experience of speaking in tongues. Seymour was very interested in what she described but was a bit cautious about the doctrines at the same time. Personally "I've been there and bought the T-shirt on that one too!" I know exactly how he felt. You want everything God has to offer, but you don't want any monkey business.

Anyway, it was now December and Parham had announced the opening of his Bible School. Mrs. Farrow passionately encouraged Seymour to attend. Motivated by her fervency and his own hunger for God he enrolled in the class.

Now, because of the strict Jim Crow laws in Houston, Seymour was forced to sit outside the classroom in the hallway. He handled the injustice gracefully and sat faithfully under the teaching. He didn't necessarily embrace every doctrine, but he did receive and understand the teaching on the baptism in the Holy Ghost and speaking in other tongues. Although he didn't personally receive the baptism in the Holy Ghost and tongues, he did agree with the theology and began teaching it himself.

Seymour heads west ~ The call to Los Angeles

After Parham's school was completed, Seymour was planning to start a new Pentecostal church in Houston in which he would preach his new revelation of the Holy Ghost. It was then that he received an unexpected letter from Los Angeles from Miss Terry Neely. Miss Neely had met Seymour when he was pastoring the church for Mrs. Farrow. She had been visiting Houston from L.A. when she attended Seymour's services and sat under his ministry. In Los Angeles she was a member of a small black church that had broken away from a denominational church. Their leader was Sister Julia Hutchinson, and Miss Hutchinson's little group was hungry for God. She and the little congregation were looking for a pastor and Miss Neely convinced them that Seymour was their man. Interestingly enough, the little church first met at the little house in the black neighborhood owned by the Asberys, Miss Neely's cousins, on Bonnie Brae Street. Yes the Bonnie Brae House was their beginning too. It was when they outgrew the house and rented a hall on Santa Fe Street that they sent for Seymour.

Believing the letter revealed his destiny, Seymour packed his bags and headed west. He arrived in California in early February, 1906. Now remember, southern California is already in a very uncommon spiritual climate. Many small moves of the Spirit are happening all over the area and great expectation is prevalent everywhere. God had been releasing more of His presence and using his vessels like Bartleman and Smale to prepare the way for two years now. A major revival was in the air.

Now, even though things initially would not work out as Seymour had planned, the stage was set. The fumes of revival were filling the air, and the fire was about to fall. "Pentecost" was about to explode in California. When he arrived he began teaching on his text:

"And they were all filled with the Holy Ghost, and began to speak with other tongues, as the Spirit gave them utterance." (Acts 2:4)

The left foot of fellowship

Now it's welcome to the "Spirit-filled" ministry. It is amazing sometimes in ministry how uncomfortable and confusing it may seem when you are indeed, in the perfect will of God. Seymour's message was met with mixed emotions. Some were blessed and encouraged while others were offended and denounced him fervently, including Miss Hutchinson. After the Sunday morning service Edward Lee and his family took him home for Sunday dinner. When they returned to the church for the evening service the church door was padlocked. Outraged, Miss Hutchinson declared that she would not allow such teaching in her church. Seymour's sleeping accommodations were in the little mission so he had no place to go. Feeling somewhat obligated, but having reservations of their own, the Lees took him home with them.

Seymour ~ A man of prayer

While at their house Seymour confined himself to his room for prayer. Then after several days of prayer, he invited the Lees to join him. Immediately their opinion of him began to change. They began telling others in the church about the prayer meetings at their house and many began attending. The word spread and the prayer meetings grew and Seymour became known as a man of prayer.

The Bonnie Brae House ~ The Fire falls

His leadership mantle became obvious to all and he was soon invited by the Asberys to move into their home on Bonnie Brae Street. The Asberys and the Lees were both black families and the Asbery home was in a predominately black neighborhood. Both Mr. Asbery and Mr. Lee were janitors by trade. In addition to living there, Mr. Asbery asked Seymour to begin regular meetings in their home as well. He accepted their offer and they began those meetings in late February of 1906. The meetings continued to grow and included hours of praying, seeking the baptism of the Holy Spirit.

Then on April 9, 1906, Mr. Lee was instantly healed when Seymour went to his house and prayed for him. Then he received the baptism in the Holy Ghost and began to speak in other tongues. The two of them then walked back to the Bonnie Brae house for the evening meeting and found the place packed out. Many were already praying so Seymour took charge and led them in songs and testimony. He then testified of Mr. Lee's experience. Mr. Lee then lifted his hands and began speaking in tongues. The congregation dropped to their knees and began crying out for the baptism. Many received it and lifted up their voices and began speaking in other tongues. Some rushed out on the porch and began prophesying and preaching. Others ran out into the street praying in tongues where all the neighborhood heard. Pentecost had come! "Bartleman's child" has been birthed.

Now the news spread even more. The crowds filled the house and the yard, and surrounded the house. The Glory of God was in and on the house. There were times of great shouting as well as times of intense quiet. Many fell under the power. Some lay out under the power for hours. God also released a strong healing anointing. Many began to testify of miracle healings during those meetings.

Seymour had to preach from the porch as people sat on the lawn and near the street. There were so many people on the porch that the porch finally collapsed.

Seymour receives the Holy Ghost
Oddly enough, up to this point, Seymour himself had not received the baptism in the Holy Ghost. It was on the third night of the outpouring, after the crowd had gone, that he finally received his breakthrough. The man that had come so far and brought the blessing to so many finally received the gift himself and began speaking in other tongues.

Time to move
Here is a quote from Tommy Welchel's book "They Told Me Their Stories."

> "The police officers were polite, yet firm. 'Either shut it down or rent a place like a regular church or auditorium. You have gotten too big to continue to meet at this home.'"

A prophetic address

Before we leave the Bonnie Brae House I want to bring this point. The street address of the house was originally 214 North Bonnie Brae Street. But after the outpouring the city changed the address numbering system and now it is 216 North Bonnie Brae Street. Now remember, the world-changing outpouring of "Pentecost" began here, not at Azusa Street. Now, look at this, the new numbers are too interesting to ignore. All through the Bible God is into numbers. Acts 2:16 reads, *"But this is that which was spoken by the prophet Joel:"*

Azusa Street

With the crowds getting bigger each night Seymour set out to find a building for the Revival. He finally located an old vacated building at 312 Azusa Street. The 40-ft by 60-ft building had originally been used for an African Methodist Episcopal Church. After they vacated it, apartments were built upstairs and the unfinished downstairs was used for storage and stables, but now it was just neglected and vacant. Nonetheless, it was just what Seymour needed: now he just needed the "money" for the rent.

Remember Sister Carney and her little Holy Ghost prayer group?

With the need to find a building heavy on his heart he prayed hard that night in the service for guidance. Immediately the Lord answered him and told him to get on a trolley right after service and go to Pasadena. Being the faith man he was he obeyed the mandate and boarded a trolley for Pasadena. At this time he was obeying God rather than man because being in the Jim Crow era as it was, it was illegal for a black man to be on the streets of Pasadena after dark. Obediently Seymour rode the trolley totally trusting the Lord and not knowing where he was going. It was after 10:00 p.m. when the Lord told him to get off the trolley.

So, there he was, a black man illegally on the streets of Pasadena late at night. The Lord then directed him to a nearby apartment.

From Tommy Welchel's book

"I'm the Man"

Meeting together for months now in the apartment of one of the members of the group, this particular evening Sister Carney and these ladies continued in fervent prayer for several hours. They were certain that God was about to do something big in the Los Angeles area.

Just after 10:00 p.m., God brought together two elements of a force that, when joined together, would usher in one of the greatest manifestations of God ever experienced by man since the birth of Christ.

Seymour walked up to the apartment that God had led him to and knocked on the door. Sister Carney remembers the time to be about 10:30 p.m. The ladies went to the door together and when they opened the door, found a black man, blind in one eye, standing before them. For many people in that day and in that area, a black man showing up at their door late at night would have been a sign to slam the door and call the police. But that night, God was in charge. The owner of the apartment, with some apprehension, asked, "Can I help you?" The answer to this simple, and somewhat fretful question would startle and astonish those gathered for prayer. After several months of fervent prayer, God responded in an unusual manner.

Seymour replied, "You're praying for revival, right?" When the ladies responded with a unanimous "yes," Seymour made a bold statement: "I'm the man God has sent to preach that revival."

Without hesitation, the ladies invited Seymour in. After some exciting chatter, he preached to them and took up an offering that was more than enough to rent the Azusa Street Warehouse.

Sister Carney, now seventeen years old, along with her prayer group, joined the group from the Bonnie Brae House and became a living part of the Glory and the history that was made in the years to come. In fact, she was there from the first rent being raised, to cleaning and remodeling the building, to padlocking the door years later when it was all over.

When the word got out that Seymour had a building, but that it was a real "fixer-upper," people quickly came from far and wide to help. A local church pitched in, plus a devout Catholic man who owned a large lumber company, and so on. They cleaned out the old manure from the stables, they painted, they put sawdust on the floor and they nailed wooden planks to crates and barrels for pews. It was a very humble facility in a skid row type setting, but they cleaned it up and prepared the place for an international revival.

They moved in and the revival services continued to be powerful, and the news of it started spreading like wildfire. Almost immediately the local newspapers began their negative press which actually only fanned the flames.

The San Francisco earthquake

As soon as they got the revival going in its new home, the devastating 1906 earthquake struck San Francisco. The quake hit on April 18, just nine days after the outpouring began at the Bonnie Brae House and a couple of days after services began at Azusa Street. There was also an aftershock in Los Angeles the next day. Needless to say people rushed to God in fear. Literally hundreds descended upon Azusa to meet God and hear about the mighty baptism in the Holy Ghost.

Frank Bartleman said the earthquake opened many hearts. He immediately printed tens of thousands of tracts entitled "The Last Call," referring to the earthquake and the hand of God. Those tracts were distributed up and down California. People's hearts were sensitive to God, and even the very wealthy came to the lower class neighborhood to experience God's power.

The Shekinah Glory

The Pisgah Saints reported that the Shekinah Glory would often roll into the meetings. It was a smoke-like substance that would begin to glow. At times it would fill the whole building.

"And it came to pass, when the priests were come out of the holy place, that the cloud filled the house of the Lord, So that the priests could not stand to minister because of the cloud: for the glory of the Lord had filled the house of the Lord." (1 Kings 8:10 & 11)

One fella said, "I would rather have lived six months at that time than fifty years of ordinary life. I have stopped more than once within two blocks of the place and prayed for strength before I dared go on. The presence of the Lord was so real."

Many people were seen dropping or falling in the street under the power as they approached the glory in the building. Oftentimes, they were first time visitors that had not experienced the revival. They would have an experience with God on the ground, and come up speaking in other tongues without anyone ministering to them.

The glory even reached Union Station, the downtown Los Angeles train station. It was less than a mile from the Mission and God seekers were arriving there from all over the world. Passengers would be seen getting off the train and walking across the platform and falling out in the Spirit and speaking in tongues. Some of them received their healing at the same time. When one of the men first saw that people were lying all over the platform he first thought that there was a disaster until he realized what was going on.

Frank Bartleman witnessed this phenomenon at the train station, and in the streets, and wrote about a blood-line of power several blocks around the mission.

Seymour's humility
It was widely reported that Seymour would frequently tarry and wait upon the Lord with his head in a box. He would put the box on his head, not caring what anyone thought, and pray until he had the witness to take it off. Many times when he took it off was when the miraculous would increase and go to another level in the service.

The anointing was so powerful in the meetings that all kinds of healings took place. Participants reported that faith for miracles became easy.

Another Quote From Tommy Welchel's Book ~ Boldness came easy
Brother Garcia summed up his experience with God at Azusa with these words:

> When you came into Azusa, you got healed. The more you attended, the more faith you had, and the more things would happen. Because your faith was building up as you saw other people believing and you believed, soon you had no doubt when you walked up to someone that they were going to get healed. After a while it was easy to have the boldness to walk up to someone and proclaim "God is going to heal you tonight!

"And now, Lord, behold their threatenings: and grant unto thy servants, that with all boldness they may speak thy word, By stretching forth thine hand to heal; and that signs and wonders may be done by the name of thy holy child Jesus. And when they had prayed, the place was shaken where they were assembled together; and they were all filled with the Holy Ghost, and they spake the word of God with boldness." (Acts 4:29-31)

Notable miracles and healings were common
The Lord poured out an unprecedented healing and deliverance anointing at Azusa Street. Devils were cast out, tumors fell off and blind eyes were opened, teeth and limbs grew back, and many got out of wheel chairs. And, we have learned from Tommy's stories that God used the teenagers extensively.

Another excerpt from Tommy's book
Remember, Sister Carney was 17 to 21 years old during the 1906 to 1910 revival.

> Tommy speaking: I asked Sister Carney about other miracles she witnessed or participated in. With a smile and a twinkle in her eyes, she talked about the mighty works of God. According to Sister Carney, many people were there in wheelchairs and cots brought in from the hospitals around the area. Often, before Seymour would come downstairs or even when he was sitting with the box on his head, Sister Carney and others would go to the sick and crippled and pray for them, and they would get their healing. She and the others would go to those in wheelchairs, pull up the footrests, pray for them, and then watch them walk off, pushing their empty wheelchairs.
>
> One of these wheelchair healings stayed with Sister Carney in a special way. One man had heavy braces on his legs and had not walked in years. She recalls that the wheelchair he was in had wheels made of wood. She prayed for him, and he was miraculously healed. His name was Brother Aubrey, and he was pastor of a big church in Los Angeles. I actually got to meet him because he would come to Pisgah to see his precious Sister Carney, because she was the one who had prayed for him when he was healed at Azusa.
>
> During one visit to Pisgah in the sixties, Brother Aubrey shared his version of the healing miracle. Sister Carney didn't say a word to him. She just walked up, pulled the footrests up, put his foot down, then got the other foot, lifted it up – remember his legs had very heavy braces on them – then laid it down. Next, she told him to get up and walk, but Aubrey told her he couldn't walk because of the heavy braces. Sister Carney responded by getting the people with him to take off his braces so he could walk. They did, and he did! He got up and walked.

I was amazed at the story and asked Sister Carney about how many miracles God had used her to personally perform. She told me that God blessed her by using her two to three times a day the three to four days she attended each week. That's six to eight miracles a week for over three and one-half years. Sister Carney explained that miracles abounded at Azusa. People with bones twisted were restored. You could hear bones popping and see arms and legs growing out.

Our talks turned from miracles performed by God through faithful saints attending the meetings to the difference in miracles when Brother Seymour was preaching. Sister Carney explained that when Brother Seymour would come down, there were even greater miracles. Seymour never had a set pattern, rather he would come down and put the box over this head and then later would take the box off when directed by God, get up and do what God told him to do.

Sometimes, he would go to a certain section of wheelchairs or to a certain section of cots – the cots were for people who had been carried in from the hospital. She explained that to her astonishment, Seymour would point at them and say, "Everyone on the cots or wheelchairs, you're healed in the Name of Jesus." Everyone on the cots or in wheelchairs would get up and walk around fully healed of whatever malady they suffered from.

Some of the greatest miracles were when the flames were above the building. Bones that were cracked and broken were totally healed.

Our conversation would turn from the miracles performed by Seymour to Seymour personally. I wanted to know about this great man, and Sister Carney was a treasure chest of information. Her story began with the box on his head.

When Seymour came down to the meeting, he would sit down and put a box on his head. At first, it startled Sister Carney. Sometimes he would sit with the box over his head for ten minutes and sometimes it would be an hour or more. Although the practice seemed ridiculous, Sister Carney realized that he was obeying God, no matter how silly or ridiculous it appeared. That apparent act of humble obedience led to mighty power when he removed the box. This box and act of humility were critical to the power God displayed through Brother Seymour.

Two stories of Seymour and healing ~ From Tommy's book

Azusa Street Mission in 1906, Courtesy "Flower Pentecostal Heritage Center

Tommy speaking: I asked if they remembered any specific miracles where God used Brother Seymour, and Sister Lankford's eyes lit up. "I recall witnessing two of the greatest miracles where Seymour was greatly used by God."

I was all ears! First, she told about the man with the wooden leg. Seymour had approached a man with a wooden leg and asked, "What did you come here for?"

The man replied, "I want you to pray for my leg. It is starting to get gangrene where the wooden leg attaches."

Seymour replied, "I'm just upset because you have the wooden leg on. It would be a challenge for God to grow a leg out when the wooden leg is attached." The man removed the wooden leg and stood before Seymour standing on his one good leg. Seymour laid hands on the man and proclaimed, "Let Thy Name be glorified. In the Name of Jesus, I command this leg to grow out. The gangrene is gone; you are healed." Seymour didn't preach that night. The miracle spoke for itself. Rejoicing was continuous as the crowd went wild. The man ran upon the platform and around the room. No one could get him to stop rejoicing and praising God.

Next, Sister Lankford told of the man with no arm. Seymour spoke with a man who had lost his arm ten years earlier through a work-related accident. The arm had been totally severed at the shoulder.

Brother Seymour asked the crowd, "Would you like to see God have a wonderful time here tonight? Some of you may remember the man's leg that grew out about a year ago."

Seymour then asked the one-armed man, "Can you work with just the one arm?"

"I'm just given minimal paying jobs and I barely make enough money to even eat."

Seymour shook his head and responded, "That's not good. Are you married?"

"Yes."

"Got kids?"

"Yes."

"This man needs to be able to make a living. This man needs to work and he needs to be able to pay his tithe. Will you tithe if I pray for you and God gives you your arm back?" Seymour said teasingly.

"Yes!"

Seymour burst out laughing. "I'm just having fun." He then slapped his hands on the shoulder itself and commanded the arm to grow out. Almost instantly it grew out. The healed man stood in total shock, then started moving his arm and feeling of it with his other hand, awed by the miracle.

A few weeks later the man came back, bringing about 200 people with him, telling many at the meeting that he had gotten his old job back. Many of those he brought with him needed healing and left that evening fully restored as people in the crowd prayed and laid hands on each of them.

God used the young people

The miracle ministry was not limited to leadership. If your heart was right with God you were allowed to move and minister amongst the people. According to Tommy, two of those youngsters were Ralph Riggs and C. W. Ward. Ralph told Tommy that he was given the liberty to go to anyone he wanted to and pray for them and every one he prayed for received their healing. Years later Riggs and Ward were early fathers in the Assemblies of God. C.W. Ward was well known Pentecostal preacher, C.M. Ward's father.

The fire of God!

" ... and the God that answereth by fire, let Him be God." (1 Kings 18:24)

"Then the fire of the LORD fell ... " And when all the people saw it, they fell on their faces: and they said, The LORD, he is the God; the LORD, he is the God." (1 Kings 18:38-39)

"For our God is a consuming fire." (Heb 12:29)

Remember the Yosemite Fire Falls and the prophetic call? "Let the fire fall!" ~ with the answer coming from above, "The fire is falling!" There were many bona fide reports of fire on the old Azusa Street building. On several occasions the fire department arrived because passers-by had reported the flames. The flames were estimated to be fifty feet high. Flames were also seen coming down to meet the flames going up. But like Moses' "burning bush" the building was not consumed. What was consumed in this fire was unbelief, lethargy, cancer, depression, etc.

John G. Lake comments on the fire in Tommy Welchel's book

> Sister Carney did go out one time to see the flames for herself. Remember, the fire department had been called on several different occasions, as passers-by would report seeing flames leaping up from the roof of the building. Finally, Sister Carney asked John Lake why the fire department kept coming and looking for the fire. He explained that the fire was coming down from heaven into the building and fire was going up from the building and meeting the fire coming down. Fascinated, Sister Carney went out, walked about a half a block and saw the awesome sight for herself. To her, this divine connection of fire coming down from heaven and going up to heaven was just further evidence of God's mighty Presence in that place.
>
> Sister Carney noted that although the Shekinah Glory was present all the time within the building, this divine connection wasn't an everyday occurrence. Whenever this connection was present, the power of God was even more intense within the meeting.

The Mighty Baptism ~ The export anointing ~ The California Contribution

Taught and caught at Azusa

"Some is taught and some is caught." Probably the most significant attribute of this mighty outpouring is how it spread like wildfire. It was extremely contagious. The revelatory teaching of "the baptism in the Holy Ghost," and the tangible manifestation of it, with the accompanying miracle and healing anointing, was imparted to preachers, teachers, and missionaries from around the world. They came from "a far country," and "the islands of the sea," to seek out this outpouring, and they got it! It is from Azusa that the Pentecostal outpouring went back to their home states, or mother countries, and then spread to the entire world.

The front gate at Pisgah in 2009

There are numerous reports of the pastors, evangelists, and missionaries returning to their home states, or foreign lands, from the revival in California and witnessing mighty outpourings of the Holy Spirit. In most cases these outpourings were not just waves of the Holy Spirit like we witness many times in revivals today. Indeed, the seeds of Azusa taken to near and distant lands proved to be lasting and continuing moves of God. They initiated the present Spirit-filled/Pentecostal/Charismatic movement. To this day it is the largest and fastest growing Christian movement in the world.

Fires of Pentecost around the world
People came to California to tap into "the outpouring from heaven" from every state and from around the world. Literally tens of thousands of people tasted of the "heavenly gift."

Before it waned it had imparted and ignited spiritual fires all across America and throughout the earth. As the doors closed to the old Azusa Street Mission in the mid 1930s, latter-day Pentecost was launched into the earth, and was spreading "like a wild fire crossing a wind-swept prairie." The outpouring at Azusa had done its work.

Give us revival again, with or without the defects!
John Wesley himself once prayed, after revival had about died out for the time,

> "Oh, Lord, send us the old revival without the defects; but if this cannot be, send it with all the defects. We must have revival!"[15]

Yes, with or without the defects, I want the excitement for God, the souls, the miracles, the hurting and sick healed, the glory cloud (presence), the power so strong people fall at the train station, the fire going up and meeting the fire coming down. In other words, the manifestation of "The Kingdom of Heaven is at hand!"

The Hundred Year Prophecy
Daddy Seymour and Charles Parham prophesied in 1909 or 1910 that in about a hundred years God was sending a revival that would be far greater than the mighty outpouring of Azusa Street. Parham was on the east coast and Seymour was in L.A. when they prophesied the same thing. Let us all stand and agree with that word for California and the nations!

Even so come, Lord Jesus!

"If My People ..."

CHAPTER 16

THE CHURCH OF GOD IN CHRIST

In the beginning of the twentieth century, The Church of God in Christ was in turmoil over manifestations of the Holy Spirit, healing, and the doctrine of sanctification. Bishop Charles Harrison Mason today is considered the founder of the denomination.

Here is an excerpt from the denomination website:

> Later, the church was reorganized during which Elder C.P. Jones was chosen as General Overseer. Elder C.H. Mason was appointed as overseer of Tennessee, and Elder J.A. Jeter was overseer of Arkansas.
>
> The turning point in Elder Mason's life came in March, 1907, when he journeyed to Los Angeles, California, to attend a great Pentecostal revival with Elder D.J. Young and Elder J.A. Jeter. Elder W.J. Seymour was preaching concerning Luke 24:49, "And behold I send the promise of my Father upon you; but tarry ye in the city of Jerusalem until ye be endued with power from on high." Elder Mason became convinced that it was essential for him to have the outpouring of the Holy Ghost.
>
> The following are excerpts from Elder Mason's personal testimony regarding his receiving the Holy Ghost.
>
> "The first day in the meeting I sat to myself, away from those that went with me. I began to thank God in my heart for all things, for when I heard some speak in tongues, I knew it was right though I did not understand it. Nevertheless, it was sweet to me.
>
> I also thank God for Elder Seymour who came and preached a wonderful sermon. His words were sweet and powerful and it seems that I hear them

now while writing. When he closed his sermon, he said 'All of those that want to be sanctified or baptized with the Holy Ghost, go to the upper room; and all those that want to be justified, come to the altar.

I said that is the place for me, for it may be that I am not converted and if not, God knows it and can convert me..."

"Glory!"

The second night of prayer I saw a vision. I saw myself standing alone and had a dry roll of paper in my mouth trying to swallow it. Looking up towards the heavens, there appeared a man at my side. I turned my eyes at once, then I awoke and the interpretation came.

God had me swallowing the whole book and if I did not turn my eyes to anyone but God and Him only, He would baptize me. I said yes to Him, and at once in the morning when I arose, I could hear a voice in me saying, 'I see...'

"I got a place at the altar and began to thank God. After that, I said 'Lord if I could only baptize myself, I would do so;' for I wanted the baptism so bad I did not know what to do. I said, 'Lord, You will have to do the work for me; so I turned it over into His hands.'

Then, I began to ask for the baptism of the Holy Ghost according to Acts 2:41, which readeth thus: 'Then they that gladly received His word were baptized,' Then I saw that I had a right to be glad and not sad.

The enemy said to me, 'there may be something wrong with you.' Then a voice spoke to me saying, 'if there is anything wrong with you, Christ will find it and take it away and marry you' ... Someone said, 'Let us sing.' I arose and the first song that came to me was 'He brought me out of the Miry Clay.'

The Spirit came upon the saints and upon me. Then I gave up for the Lord to have His way within me. So there came a wave of Glory into me and all of my being was filled with the Glory of the Lord.

So when He had gotten me straight on my feet, there came a light which enveloped my entire being above the brightness of the sun. When I opened my mouth to say Glory, a flame touched my tongue which ran down me. My language changed and no word could I speak in my own tongue. Oh! I was filled with the Glory of the Lord. My soul was then satisfied."

This new Pentecostal experience which Elder Mason found for himself, for he began to proclaim to others upon his return home to Memphis, Tennessee as a New Testament doctrine. A division, subsequently, became evident within the ranks of Elder Mason's contemporaries when Elder J. A. Jeter, the General Overseer, Elder C. P. Jones, and others regarded the new Holy Ghost experience of speaking in tongues as a delusion. Being unable to resolve their difference in the New Testament doctrine.

The General Assembly terminated by withdrawing the "right hand" of fellowship from C. H. Mason. Elder Mason then called a conference in Memphis, Tennessee of all ministers who believed in receiving the baptism of the Holy Ghost according to the Scriptures in Acts 2:1-4. Those who responded to Elder Mason's urgent call were E. R. Driver, J. Bowe, R.R. Booker, R. E. Hart, W. Welsh, A. A. Blackwell, E. M. Page, R.H. I. Clark, D. J. Young, James Brewer, Daniel Spearman and J. H. Boone.

These men of God organized the first Pentecostal General Assembly of the "Church of God in Christ." Overseer C. H. Mason was then chosen unanimously as the General Overseer and Chief Apostle of our denomination. He was given complete authority to establish doctrine, organize auxiliaries and appoint overseers.[1]

Today the organization has congregations in nearly 60 countries around the world. With a membership of over six million worshipers, it is the largest African-American, and largest Pentecostal church in the United States.[2]

Bishop Charles E. Blake, pastor of Los Angeles's 24,000 member mega church, "West Angeles Church of God in Christ," is the current presiding bishop and chief apostle of the denomination.

"If My People ..."

CHAPTER **17**

AIMEE SEMPLE MC PHERSON
&
THE FOURSQUARE CHURCH

Aimee Semple McPherson in 1927

The story of the founding of the International Church of the Foursquare Gospel and Aimee Semple McPherson is the same story.

Aimee was born on October 9, 1890, on a small farm near Ingersoll, Ontario, Canada. It was during her high school days when she attended a revival meeting conducted by the fiery young Pentecostal preacher who had been touched by the Azusa Street revival, Robert Semple, that she was convicted of her spiritual condition. She said later that she was "cold and far from

Angelus Temple in 1930

Regular Sunday attendance

God." Semple preached Pentecost from Acts chapter 2 and emphasized the word "repent." The young preacher's demeanor and message touched Aimee deeply.[1] After several days of wrestling with the idea, finally alone in her room, she threw up her hands and said, "Lord, God, be merciful to me, a sinner." Immediately the glory of the Lord filled her heart and she was "born again."[2]

The tarrying meetings

It was in 1908 that the effects of the Azusa Street Revival touched Aimee through Semple and others. The revelation and the manifestation of "the mighty baptism in the Holy Ghost" had reached Ingersoll, Ontario. A local woman was holding special "tarrying meetings" in her house for those who were seriously seeking the experience. Aimee had become increasingly desperate for the deep things of God and was praying fervently for direction. She heard in her spirit – "become a soul winner."[3]

In her pursuit of God she searched the New Testament and became convinced that she needed "the mighty baptism in the Holy Ghost." On her way to school one day she passed the lady's home that was holding the tarrying meetings and decided she couldn't go on. She went back and rang the door bell and the lady invited her in. After explaining what was on her heart, the lady started to seek God and pray with her. Aimee even prayed that God would delay school so she could tarry to receive "tongues." When she prayed that prayer, a blizzard hit Ingersoll. The storm not only prevented her from going to school but it also prevented her from returning home. She was delighted, because she was snowed-in for the weekend at the tarrying home.

It was early that Saturday morning that she arose while everyone else in the house was asleep. When she began praising Him she fell to the floor in a cloud of glory. The tongues came from deep within her. She couldn't contain herself and woke the entire house as she raised her voice and prayed in tongues. They all came rushing downstairs shouting and rejoicing for her breakthrough. One of the tenants of the house was the preacher, Robert Semple. He was staying there while he was preaching in the area.[4]

The proposal and marriage

Soon he and Aimee fell in love, and on one of his return trips to Ingersoll he proposed to her. Six months later they were married in her family's farm house. Aimee dropped out of high school to be with her husband. The two of them were very much in love. She wrote later, "He was my theological seminary … my spiritual mentor, and my tender, patient, unfailing lover."[5]

In 1910, Aimee and Robert went to China on a mission trip and it was there that they both caught malaria. Aimee got over it, but only two months after they had arrived there, Robert passed away. Now, in a foreign land, alone and pregnant with their first child Aimee was grief stricken. As she lay in her hospital bed to give birth she was overcome with misery and horror. She would often turn to the hospital wall and scream. The thought of carrying on alone was more than she could bear.

Eventually, Amiee's mother sent her the money to return home. Her tiny baby daughter was all that she had to show for her short but loving marriage.[5] As it turned out for Aimee, she never was able to enjoy that kind of relationship again. She married two more times in her life, mostly out of pure loneliness, but the relationships didn't last.

Will you go?

Through the next few years Aimee kept hearing, "Now will you go?"[6] She was preaching and teaching around the community in Sunday schools at the time but that did not silence the voice nor the fire that was in her spirit. Then in 1914 she became very sick. She was having heart trouble and stomach hemorrhages. After two surgeries she grew even worse, and finally began begging God to let her die. The doctors called in the family to inform them that she was dying. It was then that she could hear the voice booming now, "Do the work of an Evangelist! Will you go?"

The interns moved Aimee to a ward where they took care of dying patients. In her delirious state she began speaking out and calling people to repentance. She was also hearing the voice again, "Will you go?" Finally, she whispered "yes." When she opened her eyes, all the pain was gone. Within two weeks she was totally well and up and gone from the hospital.[7]

Preaching on her own

Aimee began almost at once to preach. It was now 1915. She was a natural. With her dramatics and just being a woman, she became a novelty. Women preachers were hard to find in those days. But she had the stuff and people were naturally drawn to her. She was soon drawing huge crowds. Her meetings were blessed with amazing manifestations of the Holy Spirit, and thousands received the baptism. The news of her healing ministry also spread far and wide, and people came in droves to be ministered to.

In order to minister the love of Jesus to the people, Aimee believed in using many different techniques of ministry. She used story telling, uncommon music, theater and narrated drama and so on.

The ministry went big

Between 1917 and 1923 Aimee criss-crossed America six times preaching in more than a hundred cities. Her meetings were from two days to a month in duration.[8] She was drawing huge crowds. Once in San Diego, the National Guard had to be brought in to handle a crowd of over 30,000 people. When she did multiple services people would stand in line for hours to be able to get a seat in the next service.[9]

Aimee ministering to a packed audience
Note: All Aimee photos courtesy of The Foursquare Church Heritage Archives

Called to California

It was in 1918 that Aimee was called to settle in California. God promised her and her children a home in Los Angeles. He gave her a vision of it with a rose garden and all. When she arrived there, the people gave her the land for the house and pledged the labor and materials to build it. Within months she had her promise, and it was everything in her vision, complete with the rose garden.

When Aimee arrived in Los Angeles in late 1918, the Azusa Street Revival had already waned, but it was still quite fresh in people's minds. There were many participants still hungry and hoping that God would send someone to come and revive the revival. Many believed that Aimee was that person. And to a great extent, she was. Two days after her arrival she preached to over seven hundred people. In a short time the window sills of the Philharmonic Auditorium were filled with people who came to her meetings.[10]

Now her vision was to build Angelus Temple. Most of her extensive travels in the next few years were dedicated to preaching and raising the funds for the church. By this time the media had discovered her and she was packing out the meeting halls. Many times thousands of people had to be turned away. Incredible miracles always happened in the meetings and the local press was quick to headline them. People were constantly pressing to touch her, and she would watch in horror sometimes as the police would bolt the door to protect her.[11]

At night, when she lay down and closed her eyes, she would see the people packing in to a large meeting hall that was too small for the crowd. She would see the sick overflowing the altars and think about how Jesus would handle it.

First woman preacher on radio
In 1922, during a revival meeting in the San Francisco Bay area, Aimee became the first woman to preach a sermon on radio. Then, as a result of the success of that event, she eventually bought her own radio station, "thus becoming the first woman to own and operate a Christian radio station." This also made her radio station the first Christian radio station in the world.[12]

This is a quote from the Foursquare web site

> "Through the wonder of radio, Aimee's voice became the most recognizable voice around the world. Since there were not many stations in Los Angeles at its inception, one could walk down the street, especially on a Sunday morning, hear the entire message from one open window to another, get to their destination, and not miss a single word of the sermon."[13]

Angelus Temple dedicated

In late 1923 Angelus Temple was finally completed. It was an extraordinary building that seated 5,300 people. The extravagant dedication took place on New Year's Day, 1923. The New York Times and other media gave the event full coverage. It is reported that from then on the Temple was filled to capacity three to four services each Sunday and many times during the week. The church had perfect acoustics and was the envy of many Hollywood producers.

God touches Hollywood

Aimee's messages were full of different dynamics and drama. She used costumes, props, and scenery to demonstrate her sermons in true Hollywood style. Her unique style attracted people that would normally never go to church. People that frequented some of her meetings were: Mary Pickford, Jean Harlow, Clara Bow, and Charlie Chaplin. Chaplin would later help her stage her illustrated sermons, and Aimee, in turn, showed him the truth of life.[14]

As a young man before his debut as an actor, Anthony Quinn played in Aimee's band. As a teenager Aimee took him on a Spanish crusade as her translator.

Quinn once wrote:

> "Years later, when I saw the great actresses at work, I would compare them to her … Ingrid Bergman … Katharine Hepburn … Greta Garbo .. they all fell short of that first electric shock Aimee Semple McPherson produced in me."[15]

An excerpt from the Foursquare website:

> Aimee was famous inside and outside the church. Every city where services were held usually had in attendance civic leaders, as well as pastors representing the local churches of every denomination. She made sure that Angelus Temple was represented in local parades and entered floats into the famous Rose Parade in Pasadena. Her illustrated sermons attracted even those from the entertainment industry, looking to see a "show" that rivaled what Hollywood had to offer. These famous stage productions drew people who would never have thought to enter a church, and then presented them with the message of salvation. Aimee believed that the Gospel was to be presented at every opportunity and

used worldly means at her disposal to present the Gospel to as many people as possible.

Aimee once wrote:

"You don't need to be an orator. What God wants is plain people with the Good News in their hearts who are willing to go and tell it to others. The love of winning souls for Jesus Christ sets a fire burning in one's bones. Soul winning is the most important thing in the world. All I have is on the altar for the Lord, and while I have my life and strength, I will put my whole being into the carrying out of this Great Commission."

The Church of the Foursquare Gospel

In 1922, before it was finished, Aimee called Angelus Temple "The Church of the Foursquare Gospel." Her inspiration for the name came from a vision she had while preaching in a crusade in Oakland California.

The Four Squares are:

> Jesus is Savior
> Jesus is Healer
> Jesus is Baptizer in the Holy Ghost
> Jesus is coming King

In 1923 Aimee opened L.I.F.E Bible College (Lighthouse of International Foursquare Evangelism) The name of the college was more recently changed to Life Pacific College, but it is still affiliated with the Foursquare organization.

The World-Wide organization

In 1927 the denominational organization of **"International Church of the Foursquare Gospel"** was founded by Aimee. The denomination today is a thriving move of the Holy Spirit ... planting churches and winning souls all around the world. Mighty churches such as Jack Hayford's "Church on the Way" in Van Nuys, California, are part of the growing denomination.

Today with over

> eight million members
> sixty thousand churches
> in a hundred and forty-four countries

The **"International Church of the Foursquare Gospel"** is one of the largest Pentecostal organizations in the world. Its home base is, you guessed it, Los Angeles, California.[16]

"If My People ..."

CHAPTER **18**

CALVARY CHAPEL, THE JESUS MOVEMENT, AND THE VINEYARD MOVEMENT

Chuck Smith and Calvary Chapel
As I stated earlier in this book, the stories of Calvary Chapel, The Jesus Movement, and The Vineyard Movement are all closely related.

The story of Calvary Chapel begins with Chuck Smith in 1965. Smith was a graduate of Life Bible College, the Foursquare College founded by Aimee Semple McPherson. He later left the Foursquare denomination and in 1965 took a church in Costa Mesa, California called Calvary Chapel. That church had already been planted by Pastor Floyd Nelson.

It was in 1968 that Calvary Chapel experienced the beginning of its phenomenal growth and world-wide acclaim.[1]

Meet Lonnie Frisbee ~ Hippie Preacher
Lonnie Frisbee was an eighteen-year-old long-haired and bearded hippie that was a star preacher of the Jesus Movement. Remember, I gave a brief overview of the Jesus Movement in Chapter 14.

It was said that he was not one of the hippie preachers, "there was only one." Lonnie was so well known at the time that he was featured in the 2007 Emmy-nominated film "Frisbee: The Life and Death of a Hippie Preacher." Life, Newsweek, and Rolling Stone magazines also did features on the Jesus Movement and often interviewed and photographed Lonnie for the articles.

His converts include many well-known preachers in the ministry today. Although his personal demons eventually became his demise, his powerful and charismatic demeanor influenced many young people into the Kingdom of God. His meetings were known for awesome demonstrations and manifestations of the Holy Spirit. And, of importance to the theme of this book, he was used mightily to launch two major moves of God into their destinies.

Unfortunately, although he was married to his wife Connie, Lonnie was maintaining a gay lifestyle at the same time. Once this became known, he was removed and ostracized by his leaders. He and Connie finally divorced in 1973 and, at the age of forty-three, in 1993, he died of complications of AIDS.[2]

The importance of character
I have always said that "the gifts and callings of God are without repentance," but the blessing isn't. Just because someone is anointed and moves in a powerful ministry does not mean that God endorses their lack of character. In His mercy He gives us time and space to repent. Then, if we do not repent He removes the blessing. That's why we must keep our eyes on Jesus and the Word of God and not man. Godly character is much more important to God than the anointing. Consequently character, which comes from an intimate relationship with Jesus, is essential to maintaining the anointing and the blessing.

Now back to Calvary Chapel
In 1968, Chuck Smith's church was struggling when he became impressed with Lonnie Frisbee's charismatic abilities. He invited Lonnie and his wife, Connie, into his home and connected them with his youth leader, John Higgins. Together they started a Christian commune called "The House of Miracles." John and Lonnie went out into the community to reach the youth with the gospel during the early days of the Jesus movement. The young people began coming into the church by the droves. The church, mostly through the charismatic anointing on Lonnie, was bridging the "generation gap." As pioneers of a new concept to normal church protocol, Calvary began featuring a more informal approach to worship. The church was doing outreaches on the beach and baptizing in the Pacific Ocean. They also instituted a more contemporary form of music. Maranatha Music was eventually founded by Chuck Smith for this purpose.

Today over 35,000 people attend services at the church in Costa Mesa. In addition, Chuck Smith is on daily radio and the church has an extensive media ministry. As of 2006, Calvary Chapel had over one thousand affiliate churches around the world. Its global influence is quite significant.[1]

John Wimber and the Vineyard movement

Before his destiny as the leader of an international denomination, John Wimber was the keyboard player and producer in the band The Righteous Brothers. He later joined a Quaker church and eventually became an instructor at Fuller Theological Seminary in Pasadena, California.

He joined forces with Chuck Smith in the seventies and pastored a Calvary Chapel church in Yorba Linda, California. In 1982, he became more and more convinced that the church should be operating in the healing and miracle ministry of Jesus Christ. It was this theological difference that led him to leave Calvary, with Chuck Smith's recommendation and blessing, and take up leadership of the small group of Vineyard churches already founded by Ken Gulliksen.

It was when he had Lonnie Frisbee come and preach that the Vineyard Movement hit high gear. When Lonnie gave the altar call for everybody twenty-five and under to come forward, the glory fell. When he said "Come Holy Spirit," witnesses say it looked like a battlefield as young people fell and began to shake and speak in tongues.

The Vineyard Movement then grew quickly to an international Christian organization. With an emphasis in training leaders and planting churches, the denomination also focuses on "Power Evangelism" and healing through the power of the Holy Spirit.

Excerpt from the Vineyard website

> Twenty-five years later there are more than 1,500 Vineyard churches worldwide, 600 in the US, with 8 regions actively planting churches across the country.
>
> Vineyard worship songs, documented by Vineyard Music, have helped thousands of churches experience intimacy with God. Many churches have been equipped to continue Jesus' ministry of proclaiming the kingdom, demonstrating the kingdom, and training disciples."[3]

The Calvary Chapel and Vineyard Movements are both very much a part of "The California Contribution" to global Christianity and the end-time harvest.

"If My People ..."

CHAPTER **19**

SEEKING THE "DOUBLE PORTION"

It seems that the Lord, in His plan for California, placed Grace and me in this wilderness of a place for a purpose. Although we love Mariposa, its population density makes it a hard place to build a big ministry. Until we began ministry here, everything Grace and I ever did was on a large scale. But here we are, in the remote mountains of California, sitting on the spiritual center of California ~ with our hearts bursting for an uncommon move of God.

We are beginning to see that He placed us here and planted that seed of "desperation for Him" in us, along with the anointing of perseverance to hang in there, as a strategic plan for California.

Grace and I are not conference runners or "spiritual party" seekers. We have seen enough of that "flaky stuff" to last us for a while, and some of that spirit has attended our own meetings. We know that the basis of receiving a "double portion" is one's faithfulness to the Word of God, prayer and personal devotion to Him. These are the things that are essential to build the Godly character that can receive and maintain the "filling of the Holy Spirit."

Now, with that said, we do have a "driving hunger and desperation" for the anointing power of God in our lives and ministry.

When I read in the Bible that a dead man thrown into Elisha's grave was resurrected by a residual anointing on Elisha's bones, I take particular notice. (2 Kings 13:21)

The transferrable anointing
Since the mid-90's, it seems that God has sent waves of outpourings into the earth that have had an explicit mantle of "impartation" accompanied with them. In the same spirit of Azusa Street, God has been using specific "portals" into the

earth to pour out a transferrable anointing. He then draws the hungry leaders to it to impart it to them. In turn they take it and release it in their realms of influence. When hungry ministry leaders take the time and effort to travel to a distant land to "catch a fresh wind of the Spirit," very frequently the Lord places the anointing of that outpouring on them to take home to their city and church. Today, renewal and revival fires are burning in churches and cities around the globe as a result of hungry pastors and preachers that have done just that. It is the same old principle of the Azusa Street Revival. It was the "pilgrimage" spirit that spread Pentecost to the nations.

When Grace and I hear about such an outpouring, we seriously check it out and pray for a witness from the Lord as to whether we should go and tap into it. I sincerely believe that every anointed minister of the Gospel should have the heart that is hungry enough for God to "... *turn aside, and see this great sight ...*" (Exodus 3:4)

If God is truly pouring something into the earth, Grace and I are going to do everything we can to connect with it. We know that the people that we minister to need us to have the goods. They are sick, broken hearted and hurting. We believe that hearts that truly love God and people, and consequently are truly hungry for the anointing for the right reason, will be willing to cross nations or oceans to tap into it. If Elisha had not gone on that pilgrimage with Elijah (2 Kings 2:9) he would have probably still had a ministry, but he would not have received the *"double portion."* There is something to be said for "pilgrimage."

"And ye shall seek me, and find me, when ye shall search for me with all your heart." (Jeremiah 29:13)

"... and that he is a rewarder of them that diligently seek him." (Hebrews 11:6)

In that spirit, I have outlined here some of the things that we have done, and places that the Lord has led us. It is with hearts burning for more of God that we press in.

A brief review of some of our pilgrimages seeking the "Double Portion:"

In 1991, we kneeled at John Winthrop's grave in Boston, Mass.

In 1995, we visited the Toronto Blessing twice.

In 1995, we visited the revival in Melbourne, Fla.

In 1995, we visited Rodney Howard-Browne in Anaheim, Ca.

In 1995, the river/renewal exploded and flowed in our church in Mariposa, Ca. for over a year.

In 1997, we visited the Pensacola, Florida Outpouring twice.

In 1997, the "Feast of Fire Revival" ignited in our church and ran for most of the year.

In 1998, we stood on the steps of the Bonnie Brae House in Los Angeles and proclaimed Rev 3:7.

In 1999, I visited the Grand Opening of Healing Rooms in Spokane ~ alone with the prayer team I was prayed for, anointed, and prophesied over in every room of the Old Rookery building.

In 2000, we sponsored and hosted one of the largest Native American Reconciliation gatherings in California history (32 nations/tribes represented) in Mariposa, Ca.

In 2000, our church, and our Merced sister church, Faith Mission Ministries, did a 3-day bus trip and an all-night prayer vigil in the Bonnie Brae House in Los Angeles, Ca.

In 2000, we began the 24-Hour prayer one day a week in Mariposa, Ca. It continues to this day. The vision was, and still is, for 24/7

In 2000, we led a group of California intercessors to Yosemite and spiritually re-enacted the prophetic call of The Yosemite Fire Falls ~ **Lord, let the fire fall!**

In 2000, I laid on John G Lake's Grave in Spokane, Wa.

In 2005, we kneeled at Evan Robert's grave in South Wales, UK

In 2005, we stood on the spot in the church in Bradford, England, UK where Smith Wigglesworth graduated

In 2007, we held our own revival service in Moriah Chapel in South Wales, UK (Ground Zero of the 1904 Welsh Revival)

In 2007, we celebrated the 10-year Anniversary Conference for the Feast of Fire Revival

In 2008, we visited the Lakeland, Fla. Outpouring twice

In 2009, we led another group, including Marilyn Noorda and Candi MacAlpine to the Mariposa County Courthouse to pray and decree over California. The same day we went to Yosemite and blessed the Merced River ("River of Mercy") and re-enacted the Firefalls call from Camp Curry ... **Lord, let the fire fall!** We then went up to Glacier Point where the Firefalls originated and blew the shofar and decreed over California **"The fire is falling."**

"If My People ..."

CHAPTER 20

REVIVAL COMES TO MARIPOSA
"All I know is, we were hungry!"

One of the pleasures of writing this book is to get to tell some of the stories of the awesome moves of God in our little church in Mariposa, California. Here I will tell you the story of my "offense" and repentance. This story reminds me of the principle that "God will offend your mind to reveal your spirit." We cry out for God to send revival, but many times we are the ones standing in the way.

In early January of 1995, Grace and I flew to Toronto, Canada to check out the meetings that we had heard about at the Toronto Airport Vineyard Fellowship. We planned to stay for three days. However during the first service, "yours truly," a dedicated Word of Faith preacher, was totally offended by all the manifestations and interruptions, and told Grace "Honey, we're outta here! Call the airlines and let's go home … tomorrow!" I was convinced that this couldn't be God and it was not " … *decent and in order.*"

I was serious, this was not for me, there is no way this could be God. People were manifesting all over the place, during the worship, and while the preachers were preaching. People were roaring, some were jerking and rattling their feet real fast on the floor, others were laughing loudly while others were crying or moaning. The guy next to us was draped over a chair and foaming at the mouth. It was a mess! I was a "Spirit filled" preacher that believed in the "gifts of the Spirit" and talking in tongues and casting out devils, but this was ridiculous.

I wanted to go home, "before quick!" The trouble is, God kept speaking to me these words *"Son, if the fruit is good, you make the tree good."* I argued with him and kept saying, "God, this can't be you," but I kept hearing the same thing over and over, *"Son, if the fruit is good, you make the tree good."*

The testimonies from the platform that kept coming forth from second time visitors are what the Lord was referring to. Burnt out and defeated preachers having had complete life and ministry changes from their first visit to Toronto were giving their awesome testimonies. Marriages healed, people delivered of depression and oppression, and the list goes on. I was a "Word" man, so He got me with the "Word."

All I know is, we were hungry for an uncommon move of God. So, under protest, we stayed for just a day or two, I thought. Then finally, I got it, this was a move of God. It just didn't come in the package that I thought it should have. He immediately began to show me that with a move of the Spirit, a move of the flesh almost always accompanies. Our job is to discern the difference and not "throw the baby out with the bath water." Just learn how to pastor it.

So I told Grace, "Honey, call the airline," but this time it was to postpone our departure. We had business to do with God. There was something in the way of revival in Mariposa, and guess who! We wound up staying for nine days. I watched things happen, then watched how leadership handled it. I watched them like a hawk. We also attended every leadership class they had.

Find your 2 x 4's
The next few nights when we came into the meetings I asked Grace to excuse me. I had to be alone with God. Even though there were several thousand people there I wanted to disappear in the crowd and seek the Lord without distraction. She agreed and wanted to do the same thing. So we split up.

At that time the church had just moved from their little airport church into a large international building which now I think is their permanent church. They had quickly built a wooden platform for a stage and it was quite large. It was about three to three and a half feet high and framed with 2 x 4's with a plywood deck. The front just had a makeshift curtain hanging on it. Behind that curtain was just a bunch of 2 x 4 frame work. So, nightly, for several nights, I would ease my way through all the hungry "manifesting" worshippers at the altar and make my way to the platform. When I got there I pulled the curtain back and crawled under the platform between the 2 x 4 bracings and let the curtain go. This was a time that I didn't care what they were singing or preaching. This was between God and me. In the ambience of that anointing and presence I wanted to meet with God.

> I cried "Lord, whatever is wrong in me, take it out ... and, whatever I don't have that I need, please put it in."

He took me at my word. Grace and I began a journey with God then that has changed us forever. He began anointing us for revival and revealing to us a greater revelation of Himself, while at the same time pruning us and putting us through the refiner's fire. In the weeks and years to come we developed a deeper understanding of desperation, brokenness, hunger, and humility.

I would like to tell you that revival can come some other way, but saints of God, before there can be a resurrection there must be a death. As Frank Bartleman of the Azusa Street Revival used to say, "The height of your revival will depend on the depth of your repentance."

"Except a corn of wheat fall into the ground and die, it abideth alone: but if it die, it bringeth forth much fruit." (John 12:24)

Melbourne, Florida

During our time in Toronto, we heard about an outbreak of the Toronto Blessing at Jamie Buckingham's old church in Melbourne, Florida, my home state. Grace and I were so convinced that this was a "God time" for us, and Mariposa, that we wanted to see how a local church was handling this outpouring, as compared to a global portal scene like Toronto. So, immediately after our return home, we flew to Florida for a few days of more observation and learning. As it happened, John and Carol Arnott, the pastors of the Toronto church, were there at the same time. In Melbourne we learned more and observed the same anointing in a different setting and a different dynamic.

Rodney Browne in L.A.

Then upon our return home from Florida, we heard that Rodney Howard-Browne was at Melodyland Church in Anaheim. Now remember, this is back in early 1995 when this renewal movement was new to most of us. Anyhow, the Lord told us to go to southern California and observe that outpouring from still another angle. So, we loaded our three children in the car and repacked our bags and drove south to Anaheim. The visit was life changing again. Rodney's ministry had an awesome impact on our lives.

In that meeting God did a deep and "life-changing" work in Grace. Without anyone laying hands on her, or praying for her, the Holy Spirit destroyed the yoke of shyness and timidity over her life. She was literally set free from a lifetime of bondage to those two ministry destroyers. In the months and years since God has used her anointing and testimony to set countless people free from the same two impostors. She is now a powerful speaker with a bold "seers and healing" anointing.

No personal manifestations

Now, all three of these engagements had taken place back to back. We had not been back to our own church since we left for Toronto. Nor throughout the entire three-week adventure did Grace or I receive one "manifestation." A whole line of folks could be prayed for, and everybody would go down but us. No laughter, no shakes, nothing. Not even a twitchy finger. We prayed for God to do something to confirm that we had received an impartation, but nothing came. Now, it almost looked like our pursuit was backfiring on us. We were more discouraged than when we began. The thoughts came "What is wrong with us?"

The glory falls in Mariposa!

Back at home preparing for our first service, we were soon to find out that it isn't about our own manifestations! Now, after this time of spiritual "stretching," God was about to teach us an important lesson and change our lives and ministry forever.

Grace and I were horrified that, after all the miles we had traveled, all the prayer lines we had been in, and all we have seen and been through, church would be the same as always. That was an almost unbearable thought that was gnawing deep in our spirits.

Then, without any warning, the anointing actually hit two hours before the Sunday service started. While I was at home lying on my den floor travailing and crying out to God (literally) for the service, and for an uncommon move of the Holy Spirit, it started. Grace, who was already at church preparing for service at the same time that I was travailing on the floor, prayed for a singer's sore throat in the church kitchen during pre-service worship practice. As soon as Grace raised her hand to the lady's throat **revival hit Mariposa!** The Holy Spirit "suddenly" swept through the whole building. The lady prayed for slithered down to the floor. Another lady that unknowingly walked into the kitchen hit the linoleum. The innocent bystanders, around the corner in the foyer room, where they couldn't see what was going on, got drunk and fell off the couch.

An outpouring was under way. Grace told an elder to go quickly and call Pastor Henry and tell him to quit worrying, its here! When the elder called me and said "Grace told me to tell you, quit worrying, its here!" Like a dummy I said "What's here?" He then, excitedly, gave me a briefing of what was happening.

I quickly threw my stuff in the pick-up and flew to church. By the time I arrived, the place was already in revival and people were drunk in the Spirit and out on the floor. There was uncontrollable weeping and laughing manifesting all over the building.

Spontaneous combustion had taken place. The fire was falling! The "Glory," or kabod "Presence" was tangibly thick and heavy. The little sanctuary was filled well ahead of service time and the people were already into deep worship and intimacy with Jesus. It looked like Toronto and Rodney's meetings combined.

It was especially real because we hadn't testified to the congregation of our experiences yet. This was our first Sunday home and we hadn't had a chance to tell them what we saw. The people didn't know what to copy even if they wanted to. It was a genuine and sovereign move of God! I think God did that for me as He knows that I'm not into nonsense and that I would have been suspicious if the people would have manifested after we testified. The service went for hours that day and the only two left standing at the end were .. you guessed it .. Henry and Grace.

The Full Circle ... Running the Wildest River!

Services continued that way for the rest of 1995. The joy and intoxication in the Spirit, people getting baptized in the Holy Ghost and speaking in tongues (usually without being prayed for), intimacy with Jesus, and deliverances were common during every service. The church was changed forever. Now, no longer just a Word of Faith Church, it was in the River of God. This "professional river outfitter and guide," with twenty-five years of experience running the wildest rivers of the western United States, was now pastoring a "River Church" with a "Word of Faith" foundation and flowing in the "Third Day" anointing. MORE LORD!

"If My People ..."

CHAPTER 21

The Fire Falls Again in Mariposa
THE "FEAST OF FIRE REVIVAL"

1996 ~ Afterglow ~ glory ~ hunger ... and the beginning of a flood!
1996 was a year of a mixture of awesome afterglow and ministering in a new revelation of the Holy Spirit and glory from the previous year's outpouring at Mariposa Revival Center. This was all combined with the longing and travail for another "Visitation of The Holy Spirit."

Record storm blasts California
In the meantime, by the end of the year, California experienced a series of abnormally freezing cold storms with extremely heavy snows in the mountains. The snow pack was unusually deep at relatively low altitudes. There were several feet of snow pack at the three and four thousand foot elevations with twenty and thirty foot snow drifts at the ten to fourteen thousand foot level. Then, on New Year's Eve a "pineapple express" came in off of the South Pacific that was also a very large storm. However this one was very warm and brought heavy rains all the way up to the eleven thousand foot elevations ... which is also almost unheard of in December and January.

The flood
By January 1 and 2, 1997, the state of California was in a severe state of flood. Although many of the cities like Modesto and Sacramento were hit very hard by the flooding rivers, the worst hit was Yosemite National Park, which is in Mariposa County. Yosemite Valley and the Merced River were flooded, the roads were washed out and thousands of people were trapped. A book was written about "The Hundred Year Flood." It took weeks, and ultimately rescue helicopters, to finally get all the people out to safety. Construction crews worked 24 hours a day on Highway 140, the Mariposa/Yosemite highway, for more than

a year, before they could open it to the public. California suffered with flood waters for many weeks.

A spiritual flood prophesied

On a Sunday morning, during that time of natural flooding, as I stepped to the pulpit to deliver the Sunday message, the Holy Spirit said, *"Tell the people that what is happening in the natural, I am about to do in the Spirit. A flood of My Spirit is coming to this area."* So I released that word.

February 22, 1997 ~ "The Feast Of Fire Revival" Is Born

A few short weeks after that "word" the Feast of Fire Revival broke out at Mariposa Revival Center. The Fire fell again at the little Mariposa church with even more intensity than before. However, this time the stage was set to involve more people and more places with much more of a far-reaching effect on the body of Christ in north central California.

Revival was already in the air

Grace and I and several other pastor friends from other California cities had just returned home from the Pensacola Outpouring at the Brownsville Assembly of God in Florida. We didn't all attend together but we all visited the outpouring within a week or so of each other. Although there was already a "rumbling in the heavens," the Florida experience fanned the flames. As the Holy Spirit was moving on pastors' hearts, I had asked the group of central California pastors to meet for coffee at a Merced coffee shop. My purpose for the meeting was to discuss putting together a series of meetings in the San Joaquin Valley somewhere with the unity and support of all their churches, and see what God would do. You could feel it in the air, something was about to happen. That meeting for discussion was scheduled to take place on Monday morning, February 23, in Merced.

Like Azusa Street ~ It didn't just happen!

It is interesting to note the chronological order of things. Before the Azusa Street Revival broke out in Los Angeles at the Bonnie Brae House in April of 1906 there was "a rumbling in the heavens," or as Elijah said, *"... there is a sound of abundance of rain."* Frank Bartleman, known as the architect of the Azusa Street Revival, had written Evan Roberts of the 1904 Welsh Revival for revival instructions. He was also ministering all over southern California that revival was coming soon. Rev. Joseph Swale, of The First Baptist Church of Los Angeles, had just visited Wales for three weeks with a fire in his heart to learn all he could from

THE "FEAST OF FIRE REVIVAL"

Evan Roberts. People were moving to the L.A. area because they felt something was going to happen there. Many groups were praying throughout the city. The entire city was on the verge of a great spiritual happening. The atmosphere was like Holy Ghost fumes when William Seymour arrived in L.A. God had just recently prepared him with a fresh new revelation of the baptism of the Holy Ghost and the evidence of speaking in other tongues at Charles Parham's Bible school in Houston Texas. God was revealing His plan to His people and setting their hearts on fire before He poured out the fire!

"Surely the Lord GOD will do nothing, but he revealeth his secret unto his servants the prophets." (Amos 3:7)

The Lord set the stage in Mariposa

While in Pensacola, Grace and I had met and befriended a retired married couple (while all parties mentioned were buffeting the flesh at Pensacola's anointed Barnhills Country Buffet) that were lay members of the Brownsville prayer team. They were originally southern Californians transplanted to Florida. They weren't ministers, but we invited them to come and share some testimonies of the Pensacola Outpouring in our church the next time they visited California. Through a series of circumstances unrelated to the established pastors' meeting in Merced, that date for this couple to share was set for February 22 and 23, a Sunday night and Monday night. They were scheduled to arrive in Mariposa just before the evening service on Sunday the 22nd. We thought it would just be a nice little Bible study/ministry kind of a get-together for a couple of evenings so there were no promotions or advertisements sent out.

In the meantime, I was asked to preach for one of our pastor friends on that Sunday morning, February 22, in a neighboring mountain community. The pastor was going to be out of town during the morning service. At first I said I couldn't because we felt revival was about to break out and we really wanted to minister at home that Sunday morning. However, my pastor friend persisted and needed the help, so, under friendly protest, I ministered the service for him while Grace covered the home front. As it turned out, the Holy Spirit showed up in an uncommon way as I ministered in his church. People were out "under the power" and "drunk in the Spirit" and being touched by the Holy Spirit, and joy was manifesting all over the building. The fire was falling! At the same time it was also happening at home with Grace, as she ministered to the home flock. This was definitely a time of outpouring and revival. Excited to see what was going on in his own church, the pastor friend, who had returned to his own service just before I closed it, decided to bring his flock to Mariposa that night for our service with the visiting couple from Pensacola. His church did the worship for the two services.

God knows how to do it! ~ spontaneous combustion
It was like synergy and spontaneous combustion all mixed together. The fire fell that night and the people of both churches were mightily overcome by the Holy Spirit! God showed up in a powerful way. It was explosive and contagious! People had to be carried to their cars and be driven home and put to bed. Lives were changed that night. Another revival was under way!

Now back to the pre-planned pastors meeting
Remember a group of pastors were already planning to meet in Merced (40 miles from Mariposa) Monday morning the 23rd to discuss putting together a meeting to see what God would do.

As I chaired the meeting, my pastor friend and I and the visiting man from Pensacola shared the events of the night before and suggested strongly that all of the pastors and ministers attend the second service that night in Mariposa. They did. They were not disappointed.

The Holy Spirit re-fires ministries
God showed up again and everyone was swept into the River of God. Pastors were lying on the floor of the little mountain church in uncontrollable laughter, drunkenness, and weeping. The New Wine and joy were being poured out for these men and women of God and new wineskins were being formed. It was an awesome sight to behold. The Fire was falling once more in Mariposa. And now, through a series of circumstances that only God could have orchestrated, ministries from numerous communities were connecting right at the beginning.

God gives a word
One of the pastors, John Pursell of Madera, was standing against the wall praying and observing the "glorious mess" when an unexplained wind blew across his back and neck. The same thing had happened to him a week earlier in Pensacola when God told him that, "He was using the Pensacola Outpouring for the nations." This time the Lord told him that "what He was doing in Pensacola for the nations, He was doing in this church for this region of California."

Where do we go from here?
It was toward the end of that service that night that I was walking around, through and over all the bodies on the floor and pondering what to do next. The sounds of laughter, travail, and worship were filling the air. No doubt, this was a move of the Holy Spirit. However, there was no plan to meet the next night. Who would come to an out-of-the-way church with no previous advertising during the midweek? What to do? It was then that the pastor I ministered for the day before reached up off the floor, from his drunken state, and begged me to not stop the meetings. He said "I'll have my whole church here tomorrow night if you keep it going." So I took that as my *"burning bush"* and went to the microphone and announced that the meeting would continue the next night. Everyone shouted hallelujah!

Now it's Tuesday night and the little church is packed out. God showed up again the next night, and again, and again, etc.

There were no advertisements or promotions, no well-known or planned speakers. There were just hungry people, with the catalyst of two unknown, non-ordained prayer team members from Brownsville. The little church was packed to capacity and beyond capacity every night. The prayer team had to take people into the foyer room and kitchen to pray for them. All the chairs were stacked against the wall and walking room was almost non-existent as people were manifesting all over the building.

The revival outgrew the church
It was obvious that the little church couldn't hold all the people. The revival was bigger than our church. It was also obvious that God had connected all those pastors from different cities, so, it was time to consider a bigger picture.

The revival moves through ten California cities
Another breakfast pastors' meeting was called for the coffee shop in Merced to discuss where to go from here. I set a time for the next morning and asked the pastors to spread the word with other pastors. There were forty to fifty people including the leaders and many of their wives at that breakfast. Many pastors and leaders changed their entire schedules to accommodate the move of God.

After prayer, worship, and communion, it was decided that, with Grace and me as the revival leaders, we would take the revival to all the cities that were represented by the pastors of the group. We led every service but we honored the different pastors by delegating them to deliver many of the main messages and lead much of the Holy Spirit ministry time. The first of those meetings was held in a valley town church, but again the crowds were too big. From that time on the group rented fairground buildings, community halls and university buildings for the meetings. None of the churches involved were big enough to hold the crowds. Thousands of people were touched by God during those meetings. Miracles happened, souls were saved and many lives and ministries were changed forever.

The revival went around central California for months, visiting ten cities and some of them more than once. The weekly meetings were held on Thursday, Friday, and Saturday night in each city. Each week we moved the revival to another town. At one point, more than thirty ministers and twenty churches had joined the unofficial group of "The Feast of Fire" Leadership Council. Because of its central location, the Council met almost every week in that Merced coffee shop conference room, to pray, take communion, and discuss and manage the revival.

The revival comes home
Then after almost 50 services, the pastors voted to take it back to its home in Mariposa. The meetings continued at Mariposa Revival Center for the rest of that year and well into 1998. Pastors and worship teams from the participating churches continued to support the meetings by alternating ministering with me. It was an uncommon move of God and it did an uncommon work of unity among the churches and ministries and communities in north central California. To this day, many ministries that met and bonded in relationships during the Feast of Fire Revival are very closely connected and are still working together for the Kingdom.

"If My People ..."

CHAPTER 22

WHY MARIPOSA?

A brief history of some of the historical and spiritual "firsts" in Mariposa

We all know that the great revivals and moves of God need to take place in regions that can impact the multitudes. Places like the Bay Area, Sacramento, Fresno or southern California are places that should focus on revival. So then, one might ask, why would this book about California's contribution to worldwide revival and the global end-time harvest be written from a little obscure town in the backwoods of the Sierras.

I do not propose to have all the answers, but a little history and spiritual insight might shed some light on the issue. As you read this chapter please remember the principle presented by Paul:

"Howbeit that was not first which was spiritual, but that which was natural; afterward that which was spiritual." (1 Corinthians 15:46)

Once the largest and most important county in California

Mariposa County started out in 1850 as the largest and most important county in the state of California. This was due to two basic dynamics.

First, it was one of the original major gold camps on the Mother Lode. Keep in mind that in the late 1840's and early 1850's places like San Francisco and Los Angeles were just little tiny pueblos with very little significance to them. In those days the Mother Lode towns were where all the activity was. Boomtowns like Mariposa and Hornitos had populations of tens of thousands of people. It was their gold shipments and their necessity of supplies that originally built Sacramento and San Francisco into their greatness.

Yosemite Valley ~ Mariposa County

The second, and probably most significant, reason for Mariposa's importance was John Fremont. Mariposa was his and Jessie's home base during California's first few years. We will say more about that in a little bit.

Mariposa ~ Butterfly Symbolic for Transformation or New Beginnings

The name Mariposa means "butterfly" in Spanish, which is symbolic for "new beginnings" or "transformation." Mariposa is one of the original forty-niner gold mining camps of the California "Mother Lode" gold rush era. It is situated in the foothills of the western slopes of the Sierra Nevada Mountains at the crossroads of state highways 49 and 140. The Mariposa mines were actually the south end of the Mother Lode. The Mother Lode began in Mariposa and ran 120 miles to the north. It is the home town of Yosemite National Park. Yosemite Valley and all of its waterfalls, plus the Mariposa Grove of Giant Redwoods are in the county. The town of Mariposa is less than 20 miles, the way the crow flies, from the western boundary of the park.

Contrary to what most people think about California living, today Mariposa County in its entirety is very remote and unpopulated. Even the town of Mariposa, which is the county seat, with a population of only about 1,700 people, has no stoplights. In fact, there are no stop lights in the entire county. Nor does the county, with a total population of about 18,000 souls, have any incorporated cities. There are no city police, city limits, or mayor because there is no official city in the county. There are only a few little towns in the county and they are all unincorporated. Like "the Old West," the county sheriff is the local law, and a small Board of Supervisors manages the whole county with its few small towns.

Mother of Counties ~ originally the largest county in the world

Mariposa is named the "Mother of Counties." The official county seal says "Mariposa, Mother of Counties." In 1850, when California became a state, the original Mariposa County included one fifth of the state. Its original size is still the largest county in the world. It was larger than many eastern states. Parts of the present San Benito, San Bernardino and Los Angeles counties as well as eight other entire counties were birthed from the original Mariposa County. Cities like Lancaster, Palmdale, Mojave, Santa Clarita, Bakersfield, Ridgecrest, Bishop, Mammoth Lakes, Visalia, Merced, Oakhurst and Fresno are within the original Mariposa County borders.

Yosemite Falls ~ Mariposa County

Involving twelve counties ~ the apostolic number
Counting Mariposa itself, the original county included all or part of twelve counties. It included the geographical center of California and is recorded as the largest county in world history. I believe it is of no coincidence that the county that represents the heart of California speaks of the apostolic.

Oldest courthouse in California
The Mariposa County Courthouse is the oldest operating courthouse in California, and some historians say west of the Mississippi River. It was constructed in 1854 and is still the active courthouse today with no plans for a new one.

Oldest newspaper in California
The Mariposa Gazette, Mariposa's weekly newspaper, and only newspaper, is the oldest continually operating newspaper in the state.

The Western White House
General John Charles Fremont, "the Conqueror of California," that we have discussed in more detail in a previous chapter, made his home here. He owned "Rancho de Las Mariposas," a 44,000-acre Spanish land grant that he purchased just before gold was discovered in the region. As it turned out, his ranch was 44,000 acres centered on the south end of "the Mother Lode." Being an educated and highly experienced engineer, he quickly began operations.

Fremont's Mariposa home was called the "Western White House." He was already celebrated as the catalyst in the Bear Flag Revolt and the one that, in cooperation with U.S. Navy Admiral Sloat, and then his replacement Admiral Stockton, negotiated the surrender of the Mexican army establishing California as American soil.

All during the gold rush days Fremont had already been the first appointed U.S. governor of the territory of California, plus the first elected senator for the state. In addition he was the American Republican Party's first nominee for president. Abraham Lincoln stumped for him in the election of 1856, four years before Lincoln was elected in 1860. Fremont, years before Lincoln's famous document, had actually written the first Emancipation Proclamation for the state of Missouri.

So, it is not hard to understand that in those early days in California's infancy, Fremont was one of the most influential and celebrated characters in the California arena, and that wherever he lived would be a political "ground zero."

The Mother Lode is discovered in Mariposa
Fremont brought experienced Sonorans up from Mexico to mine the gold on his ranch in Mariposa. They were the first to find the quartz ledge that ran through the heart of gold country that became known as "The Mother Lode." That was the beginning of quartz (hard rock) mining in California.[1]

The Mother Lode, as it refers to the California Gold Rush, is a vein of concentrated gold bearing quartz averaging a half mile wide and a hundred twenty miles long. Its southern end is Mariposa and its northern end is Sierraville northeast of Sacramento. It runs through the foothills, paralleling the high country, at an elevation of about fifteen hundred to three thousand feet.

The first million-dollar corporation in California
The first million dollar corporation in the state of California was the Mariposa Mining Company. It was the result of a lease transaction from Fremont to a group of San Francisco bankers for the Mariposa Mine. Incidentally, the Mariposa Mine was discovered by Kit Carson while he was in Fremont's employ.[2]

America's first authorized private mint
In 1850, near the base of Mt. Ophir, Mariposa County, John L. Moffat built the first private mint in the nation that produced government-approved coins. There were other concerns in the Mother Lode producing coins at the time but they were not official legal tender. This was a significant improvement over the inconvenience of measuring gold dust when you traded.[3]

The first Indian treaties in California
On March 19, 1851, at Camp Fremont near Mariposa Creek, the first Indian treaties with the United States Government were signed with six tribes. The treaties were later unratified by the government.

First land "Federal Park" preserved for future generations by a federal government
Mariposa's Yosemite Valley and the Mariposa Grove of Giant Sequoias (redwoods), both in the present Mariposa County, is the first land in the world that was ever preserved by its government for future generations. Yosemite was originally a federal reserve, enacted by Congress and signed into law by President Lincoln during the Civil War and placed under the administrative jurisdiction of the State of California.

In other words, it was Mariposa, California real estate, now known as Yosemite National Park, that has the distinction of being the first federally protected land in world history.

Yosemite, named "The Jewel of the National Parks," was the first of God's creation or handiwork to be preserved for all future generations to enjoy. It was not the first National Park, but Yosemite led the way. When the National Park Service was created, Yosemite was already protected by the United States government more than thirty years earlier.

The California State Mining and Mineral Museum
The California State Mining and Mineral Museum, which used to be in San Francisco, was moved to its present location in Mariposa. The museum is an elaborate exhibit of California's gold mining history as well as other minerals and gems from around the world.

SOME SPIRITUAL INSIGHTS & HISTORY

The prophetic symbolism of "The Yosemite Firefalls"
We discuss the prophetic significance of the Yosemite Firefalls in chapter 13. However in the light of the question "Why Mariposa," I believe it is important to make the connection that the Firefalls occurred in Mariposa County, the spiritual center.

Now get this picture: In 1871, only twenty-one years into statehood and thirty-five years before the fire fell at Azusa Street, man stood on Mariposa soil in the heart of California, near the banks of the Merced River, "the River of Mercy," and, I might add, in the midst of His beauty and splendor of the high waterfalls, and prophetically called the fire down. Then in 1906, God answered that call and sent latter-day Pentecost to the whole world via Los Angeles (the City of Angels) to the south. Shout amen somebody!

Cindy Jacobs and Marilyn Noorda
In 1997, respected prophetess Cindy Jacobs of Generals International, with her California/west coast coordinator Marilyn Noorda, got out a map of California to pick the center of the state. As prophetic intercessors they were strategizing a prayer structure for California and planned a gathering of intercessors from all over California to meet at that center and prophesy and proclaim for the state. As they prayed and examined the map they both put their finger on Mariposa.

The Merced River & Bridal Veil Falls ~ Yosemite ~ Mariposa County

However, due to some other circumstances, their inauguration meeting was moved to a community south of Mariposa.

I remember Marilyn telling me this story at our church when she attended one of our revival meetings back in 1997 or 1998. She said that she and Cindy had agreed that they should have prayed for the state from the Mariposa County Courthouse. Recently, when I contacted Marilyn about this book and asked for her prayers and input, she began to tell me that story again. When she began the story I finished it for her. She said "that's right," in surprise. I reminded her that she told me that story over ten years ago.

Her immediate reaction was that this book and its timing for California witnessed with her. She said "It is time, and someone has to write it," and indicated that it should come from the heart of California. She also said that with the timing of the book, and because of the times in general, it was time to pray for California from the Mariposa County Courthouse.

That gathering took place recently in July of 2009. A group of intercessors hosted by Grace and me, and led by Marilyn, met at the courthouse and prayed and decreed over the Golden State. That same day we went to Camp Curry in Yosemite and did a prophetic re-enactment of the Yosemite Firefalls. The intercessors reiterated the call "Let the fire fall!" We also prayed over the Merced River as strategic head-waters of the California water issues. Lastly, we went up to Glacier Point where the Firefalls originated and prayed and blew the shofar and decreed over California "The fire is falling!"

The Largest Native American Reconciliation event in California history

On February 24 and 25, 2001, our little church, Mariposa Revival Center, organized and hosted the largest "Spirit-filled" Native American Reconciliation meetings in California history. Representation from thirty-two tribes from across the west, and as far away as central Canada, attended those meetings. The local Mariposa Miwoks were included in the event and were honored as the host tribe to all the visiting tribes.

The event included Spirit-filled worship and ministry from the Word of God. It also included their cultural protocol, repentance and forgiveness. It was prophesied by Chad Taylor as: "A model to the nation ... Keep your eyes on Mariposa in the days ahead! Agree with them as they blaze a trail of revival for the entire nation!"

It is believed that God prophetically chose the very community where the first treaties were signed, and later unratified by the government, as "ground zero" for the beginning of the healing of the land. You can read more about this in our web at: MariposaRevivalCenter.com and click on "Honoring Native Americans."

The Feast of Fire Revival

The Feast of Fire Revival is discussed in more detail in chapter 21. However it is imperative to note in this chapter that as far as we know, besides Azusa Street itself, there has been no other move like it in the state, nor in any other western state. It was a very uncommon move of the Holy Spirit. It exploded in our little church of Mariposa Revival Center (at that time it was Sierra Faith Center), but was immediately joined by more than thirty other churches and ministries. Those other ministries represented cities in central California that were all much bigger than Mariposa. Those cities represented the counties of Stanislaus, Merced, Madera and Fresno, plus Mariposa. The combined population of the four other counties was about one and a half million souls. Yet the revival started in the woods of Mariposa.

The Nazareth syndrome

It is also interesting to note that although the revival was born in Mariposa, no other church in town would embrace it. In fact, most of them persecuted it and avoided it. We had to stand alone in the community as we were joined, and enthusiastically supported by the churches from neighboring counties. God had His way for Mariposa and the state, but He had to send the reinforcements in from the outside.

A word given by pastor John Pursell ~ Believer's Church, Madera

Place: Feast of Fire Revival meeting ~ Mariposa County Fairgrounds ~ April 19, 1997

> "There is coming a great move of God's healing power to the Mariposa area. It will begin in the churches and flow out into the streets and eventually down the mountain into the valley floor. It will be the talk of the town in Mariposa. Many people who have fought against, or misunderstood the move of God will see that God is moving in His healing power. And they will not be able to deny the move of God any longer. There will be several different churches involved in this move, and just as the Feast of Fire Revival started here this stronger move of healing and miracles will begin here also."

WHY MARIPOSA?

We here at Mariposa Revival Center continue to stand and pray for the Holy Spirit to take the pulpits of the community as well as for the State of California.

"If My People ..."

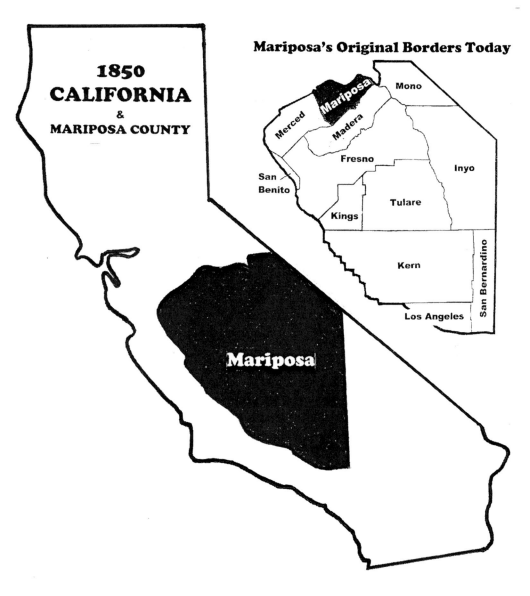

Cal & Mariposa County

CHAPTER **23**

The spirit of
MINERVA

The Great Seal of the State of California

California leads the nation that leads the world
It has been said more than once, "As goes California, so goes the nation."

California leads the nation that leads the world. That's why it is so important for the body of Christ to wake up in California and re-dig our wells of revival. There is only one thing that can turn California around … a move of God. Revival!

I believe in standing up to be heard for our Christian rights and family values, but that, in and of itself, will not fulfill what California really needs. Like Israel's Jerusalem, "the city of peace," the battle is raging in the heavenlies for the soul of California for the clear and simple reason that it has been marked by God for an uncommon influence in the world. Revival is what California needs, and the entire world needs California to get it.

Hopefully, the pages of this book reveal a mighty plan of God for this great state. With the best still ahead of us, California, indeed, has already played a key role in the end-time strategies of heaven.

The great man of God, Lester Sumrall used to say, "You can always tell what God is doing by what satan fights the hardest."

Every time God is birthing something "uncommon" into the earth, the devil is there to try to devour it.

"... and the dragon stood before the woman which was ready to be delivered, for to devour her child as soon as it was born." (Revelation 12:4)

Jesus said,

" ... satan cometh immediately, and taketh away the word that was sown in their hearts." (Mark 4:15)

And Paul tells us,

"For we wrestle not against flesh and blood, but against principalities, against powers, against the rulers of the darkness of this world, against spiritual wickedness in high places." (Ephesians 6:12)

With this Biblical principle in mind, it should be no surprise that the adversary has been up to his lowdown and evil schemes to try to pervert the state and thus divert the plan of God.

Reveal the hidden riches of California

The Lord told me the purpose of this book was to take the hidden gold of California out from under the evil cover and put it in the light for the world to see. In Matthew 5, Jesus said, *"don't put the lit candle under the bushel but on the candlestick to give out light to all"* (my paraphrase). He also said, *"A city that is set on a hill cannot be hid."*

The main purpose of this book is to bring the prophetic design of God for California into clear and visible focus. It is my heart to surface the "right stuff," and uncover it to the church to help remove our complacency. Indeed, this book is written to encourage and galvanize our intercessions. We must stir up and maintain fervency in our hearts. To do that, it is imperative that we see and remember what God has done and is doing in the state.

THE SPIRIT OF MINERVA

Now, I'm not one to give the devil more than his due, and I do not worry as much about him standing up against us as I am concerned about what the believers do about it. Jesus gave the church *"all power."* So I am more apprehensive about a complacent and lethargic church lying down than I am the devil standing up.

"For the weapons of our warfare are not carnal, but mighty through God to the pulling down of strong holds. Casting down imaginations, and every high thing that exalteth itself against the knowledge of God, and bringing into captivity every thought to the obedience of Christ;" (2 Corinthians. 10:4 & 5)

Our weapons are mighty through God. Through Him we have magnum loads, nuclear power and laser accuracy in our weapons. Compared to the awesome power of God, the devil *"can't blow fuzz off a peanut."* But if the church lies down and goes to sleep, he can take you out with a frying pan.

We do not want to exalt him, but we must acknowledge his devices. He is an adversary, he is supernatural, and he is walking about. Like the evidence of God's designs for California, the evidence of the adversary's dark counter-designs can also be found in California's early history.

The California state seal

At the very birth of California into statehood in 1850, the state seal was established. It is shown here so you can see the devil's design to try to kill the vision at its very inception.

The Great Seal of the State of California is not so "great" when you understand the spirit behind it. The devil knows he can destroy California if he can get its residents to worship a false god.

The seal features:

> The Roman goddess **Minerva**, who is the mythical (demonic) goddess of wisdom and war
>
> **A Shield** with the **head of Medusa** ~ protectress of Minerva
>
> **A California bear** ~ the official state animal
>
> **Grape vines**, representing California's wine production

A sheaf of grain, representing agriculture

A miner, representing the California Gold Rush and the mining industry

Sailing ships, representing the state's economic power

San Francisco Bay and the **Sacramento River** with the hills and **Sierras** in the background

The phrase **"Eureka,"** meaning "I have found it!" ~ the California state motto

31 stars representing California as the 31st state[1]

So who is this Minerva, and what does she stand for?

Minerva is the Roman name for the Greek goddess Athena. In their book "Releasing the Prophetic Destiny of a Nation," Dutch Sheets and Chuck Pierce call Minerva a manifestation of the Jezebel spirit.[2] She is the protectress of cities and her name comes from the root "manas," or mens. She has masculine features and is dressed in men's clothes.[3] In short, Minerva is a false god empowered by real demon spirits.

The symbol of Minerva was chosen by the first California delegation because she was not born and raised in the usual way. She sprang as a full-grown adult from the brain of Jupiter. It was a mis-guided attempt to symbolize how California sprang into statehood without the long process of being a remote territory.

According to the legend, Minerva was brash, arrogant and strong-willed. The purpose of these demon strongholds is to see that all they represent become reality.[3]

A curse

So consider this: The Great Seal of the State of California, the stamp of state authority and approval, is a demon spirit. Every drivers license, marriage license, state document and so on, is authorized by that demonic symbol. In other words, every place the California Seal is stamped or placed, a curse is referenced.

Furthermore, look at the seal - Minerva is overlooking San Francisco Bay, the homosexual capital of the world.

Minerva is also the goddess of wisdom and learning, war, commerce, and the arts. I believe that California's greatness comes from the hand of God and not from a demonic stronghold. The devil is always an imposter and he has, since the beginning, tried to place himself in the Lord's throne of worship. If his fruits ever appear good, it is a deception; they are always counterfeit. Goodness and truth are not found in him. He is a liar and the father of all lies. Through the Jezebel spirit of Minerva, satan has tried to enthrone himself over these attributes of California. Consider these:

> **Wisdom & learning:** I find it very interesting that California leads the nation in education and technology with its great University system, and all of its colleges ~ plus the technology center of the world, the Silicon Valley.
>
> **Commerce:** California's 2007 GNP (Gross National Product) was 1.7 trillion dollars, which would make it number seven in the world as its own country.
>
> **The arts**: Los Angeles and Hollywood are the media center of the world.
>
> **War**: the aerospace industry and technical weaponry production in California is substantial. Its air force bases and shipyards are also quite significant.[3]

A pastor in San Francisco once said, "My greatest challenge is making men out of wimps and ladies out of brassy women."[3]

Consider also that California gave us the hippie movement, with the summer of love and its pot smoking, free sex revolution in 1967. According to Lou Engle's book "Digging the Wells of Revival," The San Fernando Valley is the porn capital of the world.[4]

I have also been told by California prophet, Shawn Bolz, that the Golden Gate Bridge is the number one suicide spot in the country. The suiciders are drawn to the Golden Gate, but hardly none are drawn to the larger Oakland Bay Bridge.

I would say the Minerva spirit is for real. Vicki Nohrden more fully describes this spirit in her book "Breaking the Shield of Minerva." She says:

> "There is one foe spiritually seated over the land of California which I believe is in collaboration with other principalities whose agenda is designed and purposed to affect our entire nation. She's part of an antichrist system of power heads and needs to be exposed and dealt with corporately. I

believe the Lord of Hosts is presently gathering this army of trained warriors in California and through the state to arise. You find her seated atop California's gateways of commerce, the wealth and the justice system, to name a few. Her official seal stamps every marriage license, business license, driver's license, birth certificate and signed legal decree coming through the state government of California. Her impression is stamped on all state letterhead and official state and legal documents.

Her name is Minerva, also known as Athena, the Roman/Greek goddess of war, wisdom, art, schools, and commerce. Minerva is identified with Athena in Roman mythology as the goddess of intelligence, protectress of cities, and goddess of war. She's also attributed as a founder of cities. She's depicted on California's state seal watching over the waters of commerce, the gold, and the land. You'll also discover her memorialized on Battle Hill in Brooklyn, New York sharing the altar dedicated to Liberty. She stands across from, yet eye to eye with the Statue of Liberty in New York's harbor keeping watch on Lady Liberty. Known as the "Sanctifying Minerva Monument" she is strategically placed atop Battle Hill, the highest point and hilltop of our first national battleground and the highest point in Brooklyn, where our first national heroes fought and fell for American liberty and Independence. A small coincidence? I think not. Sometimes the obvious is the answer."[5]

In 1991 prophet, Dr. Chuck Pierce, founder of Glory of Zion Ministries, had a dream about Minerva's shield which he shared at the California Call to Prayer.

In the dream I was standing in the middle of a vast land, and in the dream from the heavens there began to form a shield over that particular land. Now this shield began to cover the land, and it looked exactly like a stealth bomber and the shield began to get lower and lower. Well, as the people of that land began to see the shield press down upon them, fear began to grip them, they began to scatter, and they began to go in every direction.

The Spirit of God then spoke to me in the dream and he said, "Do not bow your head to that shield." He said, "I want you to plant your feet, and keep your head high, no matter how much that shield presses down, hold your head erect." Well, it was a great test, in this dream, even because this thing was very noisy, as it began to press down lower. I looked up at the shield, and on this shield there was a word. I had no understanding of

THE SPIRIT OF MINERVA

this, whatsoever, I didn't know much about you, or anything much about the history of the state, other than the major historical facts. On the shield, as it pressed down upon me there was a word that was emblazoned upon it, and the word said, "Minerva." It kept going lower and lower and lower. Fear began to grab the land, and the people of the land, and the Lord would not let me move. When that shield began to come down so low to take over the land, and to superimpose itself over the entire portion of the land, I planted my feet, kept my head erect, and the shield when it dropped down on my head broke in two. I didn't have any idea what that meant, I just knew the dream was from the Lord. I went over to the prayer meeting and shared with the prayer meeting. I had the strangest dream last night.

I shared that with Cindy Jacobs and Cindy said, "This is the state of California. That's the shield of California with Minerva on it." And the Lord spoke to me and he said, "If I can find a people who will stand with their head erect in that state, the powers and principalities over that State will not be able to subdue the headship of the Lord Jesus Christ. Emphasis mine[6]

Well, saints, I believe the Lord has found "a people" with their head erect in California. Therefore we can declare and decree that the headship of California is the Lord Jesus Christ. Can I get some agreement?

I am sure that as a matter of semantics what Chuck refers to as the shield is actually the seal itself. I say that because in the seal, Minerva has a shield in front of her. On that shield is the head of Medusa. Medusa is the mythical fallen beauty, "the jealous aspiration of many suitors," that Minerva had punished for being seduced by Neptune, the god of the sea, in her (Minerva's) sanctuary.[7] Medusa's punishment was that her hair was turned to serpents, and her head was removed and placed on Minerva's shield. Whatever Medusa looked at was turned to stone. So, she was placed on the shield as Minerva's protectress.

An unholy trinity

So it appears that the devil has been very busy setting up an unholy trinity of evil women as a false godhead over this mighty state. That trinity is the trio of Califia, the mythical Amazon queen of the paradise island "California," Minerva, and Medusa, with Minerva now as the head of the false trinity.

Interestingly though, I must note right here that in reality, God sent strong godly men to open and establish a holy presence in the acquisition and birth of the

Golden State. The list of those men includes but is not limited to: Junipero Serra, Jedediah Smith, John C. Fremont, Kit Carson, Frank Bartleman, and William J. Seymour.

God just needs a people to stand and seek His face.

"For the eyes of the LORD run to and fro throughout the whole earth, to shew himself strong in the behalf of them whose heart is perfect toward him." (2 Chron. 16:9)

He has given us the authority over the earth, but without any power of our own to apply that authority. We must use our authority through prayer and submission to Him, to activate His power into our lives, and over every situation in the earth.

You don't come into a dark room and fight the darkness, you turn on the light. When we are in proper relationship with the Lord, we are *"the light of Christ."* Then, when we exercise His word, His light emanating from us drives out the darkness.

Over and over the Bible teaches us to go to Him. We resist the devil by going to God. Seek His face, worship, praise and pray! Only God can save a soul, cleanse a leper, or pull down a stronghold. We have all power in heaven and earth available to us, but, we must remember, it is His power. That's why the apostles prayed in Acts 4:29-30 for God to increase their boldness by stretching forth His hand to heal and do miracles.

By standing on the Word of God and continuing fervent in prayer we can then speak to the mountains (any stronghold or resistance) to "be thou removed," and the power of God will take them out. As we humble ourselves and submit to Him, the demonic strongholds come crashing down.

A demon on my daughter
One day back in the mid-eighties, I had just come into the house from the barn when I heard one of my daughters scream a blood-curdling scream. I ran to the master bedroom where I heard the commotion. I saw Grace holding our youngest daughter, Maria, in her arms and frantically confused as to why Maria was screaming in such pain. There was nothing visibly wrong with her, yet she was screaming like someone was stabbing her with a knife. Instantly, the Lord pulled the veil (like the "discerning of spirits," but this time I could literally see what was happening) and I saw a hideous creature attached to my daughter.

He was clinging to her back and physically inflicting pain on her. It was a half bug and half monkey looking thing with a monkey face. As soon as I saw it I knew it was a little demon 'spirit of pain.' The "gift of faith" immediately came on me and I said calmly but sternly, "you have to go now," it was like a knowing between us. Without argument he said "I know," and he turned loose and flew out through the closed window.

As soon as that thing left, Maria immediately fell into a peaceful sleep in Grace's arms. She was instantly pain-free too. The only thing wrong with her was a demonic attack. Grace and I prayed that that never happen again to any of our family, and it never did.

I know that was just a low-ranking principality, but he had no right in my house, and he had no argument against a believer that has a relationship with Jesus Christ. As David said, *"Who does that uncircumcised Philistine think he is?"* (I Samuel 17:26, My paraphrase)

Now listen, when that happened I was already prayed up and in good relationship with the Lord and in agreement with my wife, so I spoke with authority, and he left … end of story!

As the body of Christ, we can see the same results with the strongholds over California. All we need to do is to come together in unity and prayer, and turn on the light.

"Arise, shine!"

Psalm 133 is one of my favorites for this kind of ministry.

"Behold, how good and how pleasant it is for brethren to dwell together in unity! It is like the precious ointment upon the head, that ran down upon the beard, even Aaron's beard: that went down to the skirts of his garments; As the dew of Hermon, and as the dew that descended upon the mountains of Zion: for there the LORD commanded the blessing, even life for evermore."

When we stand in unity together with Jesus and the Word as our "center," the anointing oil flows, and God commands the blessing. Let me tell you something, when God commands the blessing, you can ship the devil's saddle home. He is through! Spiritual warfare is completed. Can I get an amen here?

Hear me, Saints, it is our decision, not the devil's, the liberals, or the politicians. If we will do our part, California goes into the hands of God.

So, as we, the body of Christ, come together and pray, and decree and prophesy, the Lord "commands the blessing!"

"Minerva, you and your cohorts have to go, now! Amen!"

Mount Diablo

I think it should also be noted here in this chapter that the highest point in the entire San Francisco Bay area is the very prominent peak, Mount Diablo, or, "devil Mountain" in English. It is a small range of mountains that literally overlooks the entire Bay Area and northern region of California.

In 1851 Mount Diablo was selected as the "initial point" for land surveys of Northern California and Nevada and part of Oregon with the Mount Diablo Base and Meridian Lines originating at its peak.[9]

That means that every legal description of property in most of California and Nevada, and part of Oregon is referenced to Mount Diablo. The language in the legal description of every piece of real estate either includes the full name of Mount Diablo, or the initials M.D. Who do you think is behind that little scheme? Mr. devil has been very busy trying to destroy the Golden State. To me that just confirms how important California is to God.

"But if he (the thieving devil) be found, he shall restore sevenfold; he shall give all the substance of his house." (Prov. 6:31)

At the cost of repeating myself, I want to re-emphasize that the Lord commissioned me to write this book to encourage and energize the body of Christ for California. He only initiates things like this when He is planning to do something uncommon. So let's commit to uncommon intercession, for an uncommon move of God in California! Shout yes with me somebody!

Saints, would you agree with me here ..
"I decree revival throughout The Golden State!"

"If My People ..."

CHAPTER 24

THE WILDERNESS TABERNACLE & AMERICA
A Very Interesting Comparison

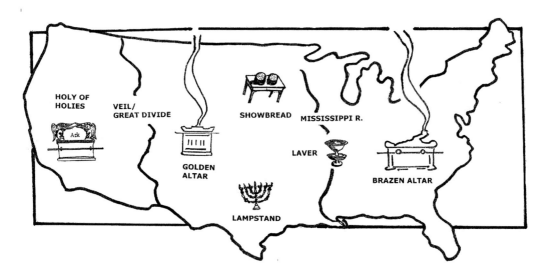

I got this nugget from Rev. Perry Stone's DVD, "AMERICA, Our Prophetic Patterns, Cycles, & Future." It is very interesting to compare the history and relationship of America with Israel. The comments below are inspired by Brother Perry, but they are my own observations and annotations.

In the above illustration you see the Wilderness Tabernacle of Moses laid over an outline of America. The Tabernacle in those days was how God dwelt among His people. Since Calvary the old Tabernacle is a clear visual example of our spiritual New Covenant approach to God. The believer is now the priest. Every object in the Tabernacle represented a different dynamic of Jesus.

> **The Brazen Altar:** The Cross ~ Jesus is our sacrifice
> **The Laver:** We are washed by the water of the Word ~ Jesus is the Word of God
> **The Lampstand:** Jesus is the light

> **The Showbread:** Jesus is the bread of life
> **The Golden Altar:** Jesus is our praise
> **The Veil:** Now removed ~ We come right into His presence
> **The Holy of Holies:** His glorious presence

The Tabernacle & America

The entrance to the Tabernacle was positioned to the east. When the priests entered on their way to the Holy of Holies, they were walking due west. As we all know, America was settled by Europeans from the East to the West.

The Brass Altar of Sacrifice ~ the eastern revivals and coal mines

The first object you encounter in the Tabernacle is the Brass Altar of Sacrifice. The main substance here is fire to consume the sacrifice. Our east coast is rich with coal. It was also the stage for the mighty revivals and great awakenings in the 18th & 19th centuries.

The Brass Laver ~ the mighty Mississippi River

The next thing you come to in the Tabernacle is the Brass Laver. The main substance in the Laver is water. In America, it is represented by the mighty Mississippi River, which is by far, the largest river in America.

The Lampstand & the Showbread ~ La., Tex. & the Great Plains

As you continue through the center of the Tabernacle on your approach to God, who is in the Holy of Holies, you come to two pieces of furniture; the Golden Lampstand, and the Table of Showbread. The Lampstand is to the south and the Table of Showbread is to the north.

The main substance in the Lampstand is oil. Interestingly enough it is represented by Louisiana and Texas, the major oil producing states.

The main substance on the Table of Showbread is bread. On the map the Showbread is represented by the wheat and grain producing states, "the bread basket of America."

The Golden Altar ~ Colo., Wyo. & N. M.

The next thing you come to in the Wilderness Tabernacle is the Golden Altar, or Altar of Incense. The main substance on the Golden Altar is a reddish incense and fire. It is a smaller altar than the first one, with a smaller fire. It is a Golden Altar, but also smaller than the Holy of Holies.

As the map illustrates, the Golden Altar corresponds to the Colorado, Wyoming, New Mexico area. Colorado means red, and the area is a gold-producing area. It also has coal.

The Veil ~ the Great Continental Divide

Just past the Golden Altar is the Veil. The Veil, or curtain, was a massive and thick material that totally separated the Holy of Holies from the rest of the Tabernacle. Here, as you can see, the Veil is positioned exactly where the Rocky Mountains form "The Great Continental Divide," also called "The Great Divide."

The Holy of Holies and the Ark of the Covenant ~ the Golden State

On the other side of the veil is the principal purpose of the Tabernacle: "The Holy of Holies," also called, "The Most Holy Place," with "The Ark of the Covenant." "The Ark of the Covenant," with its "Mercy Seat," was the dwelling place of God. It was where God dwelt among His people.

The main substance in the Holy of Holies was gold. It is of no coincidence that the map shows the Holy of Holies corresponding to "The Golden State," California. California has more gold, and has produced more gold than all the other states put together. The Mother Lode is in California. California also hosted the mightiest revival since the Book of Acts, the Azusa Street Revival. What's more, it is the source of more global moves of God than any place in history.

The Ark contained;

>The Two Tablets of Stone ~ The Commandments
>The Golden Pot of Manna ~ The bread of Life ~ The Word
>Aaron's Rod that Budded ~ Proof of Moses' & Aaron's Priesthood

The Tablets of Stone and the Pot of Manna speak of the Word of God, or, Jesus. The most preaching of Jesus Christ from any one place in the world is broadcast from California. Aaron's Rod not only budded but it also produced almonds. These supernatural events together represent God's choice and fruitfulness. California's revivals and birthing of world-changing ministries is unmistakable spiritual fruit. California is also the world leader in producing natural fruit, especially almonds. (1.33 billion pounds of almonds in the 2007-2008 crop year, 100% of America's and 80% of the world's)[1]

A word of encouragement to California

As I have cautioned previously in this book, Jesus said, *"Where much is given, much is required."* The Holy of Holies was a very special, but also a very serious place. The priest could only go in there once a year to atone for the people. That priest was a true intercessor for the people. When he did go in to the Most Holy Place, he had to be properly cleansed in his heart as well as through ritual. Otherwise, you would have to ship his saddle home. I know we are living in the age of grace and not under the law, but Jesus' words are still ringing true. As we seek to intercede for California and bring it into line with God's plans, we must always remember to cleanse ourselves continually, through repentance, prayer, and abiding in the Word.

The Wilderness Tabernacle principle and the California church

The call of intercession for the nations is foremost in California. In that light, as the Tabernacle itself represents, we decree over California a spirit of:

- √ true repentance, brokenness, humility, and righteousness
- √ that she be washed by the Water of the Word
- √ that she be illuminated by the Light of Christ
- √ that she partake of the Bread of Heaven
- √ that she present true prayer, praise & worship to Heaven
- √ that she go beyond the Veil and take her place before the Mercy Seat of Heaven

"If My People ..."

CHAPTER **25**

PRAY FOR CALIFORNIA
Travail in the Spirit

"I have found the greatest power in the world
is the power of prayer" Cecil B. DeMille

One Sunday this spring, the below story was used to illustrate a sermon on prayer at our church. When the service was over one of our elders, Fred Silva, came up to me and said, "Pastor, you need to put that story in your book." My first response was "Well, the book is about California so it doesn't really fit." But as soon as I said that I heard the Holy Spirit say, "It's a good illustration and it fits the book." I quickly repented and said, "Fred, you just spoke into the book. The story is going in, thank you!"

The day I saw prayer
In 1991, Grace and I took our family on a 10,000-mile, two-month motorhome trip, all the way around the United States. We were home-schooling our children at the time, so the trip was a history and geography lesson for them.

Our three children are adopted from birth, and at the time their ages were six, seven & eight.

When we began the trip we traveled east on the northern route across America to Niagara and New England, then drove down the east coast to Florida. From Florida we zig-zagged the southern route back to California. We visited the National Parks, walked the Freedom Trail in Boston, boiled our own Maine lobsters in a pot over the campfire at Bar Harbor, Maine, took a helicopter ride over Manhattan and the Statue of Liberty, did all the battlefields, visited D.C. and the Smithsonian, visited a southern Antebellum mansion, and did a week at Disney World.

We planned the trip to try to hit the "fall colors" in New England, and as it turned out, we hit it perfectly. Even the locals said that it was the best colors that they had seen in ten years. We even toured the Tabasco factory in Cajun country at Avery Island, Louisiana, and the Alamo in San Antonio, Texas.

In those years, we were enjoying driving horses and we drove singles and teams of horses hitched up to buggies, wagons and stage coaches here in California. We also had a "Carriage Rides" business for the tourists in Mariposa. So, on that trip we spent an awesome week with the Amish people in Lancaster, Pennsylvania. They made a lot of our harnesses, wheels, and wagon parts, and we got to meet them and see their operations.

After visiting a few relatives in my home state of Florida, we headed back west. It was something that happened on the last leg of that trip that I want to share with you.

Now, as you can imagine, these three children, outside of God, are our lives. It took us ten years of 'living hell' to break the government adoption 'curse' and finally be able to privately adopt our children.

This motorhome trip was a dream vacation and learning experience for our family. Grace and I had already been to all these places before, but now we were enjoying showing and teaching our children about them. It was an awesome experience, until we got to Houston, Texas.

Houston, Texas was a place in our lives that we experienced a bit more about prayer. There is a groan, or travail, that I believe we need to develop in our prayer lives.

As we approached Houston, our 37' luxury motorhome, which normally ran like a champ, began to shake badly. It was losing a u-joint on the drive shaft. At the same time, Interstate 10 was under construction and was all torn up. Some of it was down to a single lane and we were driving on dirt. It was a mess. My previous experiences with Houston and Interstate 10 had already prepared me that it was a nightmare even on a good day. So you can imagine the mess when it was under construction.

When we finally spotted a tire store near an off ramp, I exited and babied that motor home up to the front door of the store. We were in hopes the tire store could direct us to a mechanic that could replace the u-joint. We were praying that the u-joint would hold until we could get to a mechanic.

The way our motorhome was configured, the main door was about half way back, or about 15' behind the driver on the right side. In the far back of the rig was the bedroom where the kids were playing. I pulled the motor home up in front of the store so that the motor home door was adjacent to the store entrance and Grace could then easily access in and out of the store. After she stepped out of the motor home I stayed in the captain's chair with the motor running looking at a map, which meant the activity in and out of the store was behind me. When Grace returned and closed the motorhome door I automatically pulled out. Then, through all the construction, I finally got back on Interstate 10 heading west and looking for the place they told Grace about. After several miles of inching along with a shaking motorhome, and praying that it hold together until we could get to the mechanic, our youngest daughter, Maria, came out of the bedroom and asked Grace where Bernadette (our oldest daughter) was.

After checking the bathroom, the horror hit us like a bombshell. Bernadette was not in the motorhome. What neither one of us knew was that while Grace was in the tire store at the main counter getting information and help, Bernadette had slipped out and followed her, but saw the TV on in the adjoining waiting room and went in there. When Grace came back into the motorhome we both assumed all three kids were still in the bedroom.

Now Bernadette was eight years old, and she had above average intelligence, and we had taught our kids about keeping their wits about them and using wisdom in cases like this. But being a Salvadoran by race, and extra short in stature, and fifteen hundred miles from home, gives you a bit more of the picture.

Now we are miles across Houston, in a shaking motorhome that is threatening to break down at any minute. We are also on an overcrowded torn-up highway, with workmen and heavy equipment all around, and having to obey the frequent flag-men that are stopping and directing the traffic. Our precious daughter is miles back in a place we don't even remember the name of and don't know how to call. I'm not even real sure that I know how to find it quickly, especially coming from the opposite direction.

In that mess I had to find my way off the west bound lane and limp the rig back onto the east bound lane to start working our way back to that tire store. All the time, all we could do is pray. That's when I heard a prayer I had never heard before.

Deep travail
Grace was now up front with me in the passenger side captain's chair, in deep travail. What I heard was beyond description. I was the pastor of a "Spirit filled" church and frequently taught and preached on prayer. But that day I learned about, "effectual fervent prayer." With the deep groan and fear in my own soul, I, at least, had the distraction of having to drive and navigate. But Grace bent over in that chair and connected with heaven. She went into a deep combination of praying in tongues and a guttural groan. She couldn't see anything or hear anything but God. In a special sort of way she left her surroundings. Grace and I are full of the Word, and we have a lot of scriptures memorized, but that day we don't remember quoting any of them. We became them ... and ... we did them!

"For in him we live, and move, and have our being ..." (Acts 17:28)

"Likewise the Spirit also helpeth our infirmities: for we know not what we should pray for as we ought: but the Spirit itself maketh intercession for us with groanings which cannot be uttered. And he that searcheth the hearts knoweth what is the mind of the Spirit, because he maketh intercession for the saints according to the will of God." (Romans 8:26-27)

Grace said later that she felt like she was caught up into a bubble, with no awareness of anything but God's face. In her tremendous desperation, she had a clearer revelation than ever before that the Lord was the only one that could help and the only hope she had. She said she could "feel His face," and she knew that her breath was touching His face. She knew, or to put it a little better, there was "a knowing," that He wanted her to understand, and be assured, that she had His presence. Man, I get chills just thinking of it again!

It seemed like a lifetime, but it took me a little more than a half hour or so to finally get back to that tire store. We prayed that Bernadette would not leave the store looking for us. All the things that run through your mind at times like these are horrendous. When I finally put that motorhome door in front of the tire store again Grace shot out of there like a cannon ball. I'm getting emotional again just recalling this.

I'm reporting to you that God is good. Bernadette did go outside looking for us, and even went to the corner, but God turned her around and she ran back into the store. Now she was crying and scared, but ... a "Spirit-filled" lady in the waiting room, seeing what had happened, picked her up and held her. That lady was an angel sent from heaven just for us. She loved the Lord and held on to our Bernadette and encouraged her and prayed. Thank you, Jesus!

Needless to say, we loved on that lady and blessed her. In fact, after we got the kids back into the motorhome Grace went back into the tire store and found that lady again and hugged her and cried and cried in her arms.

That day I saw real prayer, and the power of prayer. It was so real and way past preaching. Grace hugged all three of those children all the way back to California! They probably thought she was a pest, but she didn't care. Those kids got loved on a lot before that, but they got a lot more after that! Smile!

The rest of the story
Now, the rest of the story. When we finally did get to that mechanic, and they got under the rig we were all shocked. The U-joint was totally broken. It t was completely disconnected from itself. The mechanic was amazed that we drove it into the shop. It had somehow hung-up on itself and kept us moving. With all that off-balance shaking, and the torque it takes to power an 18,000-pound motorhome, God was giving us a miracle every foot of the way. Folks, I'm just simple enough to believe that an angel had hold of that u-joint. God heard our prayer and we were in His hands!

California needs prayers like that!
Now, to the real point of my story. Saints of God, California "in the secular or natural" is lost. She has lost her way. Much sin comes out of California.

Just today I heard on the Fox News Channel that an openly gay boy was elected the prom queen at an L.A. high school. Help me Jesus!

California, county by county, is a conservative state
We all know that California votes predominantly democratic. When you web-search "Red Blue States" California will come up solid blue, representing Democratic. But if you add the words "county by county" you will find a completely different map. The map will be over 80% red. The county of Los Angeles, and the coastal Bay Area counties, where the massive population lives, votes strongly

liberal. However, as I have described earlier, most of California is rural and wilderness.

Have you ever noticed that where people live close to the land they tend to be more in tune to eternal things, and thus more conservative in their political views? There is something about nature and watching things birth, and putting your hands in the dirt and planting a seed and seeing it grow that point straight to God.

But where people live a life somewhat removed from the land they tend to be less conservative.

Now I'm not saying that every city-slicker is a heathen and every rancher is a preacher, but in general if you think about it I believe you will see what I mean. This principle is really quite visible when you look at a U.S. map that is colored "county by county."[1]

Financial crisis
The entire world is in the worst financial crisis since the crash of '29, and California is leading that parade. The state is broke and on the verge of bankruptcy. It is raising taxes, issuing I.O.U.s, and cutting services to the people. The Golden State that feeds the world and still has trillions of dollars worth of gold in the Mother Lode is in a financial crisis! It doesn't take a spiritual genius to figure out that this is a spiritual battle.

Water wars
California in general, with all of its rivers and lakes, is a water wonderland. The Lord blessed the state with an abundance of water. Nonetheless, at the time of this writing, we are in the third consecutive year of less than average rainfall and there is a fierce battle over the state's water uses. Even with the rain shortfall the water is still there, but due to spiritual forces there is a battle.

From a practical stand point the problem exists because of two basic dynamics. One is, California is an awesome place to live. That little detail is what drew millions to its shores. At the same time it is the world's number one food producer. Nevertheless, even after three years of low rainfall the California crops are still well irrigated. In the midst of the so-called water shortage if you drive up Highway 99, known as the Ag Highway, you will see 400 miles of flourishing crops. However, the battle over the water continues.

The Infamous Owens Valley War

The Water Wars have been raging in California since the scandal of the Los Angeles Aqueduct in 1913. William Mulholland, who is considered a visionary in Los Angeles and a villain in the eastern Sierras, was the master mind of the 240-mile aqueduct that brought water from the Owens Valley at the base of the eastern Sierras to Los Angeles.

Up and down the Eastern Sierras and the Owens Valley most of the old-timers still grumble about the way Los Angeles deceptively and unethically snapped up nearly all the land and water rights. Many ranchers and farmers were ruined, and there was immense bitterness. That story is dramatized in several books and the 1974 movie "Chinatown."[2]

California has been fighting over the Colorado River, the Sierras, and every other water source for years. Now, there is even a move to control your private water well on your own property.

The Delta Smelt

Today a serious water issue on the table is caused by the environmentalists (those that worship the created more than the Creator). They want to protect the little fish called the Delta Smelt. Consequently, they got a legal mandate to turn off the irrigation pumps. As a result farmers have to plow under tens of thousands of acres of prime production land on the west side of the San Joaquin Valley because they can't get the water for the crops. The effects of that are devastating to the farmers and the laid-off farm workers and their families, not to mention the entire agriculture industry and processing plants. It also affects every household in America when they go to that grocery store cash register. The sad part is that even after 3 years of low rainfall, the water is there; all they have to do is turn on the pumps. I have always said, "Never talk bad about farmers with your mouth full."

Now, for a bit of a balance here, Grace and I consider ourselves environmentalists. For twenty five-years we made our living on the "Wild Rivers" of the western United States. Furthermore, we still enjoy our horse-packing and trout-fishing expeditions into the 'High Sierra Wilderness Areas." Our lives are integrated with the pristine beauty of the wildernesses of the west. We not only took good care of the places we went, we taught our river trip passengers to do the same. On several occasions I have had clients from New York and different places call me after they spent a week with us on the river in the Grand Canyon, and laugh and tell me, "Henry, you've got me so well trained I'm still field-stripping my cigarettes and putting the butts in my pocket." Yes, we are concerned about our environment, but this "environmentalist" thing that is going on now is a spirit, and it can be very evil. It has lost all sense of right and wrong.

The developers & water
There is also a big demand and corresponding battle for water from the phenomenal growth of the cities and developments in California. Everywhere you drive these days in the Great Valley, or almost anywhere else, you see development and construction. Places that were rural just a decade ago are urbanized with malls, commercial centers, and huge shopping centers and housing projects. That all takes a lot of water.

An excerpt from Vicki Nohrden's book, "Breaking the Shield of Minerva"

> On February 16, 2007, in Camarillo, California, well known prophet Dr. Chuck Pierce delivered this word, "California will have wars over water. You won't have wars over oil. You will have war over water and you being the biggest supplier of our agriculture and our produce, the real war will come in California over water this year."[3]

Gay marriage
Recently, the State Supreme Court finally upheld the November 2008 voters on Proposition 8, which amended the state constitution to define marriage to be between a man and a woman.

The same court had previously over-ruled the people and overturned Proposition 22. In 2000 California voters adopted ballot initiative Proposition 22 (with an overwhelming 61.4% approval and 38.6% against) which prevented California from recognizing same-sex marriages. However, on May 15, 2008, the California Supreme Court struck down this initiative in a 4-3 decision, giving same-sex couples the right to marry.

Between the court's decision in May 2008, and the vote of the people taking it back again in November 2008, an alleged eighteen thousand gay marriages were performed in California. Although the court finally made the right decision to uphold the voters the second time around, they also ruled for those marriages to stand. That is an atrocity before God.

"California burning!"
Incidentally, a very short time after the State Supreme Court's decision to strike down Proposition 22 and allow gays to marry, a huge dry lightning storm went through California. The storm unleashed 25,000 to 26,000 dry lightning strikes across the state. The lightning strikes were fierce. The newspaper headlines read **"California Ablaze!"** 2,780 fires were burning at one time in California. Many homes and much property were destroyed. They had to bring in firefighters from other states and foreign countries to fight the flames.[4]

California has been anointed with a major leadership role in worldwide evangelism. God has poured out His Spirit in this state. When He gives a lot, He expects a lot.

" ... *For unto whomsoever much is given, of him shall be much required ...* " (Luke 12:48)

What happened?
My question is how did we get here? What happened? Just a few short years ago these things could never have gotten discussed, let alone voted on.

The obvious answer to my question is: "Society has gotten away from God."

So, with the gay pride movement, pornography, sex outside of marriage, unwed mothers and deadbeat fathers, abortion, and all the other corruptions in the state, we need to pray. But we can't afford patty-cake prayers. We must pray like Grace prayed for our lost daughter.

Like Hannah, after the Lord had shut up her womb, she, "... *poured out my soul before the Lord.*" (1 Samuel 1:15)

The good news! ~ God is Stirring the Waters
There is no doubt, there is a war in the heavenlies for the soul of California. But I believe "the die was cast" by God in the beginning. I am convinced that California is going to arise to its "Manifest Destiny" and be a decisive leader in the worldwide end-time outpouring.

On the very positive side of things, God has raised up a strong prayer movement in California. There are actually many sincere churches and intercessors in this state that are standing for righteousness and proclaiming the uncompromising Word of God. There are also countless very powerful "Spirit-filled" prayer groups that are on their faces stirring the waters and empowering the angels over California. Prayers and decrees are being made on the steps of the State Capitol and in all of the major cities and spiritual "well springs" (Like Mariposa and many others) in California.

In addition, I sincerely believe He wants this book written to encourage the Body of Christ and to fan the fires of the intercessors.

Arise, shine, saints! "Daddy's gonna take us Fire Fishing!"

"If My People ..."

CHAPTER **26**

FIRST, A BIRTHING IN THE SPIRIT

John Wesley said, "everything by prayer, nothing without it."

Billy Graham says there are three keys to his crusades: 1. Prayer, 2. Prayer, 3. Prayer

The Portland Vision
The great healing apostle John G. Lake had a visitation one night that was an answer to a cry of his heart. It is called "The Portland Vision." It was in Portland, Oregon, in the 1920's in a place called Mt. Taber Park, across the street from his house. Grace and I actually walked the path where the angel appeared to him.

On a midnight walk with the Lord, the Angel appeared to him on the path and took Lake's Bible and opened it to the book of Acts. He pointed to the outpouring of the Spirit on the day of Pentecost, and the other spiritual manifestations and revelations in the book and said:

> "This is Pentecost as God gave it through the heart of Jesus. Strive for this. Contend for this. Teach the people to pray for this. For this, and this alone, will meet the necessity of the human heart, and this alone will have the power to overcome the forces of darkness."

As the Angel was departing, he said:

> "Pray. Pray. Pray. Teach the people to pray. Prayer and prayer alone, much prayer, persistent prayer, is the door of entrance into the heart of God."

There is first a birthing in the spirit
The Word of God says, "Before she (Zion) travailed, she brought forth; before her pain came, she was delivered of a man child." (Isaiah 66:7)

Then, in the story of Hannah, in the first chapter of I Samuel we see that it was through prayer, fasting and travail that she succeeded in moving heaven. Hannah birthed her son "in the Spirit" before she conceived and delivered him in the flesh.

In the book of Acts we find the very familiar scripture, *"And when the day of Pentecost was fully come, they were all of one accord in one place."* (Acts 2:1)

But, saints of God, we must always remember that they were "of one accord" in the spirit of brokenness to self, in obedience to Him, praying and seeking the Lord with all of their hearts. It was in that spiritual atmosphere that the Lord was able to send the *"… sound from heaven as of a rushing mighty wind."* (Acts 2:2)

We know that we cannot make revival happen. As the preacher says, "Revival is not something man works up, but something God sends down." However, we are hungry enough to pray and fast. For many years a small group of believers has been doing spiritual warfare at Mariposa Revival Center, and praying for revival. The messages from the pulpit have focused on subjects like: revelation of Jesus Christ, hunger and brokenness, repentance, sanctification, holiness and faith in Him and His Word. Now our prayer is,

"And now, Lord, behold their threatenings: and grant unto thy servants, that with all boldness they may speak thy word, By stretching forth thine hand to heal; and that signs and wonders may be done by the name of thy Holy Child Jesus." Acts 4:29 & 30

ALL I KNOW IS, WE WERE HUNGRY
There is an intense hunger or desperation that comes from Him and its intensity is fierce at times. Like Jeremiah that had a *"fire shut up in his bones,"* it is my life's purpose and resolve to keep that hunger or fire burning forever.

I have seen many pastors with that fire burning in their bellies for a period of time only to eventually get totally burned out when it tarries. Some went back to normal dead church and even acquired an attitude against revival, while others left the ministry all together. My brothers and sisters, we cannot let this happen to our hearts.

Sometimes you just have to go fishing
I believe our job is to resolve to be intense enough to "diligently seek Him" and

to have a heart like Rachel's that told Jacob "give me a son or I'll die." We must petition God with the same intensity that says, "Give me revival or I'll die."

At the same time, to keep from dying, we need to go fishing once in a while. There are times that I can be so caught up and desperate for revival that I really believe it could kill me. This is where I believe we should take Jesus' lead and go to a mountain place, or place apart. There comes a time to go fishing, or to pull aside and do whatever a person's personal hobby or pastime might be. I believe this principle is essential to enduring "to and through" revival.

Grace and I get away from time to time with our horses to the high country. I can be in the wilderness at the ten-thousand-foot elevation with my horse tied nearby and still be dead center in the will of God as I cast the line out into that crystal clear lake. My soul rests and refreshes. And, every time I cast for a trout or look out across the snow-capped peaks admiring His incredible handiwork, my heart cries "Jesus."

You see, to me and Jesus, His name is a one-word prayer that connects straight to His heart and covers it all. Yes, it's a prayer that cries "help me catch that next fish," but He knows that my fire burns strong, and that deep longing for a move of His Spirit is the only thing that will fulfill my heart. It is in a place of refreshing like that that somehow, without losing an ounce of the desperation and hunger, He takes the pressure off and gives me the "stuff" to stay in the battle. It is in that spirit of mind that we can operate in the spirit of the Sons of Issachar (1 Chronicles 12:32) and maintain "… *an understanding of the times, to know what we ought to do.*"

A word over the body ~ The Issachar anointing

This word was spoken over me a few years ago by prophet Mary Glazier, and now I release it over the intercessors, and the body of Christ that is standing in the gap for an outpouring in California and the nations:

> "God's going to give you an understanding of the seasons and the time, my brother. You're going to have the Issachar anointing come upon you, and you're going to have a sensing of when it's time to do something and when it's time to hold your peace. You're going to have a sensing of when it's time to declare and when it's time to overlook. God's going to give you an understanding of when the fire of God needs to be fanned and when it needs to be banked … an Issachar anointing is coming upon you."

I am hopelessly convinced that the only thing that will turn this old world around is a sovereign move of the Holy Spirit ... Revival! For revival God needs people who will pray and travail without ceasing. We must stay in the battle and maintain relentless pursuit. So, He puts it in our hearts to "seek His face."

So, prayer warriors, keep the fire burning, and when it's time, go fishing!

"If My People ..."

CHAPTER 27

SO, WHAT NOW?
BACK TO THE MINISTRY OF JESUS!

Turn the light on in the church
As I keep saying, the only thing that can turn this world around is a move of God. For that to happen, our part is basically two-fold. We must pray in the Spirit of 2 Chronicles 7:14, and we must return to the apostolic ministry of Jesus Christ.

Like a bulldog on a bone!
In the spirit of Paul's heart in Philippians Chapter 3, we must re-focus on *"the knowledge of Jesus Christ our Lord ~ count everything else as dung ~ purpose to know Him and the power of His resurrection, and the fellowship of His suffering ~ we must follow after ~ this one thing.. JESUS! ~ forgetting the past and everything else as we reach forth ~ pressing for the mark of the prize of the high calling of God in Christ Jesus!"* (My paraphrase).

The message that the Lord has given me for the churches as we minister around the world is: "we must get back to the basic ministry of Jesus."

It amazes me how most churches, even "Spirit-filled" churches, are ministering much differently than Jesus did. They want Jesus' results, but they don't minister Jesus' way.

Jesus' mission statement is Luke 4:18 &19:

"The Spirit of the Lord is upon me, because he hath anointed me to preach the gospel to the poor; he hath sent me to heal the brokenhearted, to preach deliverance to the captives, and recovering of sight to the blind, to set at liberty them that are bruised, To preach the acceptable year of the Lord."

In Acts 10:38 Peter gave a summary of the ministry of Jesus when he said:

"How God anointed Jesus of Nazareth with the Holy Ghost and with power: who went about doing good, and healing all that were oppressed of the devil; for God was with him."

Remember? Jesus said in John 14:6, *" … I am the way … "* He also said in John 14:12:

"Verily, verily, I say unto you, He that believeth on me, the works that I do shall he do also; and greater works than these shall he do; because I go unto my Father."

We must remember that Jesus isn't just the way for us to get to heaven. His way of life and ministry is also the way we get others to heaven. He said in John 8:12 *"I am the light of the world."* He also said in Matthew 5:14, *"Ye are the light of the world."* Then in verse 16, He said, *"Let your light so shine before men, that they may see your good works, and glorify your Father which is in heaven."*

Now don't take me wrong when I say this, but I believe we need to do a little in-house church repair before we get so excited about our outreaches. As I said in Chapter 1, Jesus forbade a "word only" Gospel. The church isn't just important to the end-time harvest, it is key. Jesus' message to us in the book of Revelation was to the seven churches. Paul's great concern was his care of all the churches. When Jesus prayed His heartfelt prayer in John chapter 17 he said, *"I'm not praying for the world, but for the ministers."* (My paraphrase) They represent the churches and ministries that are the harvesters. That is why we must get the light (Jesus) on in the church.

The focus of Jesus' ministry, as laid out in Matthew 4:23, was preaching, teaching, and healing. His command to us in Mathew 10 was to preach and heal. In Luke 10 He commanded the seventy to heal and then preach.

Jesus didn't pray for the sick - He healed them!
If I could encourage the body of Christ in anything, it would be to re-read the four Gospels and the book of Acts with a fresh and open mind. It will change your life and ministry. One thing you will discover is that Jesus never prayed for the sick. Not once! Nor can you find the Apostles praying for the sick in the book of Acts, which happens to be the book that we, the body of Christ, are still writing.

Jesus didn't pray for the sick, He healed them. Jesus also said that He did nothing unless he saw the Father do it (My paraphrase of John 5:19 & 20 and verse 30, and 8:28 & 29). In other words, He maintained a relationship with the Father that allowed Him to hear clearly from heaven on every issue. Jesus moved in the gifts in a very simple but profound way. That's why one time He spits in a blind man's eyes, another time He makes mud from spit and rubs it in the fella's eyes and tells him to go wash in the pool, and another time He just says "receive your sight." There were three different methods that got the same results: blind eyes were opened. But notice that there was a constant in all three cases. That constant was that Jesus witnessed in His Spirit what the Father showed Him in each case, and He did that.

Our ministry should never be about "method" but about developing a relationship with Him, through the Word, that takes us to a new level of hearing from the Holy Spirit and moving in all nine of "the gifts of the Spirit."

Too many "Spirit-filled" churches are focused on the prophetic, or having a word for people, as the fulfillment of "moving in the gifts." Now, again, don't get me wrong, I believe in the prophetic and move in it myself. My wife Grace is a seer and sometimes has words and visions for almost everyone in the meeting. It is a wonderful manifestation of the Holy Spirit. We also bring the prophets into our church to speak and prophesy fresh words over our church and the people. A prophetic word can be very powerful, as it can unlock things and set people free. But, it is not central to the ministry of Jesus Christ.

What I am getting at is that too many churches are satisfied with that dynamic of the prophetic ministry. They will have church beginning with praise and worship, preach a sermon, then line the people up, or call them out, and have words for them. That's great and wonderful, but it will not attract the unsaved world to your church. What it does attract is Christians that want a "word" to make them feel good. I feel that sometimes it even borders on the Christian version of going to a palm reader or psychic to read your future.

In Matthew chapter 11:4 when Jesus confirmed to John the Baptist's disciples that He was the Christ, He told them, *"Go and shew John again those things which ye do hear and see: The blind receive their sight, and the lame walk, the lepers are cleansed, and the deaf hear, the dead are raised up, and the poor have the gospel preached to them."*

I believe that I am real safe in telling you that Jesus has shown us right here what we need to do to get the light on and bright in the church.

The world is sick and hurting and they need to start hearing the churches report what Jesus told John's disciples.

T.L. Osborn called healing "The Lord's dinner bell." Smith Wigglesworth called it "The maidservant of salvation." In Mark 7:27, Jesus called it *"The children's bread."*

In Mark chapter 1 verses 29 through 34, when Jesus healed Peter's mother-in-law, it says that by nightfall all the sick and the whole city were gathered at the door.

In Acts chapter 9 verses 32 through 35, when Peter healed Aeneas, it says that the whole country saw what God did and everybody in the region turned to the Lord.

In Acts chapter 8 verses 5 through 13, when Philip went down to Samaria, it says he preached Christ and cast out devils and healed many. The results were that *"there was great joy in the city"* and everybody turned from witchcraft to Jesus.

If that is the way Jesus and His disciples did it, why would we think we should do it any differently?

IN SUMMARY

In summary, it has been my intent, by the inspiration of the Holy Spirit, to present to the reader the divine plan of God for California through its natural and spiritual history. We have revealed the truth and uncovered the remarkable fruit that God has produced, and continues to produce, through the Golden State. California is a key player in the end-time harvest. The great Azusa Street Revival opened the gate and gave us a clear preview of even greater things to come! I truly hope that I have inspired the church to pray California into its "Manifest Destiny."

So California and the nations, let's pray and seek a fresh revelation of an old truth, "the ministry of Jesus Christ." Like one California preacher says, "Jesus is perfect doctrine." As I often tell my people, repentance isn't always turning away from the normal sins. Many times it is simply turning more towards Jesus!

And remember saints, at the wedding in Cana (John 2), Jesus provided the best wine last.

God bless America and God bless California! Can I get a loud Amen?

Lord, let the fire fall!

End

"If My People ..."

Appendix 1
RECENT PROPHETIC WORDS OVER CALIFORNIA

As California's government is on the verge of bankruptcy and the heavenlies battle for its soul, God has been speaking revival and breakthrough! I have personally talked to many spiritual leaders in California that have a strong witness that God is getting ready for something big here.

I know pastors that have recently been told by the Holy Spirit to relocate to California, to prepare for the coming move of the Spirit. Grace and I have a fire shut up in our bones that God is fixin' to move mightily here. California is revival country and it is revival time!

Below I have posted a few prophetic words over the state for your consideration. And, I'll have to say, "If they don't light your fire, your wood is wet!" Smile!

~ ~ ~ ~ ~

Dr. Chuck Pierce
Please see the word by Dr. Chuck Pierce in Chapter 1 … **"The Evil Root and the Glory Root in California."** I put it there because it speaks specifically to the heart of this book. The glory realm over California is going to overcome the evil root in California! Shout amen with me somebody!!

You may also see the Word by Dr. Pierce about Minerva in Chapter 23.

The Author's Vision
In Chapter 1 please see **The Vision** the Lord gave me in 2000. It is the basis of this book … "California, a Place of Accelerated Time on God's Clock."

~ ~ ~ ~ ~

The wording in these prophecies is unedited by us. We have merely corrected some of the punctuation.

"Prepare Yourself for the Outpouring that Has Been Prophesied By the Prophets of the Centuries"

Kim Clement

Prophesied on May 22, 2009 - San Jose, California:

The Spirit of the Lord says, "You have seen a dark cloud, you have seen a dark cloud and you have said, 'alas, why do we have this dark cloud, this foreboding cloud over us?'" But the Spirit of the Lord says, "Do you understand that a dark cloud simply means there will be an outpouring of a rain that shall come?"

And some of you have said, "This dark cloud that is over us is hiding the sun." But the Spirit says, "It is just for a season and yet the sun shall shine again, but that dark cloud is carrying an outpouring of rain that you have never experienced." The Spirit of God says, "Look, for you have said, 'Why is this cloud over us?' Stop asking Me."

A Prophetic Revival Has Begun

For God said, "Prepare yourself for the outpouring that has been prophesied by the prophets of the centuries. You are standing at the right place at the right time, for the right reason at the right season. You're in the perfect place," says the Lord.

There's a mantle all over this place; there's a mantle that God is casting. There is a mantle that God is casting just like He did when Elijah came to Elisha. He was plowing with twelve yoke of oxen and he was with the twelfth. You have come to the twelfth yoke of oxen.

And the Spirit says, "Would you say these words in the presence of an economic crisis; would you say these words when men are hearing the sounds of socialism? Would you say these words?" God said, "Since when was a church that I am building dictated to by the world? Since when was your economy reckoned by media and the spirit of prognosis?

A prophetic revival has begun. A prophetic revival has begun. What does this mean? It means God is going to do absurd things. God is going to do preposterous things. God is going to do things that men have never dreamed He would do.

In actuality, God said, "These will be very real because I am about to reveal Myself in a way that I never have in the history of mankind," says the Spirit of the Living God. "Do not laugh at these words and say, 'They are jargon.' Do not laugh at these words and say, 'He is speaking gibberish.'" The Spirit of God said, "On the Day of Pentecost they thought that they were speaking gibberish, but actually the Holy Spirit was upon them."

"What I'm Going to Do is Going to Be Called Absurd, Preposterous"

We cannot think that this is a man or a personality that has come and stirred the place. I have stirred only the Spirit of God that has said, "I have opened a door that no man can shut and those who have been shaken now shall go through this door. Kingdoms have been shaken throughout the earth. Men are crying out for something more, but can they handle the absurdity of God? Can they handle the absurdity of what God can do?"

For God said, "What I'm going to do is going to be called absurd, preposterous. It shall be called ineloquent, and they shall say of this move, 'The absurdity of it causes them to be marked as clinically insane.'" But God said, "Would you understand that it is My desire for you to enter into the realm of creativity? I am creating miracles." Men have said, "Where shall they come from?" Christ took the miracle, spat into the ground, created two eyeballs and shoved them into a blind man." God said, "Men are blind."

"A New Energy and It Shall Start in California"

"For there shall be an earthquake in California," but God said, "It shall be of a magnitude that they shall say, 'It is one of the highest ever,' and they shall say, 'How is it that men were not killed and why is it that so many lives were spared?' It shall be My sign," says the Lord.

"For out of the earth and because of this earthquake, there shall come something that shall bring a new energy and it shall start in California, and California shall not be bankrupt. It shall be the nation that shall be filled with prosperity because of what shall come from the earth," says the Lord!

God's about to do the most unusual things He's ever done!

A Door Has Opened

I saw a door opening. It was a door that had been sealed for the centuries; a door that Daniel saw, a door that Ezekiel saw. This is a door that they saw and knew that only at a certain point in time could it be opened. Now this presence that is here is for your benefit.

I am telling you as a prophet that this is a time in the history of mankind, of the Church, that men shall look back and say, "Do you remember that day in the month of May of 2009?" No, I'm not being over dramatic. I'm telling you that a door has opened. A door has opened and the serpent will try and spew out of his mouth water to create a flood.

But God said, "I will give you, My chosen, two wings which shall carry you away to a place of safety and a place of refuge. You shall not be affected by the economy, you shall not be affected by the plagues, you will not be affected by swine or bird flu or whatever flu," God says! "You shall have a divine protection and they shall say to you, 'How is it that you and your house were not affected by this? How is it that you and your business are not affected by it? How is it that you and your church were not affected by this?'"

For the Spirit of God said, "A door has opened and no man shall shut it. Therefore get ready, for this that I am going to do they shall call absurd. This that I shall do they shall say is preposterous. They shall say of this that it is not worthy of being called a move of God. They shall say that it is inappropriate, it is illogical, it is widely unreasonable."

But God said, "Tonight I poured out a mantle; I threw a mantle on you, not only you in this building, not only the youth in this nation who have strayed, but they shall come back with a vengeance."

"There is a Revelation Coming"
But God said, "As in the days of Eli, the heavens were closed. But because of the presence of Samuel, a prophetic revival, the windows opened wide. For there is a revelation coming to the Church and people shall walk in revelation knowledge and they will no longer walk in historical knowledge only, but in revelation knowledge. In other words, I the Lord will reveal Myself. I will appear Myself as I appeared to Abraham, as I appeared to Jacob. There will be appearances that shall be tangible in your homes, in your churches."

Listen now, God said, "I'm about to reveal Myself and revelation knowledge shall change the status of sin. The revelation of God shall change the status of sin," for God says, "In the presence of revelation, sin does not have the same status as it does in the absence of revelation. When Isaiah saw the Lord high and lifted up and His train filled the temple, God revealed Himself. The first thing that happened was that Isaiah said, 'I am a man of unclean lips,' and repentance took place.

"There shall be such a great revelation of God in these next ten years that people shall come to repentance without being urged to, without being preached to, and they shall say, 'We are people of unclean lips,' and they shall come into the Kingdom by the millions," says the Spirit of God!

God is about to reveal Himself in strange ways, they shall call it absurd, but His revelation, His appearances, Him revealing Himself shall change the status of sin in the Church. As God reveals Himself, sin shall have no power, and shall have no reign in marriages, in families, in churches. Unity shall be the order of the day.

Prophetic Image Expressions
Email: hope@kimclement.com
www.kimclement.com

~ ~ ~ ~ ~

"The Release of Breakthrough in California!"
(Not Another Cliche Breakthrough Word)
Shawn Bolz

April 3, 2009

Since January, something has been stirring up in California! Recently one of our friends from England came to California for a month-long "prayer journey." She entered into deep intercession for our ministry, along with one of our other team members. Days and days of intercession went by until one day, they had a "power encounter." Our friend from England saw an angel and said the angel's name was "Breakthrough." The angel had come to bring revival to California and breakthrough for our ministry, our city and the state. She had seen this angel of breakthrough at the beginning of February over a few different encounters, and when she shared this with me, I was encouraged but it did not fully register.

In the past ministry I was involved in, WhiteDove Ministries, we did a series of conferences on a similar encounter that Bob Jones and Randy Demain had with an angel of breakthrough who was instrumental in revival. Much happened, but I was not personally impacted at the time, at least not in a visible way. I was not discouraged because I saw other people, places and regions impacted. I personally just didn't have a breakthrough. I thought perhaps our friend from England was picking up on these encounters and applying them to us. However, I found out that she hadn't heard of these encounters and her encounter was completely separate from the others.

Visible Breakthrough Just Started Happening!
What caught my attention was when many things we have been praying and believing for (during the two years we've been in Los Angeles) started to happen in the two weeks following the encounter our friend had in February. We had breakthrough with our ministry's 501(c)(3) non-profit filing which is now complete; I sold my house in an impossible market I left in Alabama, and was given the money to pay the significant loss that occurred as a result of the sale; and several of our team members have had breaks in the entertainment industry. Also during this period of time, a significant breakthrough happened for one of our key leaders who's been given an incredible position to help rebuild an African nation from a governmental level and to advocate for Aids in the nations. We knew something was up!

I recently went to a conference with Randy Demain who had a previous encounter in Nigeria, while on a ministry trip in 2004, with who he also called "the angel of breakthrough." This angel had been involved with the charismatic preacher, Benson Idahosa, during the great Nigerian revivals of the 1990s. Bob Jones had a similar encounter later with similar details about this angel of breakthrough being released in America.

In February, I told Randy about our friend's encounter with the angel named Breakthrough, and he looked surprised. Randy said the presence of the angel had left him and the Lord told him that he was taking breakthrough somewhere else for a while, however, the angel of breakthrough would be back with Randy in the future! Randy said, "So that is where he is!"

Randy then began to unravel what he has seen happening when he prays for breakthrough in a church, city or region. I believe it can be summed up in the following process:

Consecration/purification of Believers.
Breaking through of promises given to Believers and the purposes for their lives, as well as for the harvesting of the harvesters. The release of Believers into all the world to bring the Kingdom and give Jesus His reward!

Our church has been in phase one and partially in the second phase of this word (although there has been evangelism and placement into the secular arena lately that has been beautiful).

Lou Engle and TheCall
On February 24, two significant things happened to us. Lou Engle and approximately 50 members of his team from "TheCall" came to my house in Hollywood to pray. We prayed over Hollywood and California, and during this time, I felt led to talk to them about the angel of breakthrough. I began to see that Lou Engle, who has been an intercessor for California for over 20 years, was about to see a breakthrough in the answers to many of his prayers. We were also reminded of a word he gave me at Harvest Rock Church in 2003. He had prophesied the following to me: "Son of California! Come home! You will be one of the main inheritors of my prayers for the last 17 years of revival in California!"

This was a few years before I moved out to California. As we reminisced about the word he previously gave me, Lou and TheCall team prayed again for us to inherit the prayers that went before us. I knew I was not only standing for myself, but for Believers in the land who have hoped for radical things to happen in their lifetimes and for California to be ripe for revival again.

On the same day we all prayed with Lou Engle, our friend from England and I shared about the breakthrough angel with our church body in Studio City, California. I loved the language because it put total emphasis on this angel being empowered to release a breakthrough so we can see Jesus and bring Him everything He deserves—the fullness of His reward!

What if God is about to break through again in a historic revival? Bob Jones had prophesied to us that by 2010 we would begin to see a measure of revival, and by 2012 revival would be historic! When I was with Lou Engle and his team, I realized that 2009 is a countdown year toward promise. I really felt this word was for them personally, but now I also see a corporate dimension to this prophetic parable. We are in a countdown year.

Staking My Dream
On February 25, I had a dream I believe is significant and specific to California (but feel free to take it if you are from another region). In the dream I went to the store and bought "22 stakes." I painted the word "breakthrough" on eleven of the stakes and also painted images of "keys and crowns." I left the other eleven stakes plain.

In the dream I went to 11 regions in California during 2009, with an emphasis on the timeframe of March through June. I presented a stake to different pastors/ministry leaders throughout California—to stake the land out for breakthrough to happen for them and for their region. The painted stake was kept for their ministry, but the plain stake was taken to a significant place in their region.

I had the ministry leader pound the plain stake into the ground to mark a covenant—declaring that in our lifetime, there would be historic breakthrough in politics, entertainment, business, education, family, and Church throughout the State of California.

In the dream I also asked the California pastors to begin to release "stories of breakthrough" on the Internet! I knew it was the Hebrews 10:24 principle: "And let us consider how we may spur one another on toward love and good deeds."

In the dream it was important that Believers in California hear from each other and spur each other toward the love of Christ as a state. I saw as we did this, God would release a strategy as contained in Hebrews 10:25, "Let us not give up meeting together, as some are in the habit of doing, but let us encourage one another—and all the more as you see the day approaching."

We are about to have historic breakthrough "revival reports" from our very state!

When I woke up I knew God was marking out territory in California, to inherit for His purposes. I knew we were entering into a "season of consecration" with a measure of breakthrough which is a "preparation season." I also knew it was going to be easier than ever to find unity among the churches that are centered around "the desire for the love of God" to visit our state.

When I awoke from the dream, I was excited to realize that the 22 stakes also represented Isaiah 22:22, "I will place on His shoulder the key to the house of David; what He opens no one can shut, and what He shuts no one can open." We had just prayed this as a release over California with Lou Engle and TheCall team. I also felt that the stakes were divided into two groups of eleven because God wants to release the Spirit of Revelation over California (see Ephesians 1:17), which is summed up by the attributes contained in Isaiah 11:1-4.

God is also going to reclaim His purpose in this land one more time. Isaiah 11:11 states the following: *"In that day the Lord will reach out His hand a second time to reclaim the remnant that is left of His people ..."* This passage represents the bringing together of God's people for His purpose.

You Are California's Breakthrough!
Whenever an area faces crises, like California is facing at this time, it's normally a set up for God to shine His marvelous light. In this time our economy is threatened, our politics are failing, our education system is in turmoil, and our families are in crises. But there is a God of breakthrough who has a Kingdom that is higher then what we see. The strategy of Heaven is to release the GOOD NEWS of who Jesus is, and of His Kingdom, to cause us not to fail but to THRIVE in love and good works. The KINGDOM of CHRISTIANS is the ANSWER for THIS SEASON in CALIFORNIA!

I encourage pastors, business owners, entertainers, politicians, educators, and families in California to come into "prayer agreement" with the Scriptures just mentioned (Ephesians 1:17, Isaiah 22:22, Isaiah 11:1-3, and Isaiah 11:11) over your family, occupation, and the land itself. One of the names of God in Hebrew is Baal-Perazim which means "Master of the Breakthrough." This is seen in 2 Samuel 5 when David defeated his enemies in a land he named after this mighty principle.

For those in Los Angeles, we just found out that in the center of the city, there is a plaque which states that 11 men, 11 woman, and 22 children came to pioneer the great City of Angels! Our city was formed with 11:11 and 22 in mind! This is just one of the dozens of signs we've seen in the natural to confirm what is happening in the Spirit.

I will be going throughout the state during the rest of the year—walking out my dream in the natural. I don't know if we will be doing this publicly or privately, but we would love to report on what is happening as we walk this out. We would also like to hear about some of the breakthrough testimonies of what happens with YOU. If you are a pastor and want to respond to this word, please contact my office at office@expression58.org. If you have had a testimony of breakthrough since January 2009, please share it with us! We will be trying to go to all 11 places (which as of yet have not been identified) during the next few months.

Pray with us for the God of breakthrough to come to California!

Expression58 Ministries
Email: office@expression58.org

~ ~ ~ ~ ~

APPENDIX 1

Evangelism Angels Come from Africa to California
Doug Addison

April 1, 2009

I went to Cape Town, South Africa on March 21, 2009, to speak at a prophetic conference with Barbara Claassen of Prophetic Breakthrough Ministries. As I landed, God began to speak to me about a radical change about to take place that would set into motion a chain reaction that would positively impact the entire earth for the Kingdom of God. Immediately I began having dreams of angels visiting me. At the conference I noticed the increase of angelic activity and the presence and power of God was extremely strong. We saw miracles take place and people healed and set free—in some cases instantly.

Power Evangelism Angel

Just before an evening session I received what I can only describe as a supernatural infusion of Kingdom Financial Strategies. As I delivered the message, the presence of a very large angel came with an anointing for businessmen and women to create finances for the Kingdom. Some refer to this as the "Joseph Anointing" which is demonstrated in Genesis 41 as Joseph interprets Pharaoh's dreams and gives him prophetic direction on how to prosper during an economic downturn. In many cases there were immediate responses as strategies for business and finances came in. My own ministry received an answer to prayer that night for a financial need.

The next session the angel was back and this time nearly the entire conference was set free and healed of broken hearts and issues with wounds from authority. The session after that the angel was present and nearly everyone present experienced a manifestation of the Holy Spirit in their body with jolts of electricity, tingling, warmth, etc. Dozens were physically healed that night and there were reports back the next day of supernatural turnarounds, including someone about to commit suicide who was ministered to and saved.

I had not seen this type of power for a while and I had never seen an angel like this. It was like a Swiss Army knife, whatever was needed for the people, the angel would release an anointing for an immediate response. I telephoned a friend of mine in the US who is a prophet named Bob Jones to ask if he was aware of an angel like this. Bob told me the angel was Power Evangelism and it was being assigned to me to come back to the US to bring about a revival.

The Gathering Angels

That night I had a spiritual experience. I don't know if I dreamed it, was really there, or it was a vision. I was driving down U.S. Highway 101 in California. I noticed at the side of the road that there were dozens of Cal-Trans workers (California Department of Transportation). I looked closer and I saw their faces turn into ancient African faces with eyes of blazing fire. They were busy scooping up handfuls of white balls of light from the grass. They were able to find these lights that had been overlooked and discarded by others. Then the fear of God came over me as I realized these were the angels that have been sent by God to gather in a great revival (Luke 10:2 and Matthew 24:31). I knew that this group of angels had come from Africa to the U.S. to bring about revival.

The Power Evangelism Angel and the Gathering Angels are now in California preparing for a great move of God that will sweep the entire earth. Their focus will be on the outcasts and people that are called by God but overlooked by the current religious system. Though this particular move from God is starting in California, it will not be limited to California but will sweep the globe. Many different types of visitations and outpourings from God are happening right now all over the earth. This is just one of them.

White Feather from Heaven

Many of the prophets at the conference in South Africa were telling me that an angel has been assigned to go back with me to the U.S. for revival. Since this is so serious, I asked God for a confirmation. At the next meeting, a white feather literally appeared in mid-air and floated down to the palm of my hand in plain view of everyone. As this happened, the power of God hit the place quite strongly. I slid out of my seat and was on the floor in an Acts 10:10 trance-type of experience. I saw the angel holding my hand and I began to receive a deep level of revelation that has not stopped since.

Sir Isaac Newton's Third Law of Motion and Revival

As I was leaving South Africa, I received a prophetic word from God that what is happening will be similar to Newton's Third Law of Motion: "For every action there is an equal and opposite reaction." The action of the angel from South Africa being given to the United States will create a reaction in South Africa of an equal proportion and there will be a reaction in the Spirit.

There will be a revival in South Africa as well as in other parts of the world. When I got home from my trip I had an encounter in which I was taken in the

APPENDIX 1

Spirit to South Africa and shown a division that God is healing. There are divine strategies being released from Heaven to help remove obstacles to unity in South Africa and around the world. Unity among Christians will be a key to sustaining any revival or move of God.

How to respond

I was really reluctant to release this article, especially after the recently derailed move of God in 2008. I am not saying this will have the same level of impact as previous moves of God or that my ministry has an exclusive right to what is happening. I do feel that I must tell people about what I experienced and begin to impart this as much as possible. In the past, I have actually downplayed many of my supernatural encounters because I don't like sensationalism, but this one is significant. As I got home, and began to do research on the internet, I saw several other ministries release articles on angelic encounters over the past few days. I have been saying for years that we are sitting on one of the biggest revivals in Church history.

What I noticed is this: as these angels and the anointing they bring are released, they take what we already have to a new level. So I encourage you to begin to ask God for more of what He has called you to do. Begin to step out and use your gifts right now. Ask God to give you opportunities to share His love. Watch as you will begin to see more supernatural signs and manifestations of the Holy Spirit as this is released.

Luke 10:2 NIV: He (Jesus) told them, "The harvest is plentiful, but the workers are few. Ask the Lord of the harvest, therefore, to send out workers into his harvest field."

InLight Connection
www.dougaddison.com
info@dougaddison.com
(800) 507-7853

~ ~ ~ ~ ~

"Prophetic Word for California: The Angel Shouted, 'The Eagles Have Landed! The Eagles Have Landed!'"
Chad Taylor

August 22, 2007

"Lift up your eyes all around, and see: they all gather together, they come to you; your sons shall come from afar, and your daughters shall be nursed at your side. Then you shall see and become radiant, and your heart shall swell with joy; because the abundance of the sea shall be turned to you, the wealth of the Gentiles shall come to you" (Isaiah 60:4-5).

Summer Revival in California
In the nine years we've been ministering in the state of California, our recent trip to Central California produced the most significant fruit. Our ministry is currently in its seventh consecutive week of revival meetings in Stockton, California, which have resulted in benchmark prophetic moments, and we are seeing the beginning stages of revival in the streets.

We've experienced firsthand what I call, "REVIVAL PRAYING." When God's people find a place of intense prayer mixed with tears, inevitably, it leads to repentance from dead works. This is usually followed by a deep resolve to reach the world that surrounds our modern parishes and churches and narrows the stark margin between the Church and the street.

I ministered at various cities and churches including a group at the Delta College Campus, one of California's oldest colleges. As I illustrated the "missing links" in today's Church that creates a general atmosphere absent of a true revival spirit, the class began to cry out to God spontaneously with tears and vehement prayers. It reminded me of a small class that I taught several years ago at the University of the Nations YWAM base in Kona, Hawaii. What started as a small strategic missions class suddenly captured the hearts of the campus as we converged on the "GO" center with revival prayers. This resulted in many going to the streets of Kona with fire and passion. Much of that continues today as many continue to carry the torch into the streets.

And our torches--our Light, was created to rule over darkness as the Lord declared eons ago, *"And God made two great lights; the greater light to rule the day, and the lesser light to rule the night....*" (Genesis 1:16). We need to be where it is dark. You see this dynamic again, "And they that be wise shall shine as the brightness of the firmament; and they that turn many to righteousness as the stars for ever and ever" (Daniel 12:3). A "shining" or "rising" always has a starting point.

PROPHETIC WORDS OVER CALIFORNIA

"As I heard the words, 'CRITICAL MASS CALIFORNIA,' I saw California as the breaking point or tipping point of a great 'Shining' across the land. Like a submarine streaking upward, towards the water's surface (as the tip of the submarine hits and breaks the waves), I see California as the tip or "ice breaker" as it shines with an effectual fervent glory."

The prophetic words I share below were released after a series of prophetic meetings at The Father's House in Stockton, California, which then led to the streets. The ministering happens weekly, Friday through Sunday, and we are scheduled through the entire month of September. We hope to continue to push through and raise a clarion call over the state.

The Pace Car of Revival is Now Taking the Track

"California is like the pace car at the Indianapolis 500, and it will begin to set the pace for radical reformation in the Church system. California will be the arrow point that pierces the old wineskin and makes way for a new dynamic of ministry and Church. You will see a first fruits of this in California as an army begins to stir herself.

As California begins to take her role as a true forerunner and trailblazer, hot spots of revival will begin to burn more brightly all over the nation. When California gets free, so a nation gets free. The pace of current breakthrough will quicken this summer and landslide into the fall and winter months. In November, we will see significant signs following as these things take place. God says, 'The oil of repentance and penance will open the floodgates of reparation as I call California's firstborn back to Me.'

Many generational legacies will begin to bear fruit as California stirs herself once again. The Mexican-Americans will find themselves in new seats of authority, governing and ruling in righteousness as delegates and ambassadors of the Lord. The royal Spanish and Mexican bloodline will find redemptive qualities for California's future, and these things will become very evident in the days and months ahead as the very land is healed from the reparative prayer of the saints. Meekness and humility will win over the hearts of the proud, and diverse and sundry streams of religious expression will come together as one to shout the walls of indifference and piety down."

California is in God's Crosshairs (and the devil's too)
"Like a nuclear reactor, California is now at critical mass. The crosshairs of God's purposes and plans are upon it. Those that labored in her vineyards for years will now reap the reward of the diligent, which is the first fruits of revival. The broken walls of her inheritance that religion and division have eroded, will now be repaired as a new strength fills the hearts of her children. Dark and dangerous plots of the enemy over Southern California will come to nothing as the Sword of the Lord and a Gideon Army fight on the side of the Lord.

Natural disaster in Central California will be extremely lessened to encourage the hearts of the laborers. Northern California will feel the refreshing winds of the Lord's presence as He strengthens her borders and removes the mountains before her. Wells that have remained shut and forgotten will give way to new rivers of righteousness and power as He heals the wounds of the land. Reconciliation will resound as you pray, releasing the fire of God.

The spirit of Ichabod will find no place to rest in California as she passionately pursues His heart for the lost and the poor. Places of worship will now be called, 'Cities of refuge' for the downcast and the rejected as an underground harvest begins to step from the cave into the light. Faces etched with destiny will shine with His glory despite tattoos and outward signs of their persecution. Like David, they will dance in the streets and war in the highways and byways for a people yet to see His glory. RADICAL is written on their hearts as they pursue His plan with unshakable resolve."

The Cup of the Prophet is Over California
"He that receiveth a prophet in the name of a prophet shall receive a prophet's reward;" (Matthew 10:41).

"Because of California's ability to accommodate the prophets of the Lord, a prophet's reward is upon her. A prophetic prosperity will fill her coffers and overflow her bosom as she gives birth to the prophetic word sown inside of her. Current trends in real estate and land ownership will set a new standard in California and the nation, as God prepares her borders for His arising in

His people. As in the pages of Acts, "Lands and Houses" will be released at a blurring rate and the finances from this divine release and blessing will supply the frontlines of revival around the world. Great missionary endeavors will come from California unlike any other time in recorded history as the gates of prosperity are opened.

Pray intercessors, Pray! The battle is intensifying over you and the price will not be light as you stand in the gap for a generation. The timing has come into maturation and the bells of grace are sounding over your heads--lift them up, for the deliverance of the Lord is here!"

The Angel Shouted, "The Eagles Have Landed! The Eagles Have Landed!"

I heard this crystal clear in the spirit as I received this prophetic word, "THE ANGEL SHOUTED, 'THE EAGLES HAVE LANDED! THE EAGLES HAVE LANDED!'"

"California is a great eagles nest that is preparing to propagate the Word of the Lord in a very unique and significant way. I also saw the eagle as the symbol of the United States and its governing body. California would once again become the 'point man' in 2008 as the elections come to a head.

The prophetic company assembled in California's borders would become an epicenter of historic prayers predetermining the future of a nation. A divine highway is coming to completion in California--a landing strip will be receiving prophetic ministries from around the world and into its borders. California will quickly become a 'prophet's upper room,' and the blessings of the Lord will overtake her. Her land will flourish and her banks will overflow as in times of harvest like Israel's crossing over the Jordan.

The distinct sounds of worship will be heard in her cities. San Francisco will not be just sounding brass or clanging symbols, but rather a distinct call to battle will be sounded out, rallying the army into action. For a time of reckoning and reconciliation is upon you and you will see the Lord in the land of the living."

In 2 Kings 6:16-17, Elisha was in Dothan, and he said, *"Do not fear, for those who are with us are more than those who are with them."* And Elisha prayed, and said, *"LORD, I pray, open his eyes that he may see. Then the LORD opened the eyes of the young man, and he saw. And behold, the mountain was full of horses and chariots of fire all around Elisha."*

The Lord Said, "I Am Leaving My Heart in San Francisco"

As the old song pays tribute, "I left my heart in San Francisco," I heard the Lord say, I am leaving MY HEART in San Francisco. A redefining moment is upon you, O great city. As you once burned into the night and ships from afar saw your demise, now watch and see as I arise and shine, declaring a new day of liberty. Ships from afar shall once again see the night sky burning bright, but now it will be the fires of My Spirit as a lamp to your feet and a light to your path. I will now light the torches of My passion and purpose and like an Olympic runner, your streets will see it and be glad."

I say something unique in the months of June, July, and August. For those months shall be as three days to Me, says the Lord, and I will open the graves of your destiny and call Lazarus forth. The stone of judgment shall be rolled away, and you shall stand in victory as the reproach of your youth is remembered no more. An army of the destitute and despised will stand in My glory with fire in their eyes as the Spirit of the Lord is poured out without measure. That which has been your greatest shame shall now become your greatest glory as I testify My grace in you.

Watch and see, even from the Golden Gate, My Glory will be seen. Many will stop to behold a sign and a wonder and lift up their eyes to Me, for this purpose will it be. I am even now removing those that oppose, and a great turning will transpire as the seats of authority are occupied by those that pray. Righteousness will prevail, and the gates of hell will not, as a new day is declared in you, and many will see it and rejoice."

I am leaving My heart in San Francisco, says the Lord, I am leaving My heart in you. What was once stone is now flesh and will be filled with the knowledge of the Lord.

Consuming Fire Revival Network
Email: info@consumingfire.com
Web: www.consumingfire.com

"If My People ..."

Appendix 2

FROM CALIFORNIA DEPARTMENT OF FOOD AND AGRICULTURE CHART

Livestock, Dairy, Poultry and Apiary
Cash Income 2007

Source of Income	2007 (Dollars)
Aquaculture	14,291,000
Chickens, All	712,943,000
Cattle and Calves	1,784,101,000
Eggs, Chicken	323,708,000
Hogs and Pigs	31,549,000
Honey	14,144,000
Milk and Cream	7,328,474,000
Turkeys	42,610,000
Wool and Mohair	195,712,000
Other Livestock	2,810,000
Other Poultry	70,650,000
Total	**10,734,914,000**

Top 5 Agricultural States in Cash Receipts, 2007

State	Rank	Total Value Billions of Dollars
California	1	36.6
Texas	2	19.1
Iowa	3	19.0
Nebraska	4	14.6
Minnesota	5	12.5

Crop and Livestock Commodities in which California Leads the Nation

Almonds	Eggplant	Lettuce, Romaine	Pistachios
Apricots	Escarole/Endive	Melons, Cantaloupe	Plums
Artichokes	**Figs**	Melons, Honeydew	**Plums, Dried**
Asparagus	Flowers, Bulbs	Milk	**Pomegranates**
Avocados	Flowers, Cut	Milk Goats	Raspberries
Beans, Dry Baby Lima	Flowers, Potted Plants	Nectarines	**Rice, Sweet**
Beans, Dry Large Lima	Garlic	Nursery, Bedding Plants	Safflower
Beans, Green Lima	**Grapes, Raisins**	Nursery Crops	Seed, Alfalfa
Bedding/Garden Plants	Grapes, Table	**Olives**	Seed, Bermuda Grass
Broccoli	Grapes, Wine	Onions, Dry	**Seed, Ladino Clover**
Brussels Sprouts	Greens, Mustard	Onions, Green	Seed, Sudan Grass
Cabbage, Chinese	Hay, Alfalfa	Parsley	Seed, Vegetable and Flower
Cabbage, Fresh Market	Herbs	Passion Fruit	Spinach
Carrots	Jojoba	**Peaches, Clingstone**	Strawberries
Cauliflower	Kale	Peaches, Freestone	Tomatoes, Processing
Celery	Kiwifruit	Pears, Bartlett	Turnips
Chicory	Kumquats	Peas, Chinese	Vegetables, Greenhouse
Cotton, American Pima	Lemons	Peppers, Bell	Vegetables, Oriental
Daikon	Lettuce, Head	**Persimmons**	**Walnuts**
Dates	Lettuce, Leaf	Pigeons and Squabs	

California is the sole producer (99 percent or more) of the commodities in bold.
http://www.cdfa.ca.gov/statistics/files/CDFAResourceDir08_final.pdf
A list (not shown) of California in the top five of production would be much larger.

Epilogue 1
CALIFORNIA ~ "A STORY STILL UNTOLD"

There is much more to the spiritual story of California. This first edition of "God, Gold & Glory" has been written to get the ball rolling. As one prophet said, "Henry, don't wait to get all of the spiritual history of California. Get this first edition out and let the people help you write 'the revised edition' later." He said, "It is California's time and NOW is the time for the book to be released."

So, we are asking the readers to let us know, by email or snail mail, about any major moves of God in California that were not included in this book.

Our church website
We will also try to maintain updated dedicated sections in our website about:

- Current prophetic words over California
- A current list of all organized prayer groups in the state with contact information
- Articles of major spiritual happenings in the state

Mailing: Mariposa Revival Center ~ P.O. Box 1269 ~ Mariposa, Ca. 95338
Email: hisword@sierratel.com
Web: www.MariposaRevivalCenter.com

Epilogue 2
RE-DIG YOUR WELLS

I wrote this book as an encouragement to the body of Christ. It is not meant in any way to be offensive or demeaning to any other region in the world. I sincerely did my best to be guided by the Holy Spirit to present the facts and spiritual parallels as He gave them to me.

A prophetic down-load

Just before I began to write this book I had received several prophetic words over me about writing it. I had the witness in my spirit but I couldn't get it all together in my mind on how to start. Then one evening in late December, 2008, just after returning home from several weeks of itinerant preaching in Wales, England and Hawaii, it happened. As I sat down to watch the evening news, the Lord started an immediate down-load. It came at a time that I wasn't even thinking about a book, but instantly it was like a gusher. Most of the chapter subjects in this book came to me right then in a matter of minutes. I literally scrambled out of my chair to grab some paper to write on.

With that outline of subjects, which came straight from heaven, I had the backbone of the book. The next few months were then spent researching and writing those chapters.

Now, with that said, if you live in a state or region in the world that has been very fruitful spiritually, I would say let this book challenge you, or someone you know, to chronicle it. Just off the top of my head I can think of several states that have been hot-spots for the Lord. Surely, my old home state of Florida would be a candidate, as well as Oklahoma, Texas, and Missouri, just to name a few.

It would be an added blessing to us if this book prompted others to write and chronicle the moves of God from their state, region, or nation. I believe we all need to re-dig those old wells to encourage the body of Christ and fan the fires of revival around the world.

A DECREE AND PROPHECY OVER CALIFORNIA

In the spirit of Job 22:28 and Ezekiel 37:4-14, we the body of Christ come together in agreement and unity, and decree and prophesy that …

- Holy Spirit, You are welcome in California

- The spirit of 2nd Chronicles 7:14 & 15 will increase mightily in the California church

- The adversary will be exposed and the evil veil will be removed from California

- The Glory realm will overcome the evil root in California

- We say to Minerva and her cohorts, "Be thou removed from California, and be thou cast into the sea"

- We decree that California is divorcing the spirit of baal, and renewing its covenant with God

- A new "gold rush" ~ "revival" ~ is coming to California

- California will fulfill its "Manifest Destiny" in the Lord

- California will arise to the voice of the prophets

- "The Vineyard of the Lord" ~ "the Land of Milk & Honey" ~ "the Mother Lode" ~ and "The Golden State" ~ will increase as terms of spiritual reality in California

- Hollywood will repent and earn the title "Holy Wood"

- California's apostolic anointing will increase as a mighty blessing to all nations of the world

- California will lead the nation that leads the world in the end-time harvest

- The nations will agree that they need to stand and pray for the Golden State

- Jesus is Lord over California!

AMEN!

ABOUT HENRY & GRACE FALANY

Henry & Grace Falany

Henry & Grace Falany founded Mariposa Revival Center in 1989. The ministry is located in Mariposa, California. Mariposa is a mountain community located on the Mother Lode of the historic 1849 California Gold Rush. It is also the home of Yosemite National Park.

Since its inception, the Falanys have guided the church to focus on preaching the uncompromised Word of God, ushering in the "presence of the Lord" through worship, restoring the Tabernacle of David through uncommon prayer endeavors, an extensive and expanded Feed the Poor program, and restoring the healing and deliverance ministry of Jesus to the body of Christ and the world.

They have also been used by God to spark revivals and spontaneous uncommon moves of the Holy Spirit in numerous churches besides their own. In one such movement, "The Feast of Fire Revival," as many as 20 regional churches and more than 10 other ministries came into unity and were swept into the revival. Without advertisement or any pre-planning, a two night meeting exploded into a powerful move of God that touched thousands of lives. It went to ten cities and lasted for most of the year.

With revival shut up in their bones, the Falanys are also itinerant church and conference speakers around the country and internationally. Called a Mom & Pop in the Kingdom, they also minister to leaders. Pastor Henry has often been called a pastor to pastors.

Henry has always been an American history buff and has read and studied much on the American Revolution, the Civil War, and the westward expansion. He has also been a revival enthusiast and has read and studied the major revivals of history.

Henry and Grace travel and minister with an apostolic anointing and experience many healings and miracles in their meetings. To help spiritual revelations come alive, Pastor Henry's preaching is often salted with a lot of country humor and interesting illustrations. This is often based on stories of his many life experiences in the great western outdoors, and southern swamp and bayou upbringing.

Grace moves in a strong seer's, deliverance, and healing anointing. The Lord frequently gives her clear prophetic visions and words for the people to whom she ministers. Her ministry edifies, encourages, and confirms many, while others are totally set free. Frequently, the local pastors testify of how her prophetic visions and words are so accurate and how they manifest and come to pass.

Henry's ministry usually features fiery prophetic messages to the church, as well as an uncommon healing anointing. It has also been said that he has a unique "convincing" gift that affirms and activates the people with a "You and God can do it" spirit. God uses him to take the people to the next level in their personal ministry and walk with the Lord.

ABOUT HENRY & GRACE FALANY

The Falanys also teach and train healing classes in churches around the world.

Henry was inducted into "Who's Who in California" in 1984.

They have three adopted children who all love the Lord ~ Bernadette; born in 1983 is Salvadoran and married to Trent ~ Travis; born in 1984 is Mexican, and Maria; born in 1985 is Dutch-English. They have one (so far) beautiful granddaughter, Bayleigh, born in 2003. She is Bernadette and Trent's daughter and she is Grandpa's riding and fishing buddy!

Lower left: Bayleigh, Bernadette & Trent Davis Lower right: Maria Falany ~ upper left: Travis Falany

For 25 years prior to pioneering their ministry, the Falanys pioneered and conducted White Water River Expeditions, Incorporated. As world renowned "outfitters and guides" WWRE became one of the world's largest river running companies. They outfitted people from all over the world on several days to week long, 300 mile, white-water rafting and camping expeditions. They conducted trips on the Salmon & Middle Fork of the Salmon River (River of No Return) in

Idaho, the Colorado River in the Grand Canyon, and all the major wild rivers of the western United Sates.

In the mid 1970's, they also founded and operated Lighthouse Reef Expeditions, a deluxe island camping and scuba diving and sport fishing adventure in remote areas of the Caribbean. That operation was off the coast of Belize, Central America.

In addition, they owned and operated Grace 'N Oaks Ranch, a horse breeding ranch in Mariposa, California. With over 55 horses in their brood stock, they showed and campaigned several "working cow horses" and "cutting horses" to state, national, and world champions.

Now, as pastors and international preachers, they still take occasional breaks with horses and mules. During the summer and fall they frequently pack train into the High Sierras to "ride the high country," camp, fish, and enjoy God's handiwork.

SOURCE NOTES

Chapter 1: The Seed of Original Intent
1. Will "Hollywood" Conquer the World,
   http://www.geocities.com/americanreflections/Will_Hollywood_Conquer_the_World.html?
2. Heaven Invading Hollywood, by Joshua Mills
3. Heaven Invading Hollywood, by Joshua Mills
4. http://en.wikipedia.org/wiki/Grauman's_Chinese_Theatre

Chapter 4: California: Young Land of Abundance and Greatness
1. "California Agricultural Resource Directory 2008–2009"
2. http://www.cdfa.ca.gov/statistics/files/CDFAResourceDir08_final.pdf
3. Personal interview with Jim Covel, Senior Manager of Guest Experiences, Monterey Bay Aquarium, June 09
4. Historical display at Fishermen's Wharf ~ Monterey
5. http://eastbay.bizjournals.com/eastbay/stories/2008/06/23/daily24.html

Chapter 5: America by the Hand of God
1. http://en.wikipedia.org/wiki/Mayflower_Compact
2. The Light and the Glory, by Peter Marshall & David Manuel, Pg. 149
3. The Light and the Glory, by Peter Marshall & David Manuel, Pg. 184
4. The Light and the Glory, by Peter Marshall & David Manuel, Pg. 166
5. The Light and the Glory, by Peter Marshall & David Manuel, Pg. 185
6. http://en.wikipedia.org/wiki/City_upon_a_Hill

Chapter 6: California by the hand of God
1. Geoffrey C. Ward ~ The West, An Illustrated History, Pg. 30

Chapter 7: Meet Jedediah Strong Smith ~ God's Mountain Man
1. http://www.christnotes.org/dictionary.php?dict=sbd&id=2296
2. http://en.wikipedia.org/wiki/Jedediah_Smith
3. http://www.jedediahsmithsociety.org/bioforstudents.html
4. http://www.geocities.com/cott1388/jedidiah.html
5. http://www.geocities.com/cott1388/jed-cal.html
6. http://www.christianhistorytimeline.com/GLIMPSEF/Glimpses/glmps143.shtml

7. http://www.jedediahsmithsociety.org/images.html

Chapter 9: JOHN CHARLES FREMONT

1. Fremont: Eagle of the West, by Midge Sherwood, pg 37
2. Fremont: Eagle of the West, by Midge Sherwood, pgs 482-7
3. Fremont: Eagle of the West, by Midge Sherwood, pg 13
4. Fremont: Eagle of the West, by Midge Sherwood, pg 12
5. Fremont: Eagle of the West, by Midge Sherwood, pg 481
6. Men to Match My Mountains, by Irving Stone, pg 74
7. http://www.longcamp.com/kit.html
8. Fremont: Eagle of the West, by Midge Sherwood, pg 138
9. http://en.wikipedia.org/wiki/Manifest_Destiny

Chapter 10: Eureka!

1. http://www.enotes.com/topics/gold-rush
2. Men to Match My Mountains, by Irving Stone, Pg 111
3. Men to Match My Mountains, by Irving Stone, Pg 112 and http://en.wikipedia.org/wiki/Lu%C3%ADs_Mar%C3%ADa_Peralta

Chapter 11: The World Rushed In

1. http://en.wikipedia.org/wiki/California_Gold_Rush
2. http://www.calgoldrush.com/resources/photos/timeline_01.html
3. http://www.calgoldrush.com/

Chapter 14: California's Apostolic Mantle

1. California Chamber of Commerce website
2. http://en.wikipedia.org/wiki/Assemblies_of_God
3. http://ag.org/top/About/history.cfm
4. http://healingandrevival.com/BioCSPrice.htm
5. http://www.mentoring-disciples.org/mears.html
6. http://www.westa.org/about_west.html
7. Quoted from an email posting from Lou Engle's ~ TheCall CA - November 1, 2008 - Qualcomm Stadium, San Diego
8. http://open-encyclopedia.com/Billy_Graham
9. http://open-encyclopedia.com/Billy_Graham
10. http://www.seekgod.ca/fuller1.htm
11. http://en.wikipedia.org/wiki/Bill_Bright
12. http://en.wikipedia.org/wiki/Crystal_Cathedral
13. Dictionary of Pentecostal and Charismatic Movements, Pg. 909
14. https://www.ywam.org/searches/searchintloff.asp
15. https://www.ywam.org/contents/abo_introduction.htm
16. https://www.ywam.org/contents/abo_wha_founder.htm
17. http://en.wikipedia.org/wiki/U.S._Center_for_World_Mission

SOURCE NOTES

18. http://en.wikipedia.org/wiki/Ralph_D._Winter
19. Zhttp://thecall.com/Groups/1000039667/TheCall/New_Call/Call_Cam/Call_Cam.aspx
20. Email posting from Wiley Drake Ministry, "Southern Baptist Leader Rick Warren," Posted 6/29/09
21. http://en.wikipedia.org/wiki/Rick_Warren

Chapter 15: Fire on Azusa Street

1. Into the Fire by Che Ahn, Pg 23
2. Quoted from Digging the Wells of Revival, by Lou Engle, Pg 83
3. My Story: "The Latter Rain," by Frank Bartleman, Pg 12
4. My Story: "The Latter Rain," by Frank Bartleman, Pg 13
5. Azusa Street, by Frank Bartleman, Pg 7
6. My Story: "The Latter Rain," by Frank Bartleman, Pg 15
7. My Story: "The Latter Rain," by Frank Bartleman, Pg 16
8. My Story: "The Latter Rain," by Frank Bartleman, Pg 16
9. Azusa Street, by Frank Bartleman, Pg 28
10. Into the Fire, by Che Ahn, pg 97
11. My Story: "The Latter Rain," by Frank Bartleman, Pg 16
12. My Story: "The Latter Rain," by Frank Bartleman, Pg 15
13. http://en.wikipedia.org/wiki/Jim_Crow_laws
14. http://www.azusastreet.org/WilliamJSeymour.htm
15. Azusa Street, by Frank Bartleman, pg 43

Chapter 16: The church of God in Christ

1. http://www.cogic.com
2. http://en.wikipedia.org/wiki/Church_of_God_in_Christ

Chapter 17: Aimee Semple McPherson & The four Square church

1. God's Generals, by Roberts Lairdon, pg 237
2. http://www.foursquare.org/landing_pages/8,3.html
3. God's Generals, by Roberts Lairdon, pg 237
4. God's Generals, by Roberts Lairdon, pg 238
5. God's Generals, by Roberts Lairdon, pg 239
6. http://www.foursquare.org/landing_pages/8,3.html
7. God's Generals, by Roberts Lairdon, pg 243
8. God's Generals, by Roberts Lairdon, pg 244
9. http://www.foursquare.org/landing_pages/8,3.html
10. God's Generals, by Roberts Lairdon, pg 249
11. God's Generals, by Roberts Lairdon, pg 251
12. http://www.foursquare.org/landing_pages/8,3.html
13. http://www.foursquare.org/landing_pages/8,3.html

14. God's Generals, by Roberts Lairdon, pg 255
15. God's Generals, by Roberts Lairdon, pg 255
16. http://www.foursquare.org/landing_pages/2,3.html#annual

Chapter 18: Calvary Temple, the Jesus Movement and the Vineyard movement
1. http://en.wikipedia.org/wiki/Chuck_Smith_
2. http://en.wikipedia.org/wiki/Lonnie_Frisbee
3. http://www.vineyardusa.org/site/about/vineyard-history

Chapter 22: Why Mariposa
1. California Division of Mines & Geology, Bulletin 193, page 5
2. California Division of Mines & Geology, Bulletin 193, page 89
3. http://www.yosemite.ca.us/library/call_of_gold/mint_mining_code.html

Chapter 23: The spirit of Minerva
1. http://en.wikipedia.org/wiki/Minerva
2. Releasing the Prophetic Destiny of a Nation, by Dutch Sheets and Chuck Pierce, pg 141
3. Storming Hell's Brazen Gates, by Dick Bernal, Pg. 19
4. Digging the Wells of Revival, by Lou Engle, Pg. 8
5. Breaking the Shield of Minerva, by Vicki Nohrden, Pg. 17
6. Breaking the Shield of Minerva, by Vicki Nohrden, Pg. 19 & 20
7. http://en.wikipedia.org/wiki/Medusa_(mythology)#Modern_interpretations
8. http://www.waymarking.com/waymarks/WM4HAB

Chapter 24: The Wilderness Tabernacle & America
1. http://westernfarmpress.com/tree-nut-crops/almond-price-0108/

Chapter 25: Pray for California
1. http://www.usatoday.com/news/politicselections/vote2004/countymap.htm
2. http://www.foxnews.com/wires/2006Dec05/0,4670,WaterWars,00.html
3. Breaking the Shield of Minerva, by Vicki Nohrden, Pg. 6
4. http://en.wikipedia.org/wiki/Summer_2008_California_wildfires

Henry & Grace Falany are founders and pastors of their local church. They are also itinerant ministers with a sound apostolic and prophetic anointing.

The Falanys minister in a powerful healing and miracle anointing. Their revivalist hearts are contagious and they lift and encourage congregations around the world.

In addition, as a "Mom and Pop" in the Kingdom, the Lord has used them frequently in the spirit of fellowship to support and inspire the local leaders.

If you would like to invite them to your church or city please visit:

www.MariposaRevivalCenter.com
Email: hisword@sierratel.com

Or call the church at:
209-966-5090

~~~~~~~~~~~~~~~~~~~

If this book has been an encouragement to you we would like to hear about it. Also, for information about this book, or to order more books, please visit:

www.GodGoldandGlory.com

Or email us at:
godgoldglory@sti.net

Henry, Grace & Bayleigh ~ High country pack trip

The Falany's Caribbean Island Expeditions ~ Belize

One of the Falany's 40ft. rafts ~ Grand Canyon

Henry & his horse J.C.

The Falany's 1980's brochure catalogue front cover